"In digestible and elegant prose, easy to r
and Moodliar show brilliantly how runav.   ....g. ...
militarism (with its nuclear threat) create the perfect storm that threatens
human survival. With many ah-ha moments, they make an urgent call,
based on solid evidence, for a 21st century movement to abolish carbon
emissions and nuclear weapons, taking inspiration from the movement to
abolish slavery. They make the impossible seem not only possible, but essential. Read it and jump into the movement waters that will nourish your
soul and might just save the planet."

Medea Benjamin, *cofounder of Code Pink and Global Exchange,*
author of War in Ukraine,
winner of Gandhi and Martin Luther King peace prizes

"An eloquent call for abolition of fossil fuels and militarism, very soon.
Dying for Capitalism is carefully reasoned and informed, spelling out what
we can and must do, without delay."

Noam Chomsky, *University of Arizona,*
Emeritus Professor, MIT

"Our planet Earth lies in the tightening grip of giant corporatized destruction with no firm stop signs. Derber and Moodliar deliver the indictment
and verdict in many dimensions, showing the urgency of universalizing the
resistance beyond protest and demands. They call for nothing less than unified action, propelled by the younger generation towards displacing cor-
poratism and militarism with transformative structures taking ever deeper
roots. This motivating book, marked toward the survival of all species,
should be in every high school and college classroom."

Ralph Nader,
author, activist and consumer advocate

"This must read cogent book dissects the interconnected systemic crisis
bringing us to the brink of extinction. Dying for Capitalism illuminates the
threads of the poly-crisis driven by extractive capitalism, ecological destruction, and entrenched militarism. Read it and weep – and then roll up your
sleeves and engage."

Chuck Collins, *co-editor,*
Inequality.org at the Institute for Policy Studies;
author, Altar to an Erupting Sun

"This book is original and essential reading. As this and upcoming generations contend with a web of existential, hand-me-down crises, Dying for
Capitalism reveals root causes and solutions. I will be assigning this book to
my students as a major resource for navigating the political and grassroots
community work that is now both their burden and charge."

Jonathan White, *Associate Professor of Sociology,*
Bentley University

"Few could be free so long as what 19th century abolitionists called 'The
Slave Power' remained standing. Derber and Moodliar call us to face up
to today's abolitionist task with the courage of our forebears, and lay out a
series of original and urgent strategies."

Ben Manski, *Assistant Professor of Sociology,*
George Mason University

Dying for Capitalism

This is an original, accessible book for scholars, students, activists, and the general public on the greatest crisis the world has faced. The authors challenge the widespread notion that a green and peaceful set of technological reforms in the current economic and political system – perhaps a "green capitalism" – can prevent disaster. *Dying for Capitalism* analyzes the "triangle of extinction" that links capitalism, environmental destruction, and militarism as a system that cannot sustain life on the planet. The authors analyze how the extinction triangle evolved historically, how it functions globally as integral to the world capitalist order, and how the United States has become the dominant "extinction nation." They also show how recent anti-democratic and anti-scientific cultural and political forces intensify denial of the threat and subordinate health and survival to profit and extreme concentrated power.

The book offers a "slender path" of social and political transformation that can prevent catastrophe. The path requires moving beyond current ruling systems. But possibilities of survival arise from action at local, state, regional, and global levels through multiple strategies and movements that already exist. The authors draw on the history of abolitionism and emancipation from slavery in the United States to show how a system that appears unchangeable can be transformed, while describing organizations, movements, and practices that are models of hope and a shift from the triangle of extinction to the "circle of creation."

Charles Derber is a Professor of Sociology at Boston College and a noted public intellectual who has written 25 books, including several best-sellers reviewed in the *NY Times*, *Washington Post*, *The Boston Globe*, and other leading media. His books include *Welcome to the Revolution*, *Sociopathic Society*, *Corporation Nation*, *People Before Profit*, *The Pursuit of Attention*, *The Wilding of America*, and *Greed to Green*. With Suren Moodliar, he is a co-editor of the Routledge book series Universalizing Resistance. Derber, a life-long activist, has done hundreds of radio, television, internet, and film interviews by prominent media and commentators.

Suren Moodliar is a scholar and activist who helped found and manage encuentro5, a movement-building center in Boston. He is also managing editor of the journal, *Socialism and Democracy*. He is co-author of *A People's Guide to Greater Boston* (2020). He also co-edited and contributed to *Turnout! Mobilizing Voters in an Emergency* (2020) with Charles Derber and Matt Nelson, and to *Internationalism or Extinction* (2020) and *Chomsky for Activists* (2021) with Charles Derber and Paul Shannon. In the 1980s, Suren supported the national liberation movement in his home country, South Africa. He has also participated in public health, peace, solidarity, and pro-immigrant movements and labor organizations.

Universalizing Resistance
Edited by Charles Derber and Suren Moodliar

The modern social sciences began in the late 19th century when capitalism was establishing itself as the dominant global system. Social science began as a terrifying awakening: that a militarized, globalizing capitalism was creating the greatest revolution in history, penetrating every part of society with the passions of self-interest and profit and breaking down community and the common good. The universalizing of the market promised universal prosperity but delivered an intertwined sociopathic system of money-making, militarism and environmental destruction now threatening the survival of all life itself.

In the 21st century, only a universalized resistance to this now fully universalized matrix of money, militarism and me-firstism can save humanity. History shows that people can join together under nearly impossible odds to create movements against tyranny for the common good. But when the world faces a universalizing system of madness and extinction, it takes new forms of resistance moving beyond the "silo" movements for social justice that have emerged notably in the US in recent decades: single-issue movements separated by issue, race, gender, social class, nation and geography. The story of what universalized movements look like, how they are beginning to be organized, how they "intersect" with each other against the reigning system of power, and how they can grow fast enough to save humanity is the purpose of this series.

The series is publishing works by leading thinkers and activists developing the theory and practice of universalizing resistance. The books are written to engage professors, students, activists and organizers, and citizens who recognize the desperate urgency of a universalizing resistance that can mobilize the general population to build a new global society preserving life with justice.

Chomsky for Activists
Noam Chomsky

**Dying for Capitalism: How Big Money Fuels Extinction
and What We Can Do About It**
Charles Derber and Suren Moodliar

For more information about this series, please visit: www.routledge.com/Universalizing-Resistance/book-series/RESIST

Dying for Capitalism

How Big Money Fuels Extinction
and What We Can Do About It

Charles Derber and Suren Moodliar

Routledge
Taylor & Francis Group

NEW YORK AND LONDON

Designed cover image: Suren Moodliar

First published 2023
by Routledge
605 Third Avenue, New York, NY 10158

and by Routledge
4 Park Square, Milton Park, Abingdon, Oxon, OX14 4RN

Routledge is an imprint of the Taylor & Francis Group, an informa business

© 2023 Taylor & Francis

The right of Charles Derber and Suren Moodliar to be identified as authors of this work has been asserted in accordance with sections 77 and 78 of the Copyright, Designs and Patents Act 1988.

Library of Congress Cataloging-in-Publication Data
Names: Derber, Charles, author. | Moodliar, Suren, 1962- author.
Title: Dying for capitalism : how big money fuels extinction and what we can do about it / Charles Derber, Suren Moodliar.
Description: New York, NY : Routledge, 2023. |
Includes bibliographical references and index. | Summary: "This is an original, accessible book for scholars, students, activists, and the general public on the greatest crisis the world has faced. The authors challenge the widespread notion that a green and peaceful set of technological reforms in the current economic and political system, perhaps a "green capitalism", can prevent disaster"-- Provided by publisher.
Identifiers: LCCN 2023000952 (print) | LCCN 2023000953 (ebook) | ISBN 9781032512792 (hardback) | ISBN 9781032512587 (paperback) | ISBN 9781003401483 (ebook)
Subjects: LCSH: Economic history--21st century. | Capitalism--Social aspects. | Capitalism--Environmental aspects. | Climatic changes--Social aspects. | Climatic changes--Economic aspects.
Classification: LCC HC59.3 .D457 2023 (print) |
LCC HC59.3 (ebook) | DDC 330.9--dc23/eng/20230117
LC record available at https://lccn.loc.gov/2023000952
LC ebook record available at https://lccn.loc.gov/2023000953

ISBN: 978-1-032-51279-2 (hbk)
ISBN: 978-1-032-51258-7 (pbk)
ISBN: 978-1-003-40148-3 (ebk)

DOI: 10.4324/9781003401483

Typeset in Bembo
by KnowledgeWorks Global Ltd.

Contents

Introduction

The Greatest Emergency of All Time

A group of young British activists have started a movement called *Extinction Rebellion*. They are advocating the abolition of all new fossil fuel emissions virtually immediately, by 2025. When pushed for more "realistic" solutions by reporters covering their protest, one young activist, Liza Woolf, came forward, speaking with grief and fury:

> What is it that you are asking me as a 20-year-old to face and to accept about my future and my life? … This is an emergency. We are facing extinction. When you ask questions like that, what is it you want me to feel?[1]

The reporters had no answer to her tears.

The rest of us have to answer her.

Indeed Liza's plea is sounded everywhere. On Indigenous People's Day 2021, in the run-up to the international climate conference in Glasgow, indigenous activists called on President Biden to declare a climate emergency. Siqiñiq Maupin of the Iñupiat nation described the relocation of 12 flooded villages in Alaska, while going on to state:

> People are dying right now from the pollutants, the toxins, the climate catastrophes that are happening, and we have to stop the harm.[2]

As 2021 drew to a close, Tim Weatherbee of Mayfield, Western Kentucky, added his voice to Liza's and Siqiñiq's. A powerful and unseasonal tornado had torn through his home state, killing dozens, many dying in their workplaces, destroying upwards of 15,000 buildings, and Weatherby noted the unusual circumstances:

> It's not normal to get a tornado in December, but then it's not normal for it to be 73 degrees at night …. People think about today, not tomorrow, and it's only going to get worse.[3]

DOI: 10.4324/9781003401483-1

By the time of the UN Framework Convention on Climate Change's Conference of the Parties held in November 2022, it took a 10-year-old Ghanaian, Nakeeyat Dramani Sam, to synthesize the claims of Tim, Siqiñiq, and Liza and ask the global decision-makers and on behalf of climate change's present victims a sharper question after noting that time is running out. Noting the droughts and floods that have hit her region, she made the connection to climate change:

> There is less than 86 months to go before we hit 1.5 [Celsius] .... So I appeal to you, have a heart and do the math, it is an emergency!

But Nakeeyat went further and harnessed the sense of emergency to actual obligations and matters of justice:

> "I put a simple question on the table," she said. "When can you pay us back? Because payment is overdue."

As she concluded her remarks, she held up a sign stating simply, "PAYMENT OVERDUE."[4]

★★★

To be sure, the world has entered a new stage threatening the very survival of humanity and all life species because of run-away climate change and endless militarism in the nuclear age. Both climate change and war now threaten extinction. Moreover, other threats in the DNA of our economic system multiply the extinction perils; the drive for endless profits and production is depleting scarce vital resources and extinguishing thousands of life species in an unprecedented existential crisis of biodiversity. The same forces help drive global pandemics such as COVID-19, which is also a global existential risk. These once unbelievable perils are a creation of our own hands – and of the leaders and systems we are taught to cherish.

A "triangle of extinction" that connects environmental death with war and capitalism – creates an emergency that humanity-as-a-whole has never faced before. The triangle operates with the greatest force and danger in the United States – and it needs to become the subject of conversation and activism of all Americans as well as all nations. The Earth Strike movement, a grassroots group focused on climate change, works to promote consciousness and activism about looming destruction of the earth.[5] Among its actions are a general strike to save the planet. In coordination with unions against both governments and corporations, Earth Strike has carried out multiple global actions since 2019, including close coordination with labor unions on a May Day protest in 2019, leading up to a September protest on the anniversary of Rachel Carson's book, *Silent Spring*, which prophesized the devastation of the environment.

Likewise, the Sunrise Movement has been catalyzing a massive group of climate activists in the United States, involving many young people, indigenous nations and people of color, by holding wealthy elites accountable for sacrificing the future of everyone. Sunrise challenged Biden's climate programs as far from adequate, sitting-in against Democratic Senators in July 2021 and calling for $12 trillion over ten years in green jobs and infrastructure, helping push the Democratic Party and President Biden to focus on the emergency and demanding new investment for resilient new infrastructure and climate adaptation. By late 2022, albeit with an unfavorable political arithmetic, elements of the Sunrise agenda made it through both houses of the US Congress in the form of the awkwardly named, Inflation Reduction Act.[6]

And we now also have "Birth-strikers," women who refuse to have children because of the climate-devastated world they would occupy. A 33-year-old Blythe Pepino, a British founder of BirthStrike and a songwriter who began to read extensively about climate change, became more and more anxious after seeing government inaction. She felt she had to act, helping found BirthStrike and declaring the group's primal fear:

We're too afraid to bring children into the world with future that's forecast.[7]

Alexandria Ocasio-Cortez, one of America's most influential progressive Democrats in Congress, and a self-proclaimed "democratic socialist," says she understands the birthstrikers, commenting on Instagram Live:

It is basically a scientific consensus that the lives of our children are going to be very difficult, and it does lead young people to have a legitimate question: is it OK to still have children?[8]

Meanwhile, the Bulletin of Atomic Scientists, a global community of nuclear physicists and other influential scientists, have moved their "Doomsday Clock" that they created after World War II closer and closer to midnight. Since the invention of the nuclear bomb, their Doomsday Clock has been set each year as a symbol of the looming end of the world, with the scientists changing the time reflecting their best estimates of the changing risk of total destruction. For the first time, in 2015, they began including the risks of climate change to the risks of blowing up the world in a nuclear war. In 2019, they moved the time on the clock to two minutes before midnight, noting that

We are like passengers on the Titanic, ignoring the iceberg ahead in terms of climate and nuclear threats.[9]

Entering 2022, the clock stood at 100 seconds before midnight, reflecting accelerating climate and military extinction threats. In August 2021, the UN latest IPCC climate report, called *"code red for humanity,"* showed that the climate meltdown is already here and we cannot stop massive climate damage; instead, we have about ten years to make drastic changes to try to save civilized life on the planet. While such alarms by scientists have catalyzed a more widespread and fearful public awareness of the terrible damage already baked in, reinforced by the huge numbers of research studies and activist protests about the climate change crisis and nuclear war dangers, none of this has awakened a visceral or political response proportional to the catastrophic threat.

For some, awareness of the extinction threat has produced a technological turn – the hope that new inventions and the rapid pace of technological change may help us solve the terminal threats. For example, the promise of fossil fuel-free and radioactive-free nuclear fusion energy periodically makes headlines. However, even in the most optimistic scenarios, commercial production of fusion energy is at best decades away. If humanity is to survive to enjoy the benefits of this allegedly limitless energy source, it will have to alter the way it organizes its economy and its approach to economic growth along the lines that we spell out in this book.[10]

As 2022 drew to a close, the war in Ukraine was correctly seen as increasing the likelihood of nuclear annihilation – with observers noting that the "usual methods for managing conflict between the United States and Russia in the Cold War have fallen into disrepair, and it is not clear that anything has replaced it." Similar observations may be made for the novel and rapidly evolving Taiwan-centered confrontation between the United States and China.[11] On January 23, 2023, the Clock was moved to 90 seconds before midnight, the closest to apocalypse since its creation in 1947.

Bang, Crunch, Shriek, and Whimper: Varieties of Existential Threat and Extinction

Because extinction is the most terrible and deadly destiny that humans now face, we need to be clear about the various forms of existential risks from which humanity cannot meaningfully recover. We need to begin then with some definitions that offer as much clarity as possible about the apocalyptic threats we face.

Most discussions of climate change and nuclear war do not offer theories or even a definition of extinction. They simply tend to take the "common sense" view that extinction means the worst outcome that nuclear war and climate change might produce: the elimination of humans and other life species from the planet.

An Oxford philosopher, Dr. Nick Bostrom, has developed a more rigorous definition of extinction. He argues that the commonsense view is too limited. It fails to recognize that there are many forms of existential risk and extinction that need to be named, understood and confronted. His definitions not only include total elimination of all life but also extend to a much wider set of catastrophic futures that humans now face.[12]

Bostrom offers the following definition:

> Existential risk – One where an adverse outcome would either annihilate Earth-originating intelligent life or permanently and drastically curtail its potential.[13]

Note that he includes not only risks of total annihilation of all life but of threats that would "permanently and drastically curtail" the potential of humanity for growth and further positive development. He is offering a definition that includes total extinction but extends to a variety of other existential risks. But he's not just lumping into his definition every kind of catastrophic risk. He distinguishes existential or extinction risks from catastrophic "endurable" risks as follows:

> Existential risks are distinct from global endurable risks. Examples of the latter kind include: threats to the biodiversity of Earth's ecosphere, moderate global warming, global economic recessions (even major ones), and possibly stifling cultural or religious eras such as the "dark ages", even if they encompass the whole global community, provided they are transitory (though see the section on "Shrieks" below). To say that a particular global risk is endurable is evidently not to say that it is acceptable or not very serious. A world war fought with conventional weapons or a Nazi-style Reich lasting for a decade would be extremely horrible events even though they would fall under the rubric of endurable global risks since humanity could eventually recover.[14]

Bostrom identifies four categories of existential risk, which include not only total destruction but also permanently prevent the development of humanity toward its full potential and fulfillment, a state he calls "posthumanity, meaning a new stage of history where humans are either extinct or have lost the sensibilities we define as "human":

Bangs – Earth-originating intelligent life goes extinct in relatively sudden disaster resulting from either an accident or a deliberate act of destruction.

Crunches – The potential of humankind to develop into posthumanity is permanently thwarted although human life continues in some form.

Shrieks – Some form of posthumanity is attained but it is an extremely narrow band of what is possible and desirable.

Whimpers – A posthuman civilization arises but evolves in a direction that leads gradually but irrevocably to either the complete disappearance of the things we value or to a state where those things are realized to only a minuscule degree of what could have been achieved.[15]

Bostrom offers examples of each category.

An example of Bangs would be global nuclear war suddenly killing all life, consistent with the most common view of extinction. Interestingly, Bostrom, writing in 2002, adds the possibility of global pandemics becoming Bangs:

> What if AIDS was as contagious as the common cold?
>
> There are several features of today's world that may make a global pandemic more likely than ever before. Travel, food-trade, and urban dwelling have all increased dramatically in modern times, making it easier for a new disease to quickly infect a large fraction of the world's population.[16]

He was writing 17 years before COVID-19 erupted. At this writing, he might consider it a catastrophic but "endurable" rather than existential or extinction risk, but it remains unclear whether the virus could mutate or interact with other rising deadly viruses such as Highly Pathogenic Avian Influenza to permanently alter social interaction or a society consistent with full human potential. If that were to happen, it would become an "existential risk," and possibly a Bang or Crunch.

Bostrom also notes that "runaway global warming" could become a Bang. Based on current evidence since his 2002 analysis, he would almost certainly see it as an extinction risk that should be classified as a potential Bang or, if the world acts more decisively than now seems likely, a possible Crunch.[17]

An example of other Crunches, closely related to global warming is what he calls "Resource depletion or ecological destruction":

> The natural resources needed to sustain a high-tech civilization are being used up. If some other cataclysm destroys the technology we have, it may not be possible to climb back up to present levels if natural conditions are less favorable than they were for our ancestors, for example if the most easily exploitable coal, oil, and mineral resources have been depleted.[18]

It seems clear that, if writing today, he would alter this paragraph and focus on climate change as well as "resource depletion." He would likely view the depletion of oil and coal as not an existential risk but a basis for a new clean energy economy that might limit climate change to a Crunch rather than a Bang.

Examples of Shrieks include a "repressive totalitarian global regime":

> One can imagine that an intolerant world government, based perhaps on mistaken religious or ethical convictions, is formed, is stable, and decides to realize only a very small part of all the good things a posthuman world could contain.[19]

Here, we see an existential risk that would not extinguish human life but could potentially permanently curb the potential for human development and growth that he calls "posthumanity." Orwell's 1984 would constitute Bostrom's Shriek.

An example that Bostrom argues of Whimpers – one that current space wars and colonization are making more likely – is what he describes as a "colonization race."

> Our "cosmic commons" could be burnt up in a colonization race. Selection would favor those replicators that spend all their resources on sending out further colonization probes.
>
> Although the time it would take for a whimper of this kind to play itself out may be relatively long, it could still have important policy implications because near-term choices may determine whether we will go down a track that inevitably leads to this outcome. Once the evolutionary process is set in motion or a cosmic colonization race begun, it could prove difficult or impossible to halt it. It may well be that the only feasible way of avoiding a whimper is to prevent these chains of events from ever starting to unwind.[20]

Of course, we have seen a version of such existentially risky colonization in the history of Western militarist colonial nations both in Europe and, especially since World War II in the postcolonial, intensely militarized US state. We shall see that US militarism and endless wars remain the most dangerous risk of ending the world through nuclear war.

Beyond his colorful classification of varieties of existential risks and extinction, Bostrom offers two other relevant arguments. One has to do with the history and future of existential and extinction risks. There have been five prior extinctions, all before the existence of humans. He argues that the invention and use of the nuclear bomb in 1945 started a modern sixth extinction stage, in which humans both exist and play a role in creating new existential risks. He argues that these risks are multiplying with natural, technological and socioeconomic and political developments that will make the future ever more vulnerable to all his classes of extinction.

This leads to a second idea that he does not highlight but seems to recognize. In the sixth extinction, where humans exist, we can foresee what might be "systemic extinction." This would emerge when humans design the world, whether deliberately or not, for total repression and destruction, as seen in his notion of a Shriek extinction based on elites constructing a global totalitarian regime.

Systemic extinctions are existential risks that arise from the major institutional systems – whether economic or political – created by humans. Bangs of global nuclear war and run-away climate change would represent systemic extinction. They arise out of military and "security" systems as well as fossil fuel driven capitalist societies leading toward both of these forms of "Bangs." Indeed, our book focuses on "systemic extinction," and, more specifically, on United States and global capitalism that we argue is destined to create inevitable extinction unless we undertake urgent systemic change.[21]

Extinction Denialism

Despite the growing and more widely discussed prospects of extinction, and the rise of "systemic extinction," we are witnessing, in many conservative movements around the world and, in extreme form in the Republican Party of the United States, what can be called Extinction Denialism. The denial of man-made climate change in the Republican Party leadership has led the world-famous critic, Noam Chomsky, to argue that

> We might stop for a moment to ponder on most extraordinary fact. A major political organization in the most powerful country in the world's history is quite literally dedicated to the destruction of much of life on earth. That might seem to be an unfair comment but a little reflection will show that it's not.[22]

Donald Trump became the emperor without clothes here, openly ridiculing climate change and arguing – in relation to extinction by nuclear war – that "it makes no sense to have nuclear weapons if we aren't ready to use them."[23] During the deep freeze of the Midwest in early 2019, something climate scientists showed was extreme weather predicted by their climate change models, Trump saw it as a huge joke about the fear of climate change, saying "we could use some more global warming right now." In 2017, Trump also ordered all agencies of the federal government to expunge the words "climate change,"[24] punishing any employee using the words.

Extinction denialism includes tendencies among both conservatives and liberals to diminish the concerns about nuclear war that were present in the public discourse during the Cold War. And the denial of the existential dangers of unfettered economic growth and profit-seeking in a finite world is even deeper. Such denial is central to sustaining the profits and power of the "masters of the universe" running the global capitalist system's largest banks, corporations and states. This hints that extinction, much like racism, is "systemic," a function not just of rotten leaders but of the way we organize our ruling economic and political institutions. And the denial is systemic too, built into not just the Republican Party but much of the corporate and political world, as we show in later chapters.

Millions of people, nonetheless, are beginning to wake up, especially, in the United States, after the election of President Biden and President Trump's defeat. A new awakening about climate change began to spread not only among activists fighting pipelines and fracking but among millions of ordinary Americans supporting Biden's climate agenda. The astonishing extreme weather of 2021 – filled with once-in-a-millennium floods, record drought, fires, and record heat – reaching 130 degrees in Death Valley and a record 121 degrees in British Columbia, Canada – made many realize climate disaster is not a future threat; it is here in spades right now.

Western opinion polls in 2021 showed rapidly growing concern among the majority of Americans about climate change.[25] But even for the emerging majority scared by the experience of the COVID-19 pandemic and now frightened by the extreme weather, climate change for the majority does not deeply intrude into their daily thoughts or behavior – or propel them into urgent political action. Even for those believing in human-caused climate change and a possibility of major nuclear or cyber conflict, or a pandemic that races out of control, the extinction nightmare is more a cognitive concern than a gut-level obsession. And for many, including politicians, who back a political response, it is often too slow; as climate author and activist Bill McKibben has said on climate, "winning slowly is the same as losing."[26]

Ask yourself these four questions about your reaction to the extinction threat, whether of climate change or nuclear war:

- Does it keep you up at night?
- Do you cry about it?
- Does it make you ask whether it's moral to have kids?
- Does it mobilize you to act politically to save life on the planet?

You can be aware of the truth of climate change and the nuclear threat – and the perils of run-away capitalist growth – and still answer "no" to any or all these questions. If so, you are still living in a kind of Extinction Denialism. If would be as if you were told you had cancer, but don't respond as if the knowledge made any difference. Or you simply can't deal with it emotionally or feel you'll be dead by the time extinction truly kills us. Either way, that's a way of being in denial. There is a spectrum of denialism ranging from complete disbelief, to partial awareness, to full cognitive understanding without the knowledge getting into your gut and driving you to urgent action. *Unless you act, you are in denial!*

While elites in many nations, including President Biden in the United States and President Xi in China and leaders in Europe, recognize the existential threat and are proposing major new climate and COVID-19 agendas, they are not sounding the emergency alarm and activating the all-out emergency public mobilization and far-reaching agenda that is required. Leaders have to encourage a culture where people answer "yes" to the four questions above, but that would have big consequences. It would threaten ruling elites and the system of power they benefit from in the here and now.

We have seen this movie before. British journalist and influential climate change author, George Monbiot notes that ruling elites historically have typically been more likely to promote than prevent collapse because of the short-term gains for themselves, writing that one scholar:

> The social science professor Kevin MacKay contends that oligarchy has been a more fundamental cause of the collapse of civilizations than social complexity or energy demand. Control by oligarchs, he argues, thwarts rational decision-making, because the short-term interests of the elite are radically different to the long-term interests of society. This explains why past civilizations have collapsed "despite possessing the cultural and technological know-how needed to resolve their crises". Economic elites, which benefit from social dysfunction, block the necessary solutions.[27]

Ruling elites – what we now call the 1% – perpetuate systems that will eventually destroy them and everyone else, to protect their short-term interests. Monbiot notes that:

> The oligarchic control of wealth, politics, media and public discourse explains the comprehensive institutional failure now pushing us towards disaster. Think of Donald Trump and his cabinet of multi-millionaires; the influence of the Koch brothers in funding rightwing organisations; the Murdoch empire and its massive contribution to climate science denial; or the oil and motor companies whose lobbying prevents a faster shift to new technologies.[28]

The denialism of much of the corporate 1% and their conservative political allies, especially the Trumpist GOP, is still on full display. Virtually all GOP leaders and millions in their base – as well as their apologists on Fox News, such as Tucker Carlson who rails against climate policy as socialism and COVID-19 vaccines as government tyranny – continue to deny man-made climate change. They demonize and ridicule the Biden climate and COVID-19 proposals as well as the activists seeking even bolder action on climate, nuclear war or even COVID-19. And conservative leaders in Brazil, the Philippines, Hungary and many other countries continue rule with their own versions of denialism.

Moving beyond extinction denial is the first step in any movement to save all life. It is an integral part of the new politics of extinction that can preserve the planet. It is also the first step away from collective insanity. To deny the threat of extinction of all life at this stage of history is delusional and unbelievable – it reflects a madness that goes beyond anything even George Orwell could imagine. It also indicates how the widely viewed rationality of capitalism is ultimately irrational – a system dependent on maintaining madness to perpetuate itself.

Earth's survival is going to depend on the resonance of the emergency calls by people like the now world-famous teen climate activist, Swedish teenager, Greta Thunberg, who thunders at adults that "you are stealing our future." She won't eat meat, fly in a plane, or do anything else that creates major carbon emissions. She leads school strikes by kids that have mushroomed round the world – with revolutionary calls to her generation aiming not only to mobilize millions of children and teenagers but also shame genocidally complicit adults, especially wealthy elites, into emergency action:

- You only talk about moving forward with the same bad ideas that got us into this mess, even when the only sensible thing to do is pull the emergency brake. You are not mature enough to tell it like it is. Even that burden you leave to us children ...
- Our civilization is being sacrificed for the opportunity of a very small number of people to continue making enormous amounts of money ... It is the sufferings of the many which pay for the luxuries of the few ... You say you love your children above all else, and yet you are stealing their future in front of their very eyes ...
- We cannot solve a crisis without treating it as a crisis ... if solutions within the system are so impossible to find, then ... we should change the system itself.
- We have not come here to beg world leaders to care ... We have come here to let you know that change is coming, whether you like it or not. The real power belongs to the people ...[29]

Money and Madness: Talking about Capitalism

With the fresh eye of a teenager, Thunberg is onto the role of money, profits, and corporate elites in driving extinction. She is ahead of most adults. While some parts of the environmental movement and antiwar movement have discussed the climate dangers of corporate capitalism, the idea that capitalism fuels extinction is mainly off the table. Indeed, many American liberals as well as conservatives view US-style capitalism as the solution rather than the problem, the only system capable of bringing technological innovation or global integration in a way that can ultimately prevent extinction. Even those who see a connection between capitalism, climate change, pandemics, and war may be reluctant to talk about capitalism, believing that any focus on changing our economic system is such a long and difficult proposition that to focus on it will simply drag out and intensify the extinction threat. And many progressive Americans, who worry about climate change, recognize that just a mention of the word "socialism" will turn off millions of people, with leaders such as Trump and many Republican politicians today using it as the bogey-man of all evil and the end of freedom.

The social critic Naomi Klein titled her best-seller on climate change, *This Changes Everything.*[30] When all life is threatened with being snuffed out, something people have never before experienced in human history then, yes, it does change everything. And that includes changing what we can and must talk about, including the formerly sacred subject of capitalism. Since the economic system is so deeply intertwined with the extinction threat, everything about our economics and politics is now on the table – and as extinction looms closer and larger, subjects like changing capitalism itself, even in capitalist America, will no longer remain taboo.

We see it even in the United States, where talking critically about capitalism is harder than in most other countries. Yet millions of US young people have already opened their hearts and minds to a critical conversation about capitalist economics and saving the planet. This new conversation must catch fire and create transformative action now because it is already almost too late.

Capitalism and Survival

In the chapters that follow, we flesh out in some detail why corporate capitalism, particularly the neoliberal type in the United States, now threatens survival and makes extinction perils systemic, for five reasons briefly mentioned below.

First, capitalism is a system organized around *profit as the central goal.* Any effort to put other goals above profit, including social and environmental protection, is in tension with capitalism itself. As a system breeding ever more inequality, class divisions between billionaires and struggling workers take on a more *life-and-death* quality. This helps de-sensitize decision-makers to the broader extinction of all life through climate change or war.

Second, maximizing profit requires removing *limits to growth.*

Any company that puts limits on its growth will eventually reduce profit margins and succumb to competitors who seek maximum growth. Yet because we live on a finite planet, a system that cannot accept limits to growth, and is always hungrier to extract oil and exploit more workers, is incompatible with human and planetary survival.

Third, maximizing profit has always required capitalist wars. European colonial wars led to mass death but did not create the threat of total life extinction. But with World War II, invention of the nuclear bomb made war itself an extinction threat, because any war can now escalate to nuclear conflict, a major threat of extinction.

Fourth, capitalism seeks to privatize and sell virtually everything in global markets – both are inherently destabilizing imperatives. But a sustainable and peaceful society requires *massive investment in public goods*, which are aimed at maximizing the well-being and health of people and all life species rather than maximizing profit. The ultimate public good is sustaining human survival itself.

Fifth, capitalism generates consent – and vests itself with moral legitimacy – by calling the market the source of freedom and cultivating fear and hatred of government. But survival now requires *an affirmative view of expansive government and public goods at all levels*; it is the only way to create essential public goods.

The United States and Survival

Extinction is a global threat, rooted in a globalizing capitalism system, as well as the global political elites and culture tied and subject to that system. But while global systems continue to grow, we also continue to live in world of national states. While extinction is inherently a global crisis, every country plays its own role in shaping the threat and prospects for sustaining survival of life.

The hard truth is that the United States is the leading "extinction nation," a fact that every American needs to understand in his or her gut. More than any other nation, American policies are fueling the existential threat to human civilization. The United States lead the race to extinction partly because it is indisputably the most powerful nation on the planet. It has a larger role than any other nation in setting the global rules of the game. America's unique brand of capitalism, neoliberalism, also plays a central role. It requires US elites *to* slash public goods, cut taxes, reduce welfare, deregulate corporations, sell off public lands, and other policies that make neoliberalism an engine of extinction dangers.

Aggravating matters – all these rollbacks fuel far-right forces of reaction, the very alienated and aggrieved voices animating Republican political projects in the United States *and* the world over. While the United States is a declining hegemon or empire, its politics, and ideas still have enormous impacts on the world as a whole. As the threat of US authoritarian and fascist movements – exploding in the January 6 attempted coup and continuing in the ongoing Trumpist Republican Party attack on democracy itself – took center stage in the United States, parallel Far Right movements emerged throughout much of the world. The extinction threats of climate and war are paralleling and intensifying the threat of the extinction of democracy in the United States and elsewhere. Indeed, these two categories of existential threats are intertwined, feeding and fueling each other, as we show later in this book.

In the final chapter, we address how it is that the Far Right, an enduring presence through much of American history (and subject of several books by Derber) may be countered by a Front for Survival, one which is global in scope but necessarily also anchored the United States.

The good news for the United States is that as the country most responsible for endangering survival, it has great power to turn things around. This is not to say that the United States can solve the crisis because that will take new and powerful global change: the rise of new global social justice movements, cooperation, treaties, and governance. But global solutions are not likely to happen fast enough without the US seizing the moment, something that many Americans hope the Biden Administration will do, pushed hard by millions of new activists in popular movements for justice, democracy, and survival itself.

In Part I, we offer an analysis of how the history and spread of global capitalism are putting us on the road to disaster. In Part II, we turn to the United States, showing how it is the most powerful country putting the pedal to the extinction medal. And finally, in Part III, we look to the solutions, focusing on the new "abolitionist" movements, briefly discussed below.

Toward a New Abolitionism

Survival requires a new abolitionist movement. The famous US 19th-century abolitionists, such as Frederick Douglass, the former slave who became the most famous orator of his era, and William Lloyd Garrison, organized to abolish slavery centering their efforts, first and foremost, on the suffering and rebellions of the enslaved themselves. We now need to abolish carbon emissions and nuclear weapons, and transform the economy driving them and perpetuating other extinction threats including those of over-production and rapidly shrinking biodiversity. And, while this seems a nearly impossible dream, much like the abolitionist call for ending slavery, it is potentially within our reach. Indeed, the United Nations and the US Democratic Party have already called for abolishing the creation of fossil fuel pollution by 2030. And a significant number of scientific and grassroots peace groups have been organizing for several decades to eliminate all nuclear weapons on earth. Moreover questions about the morality and legitimacy of an economic system producing billionaires while neglecting the needs of most working people for basic housing, health care, and a living wage have begun to energize a new politics among young people women, people of color and progressives throughout the world.

The United States must play a major role, but other nations have already advanced their own abolitionist movements – and may be the leaders in global abolitionism. But it cannot succeed without US engagement, and there are signs from history that US abolitionism is possible. Indeed, none other than President Ronald Reagan in 1984 called for the abolition of nuclear weapons:

> After his reelection in 1984, President Ronald Reagan sat for an interview with Time magazine. "I just happen to believe that we cannot go into another generation with the world living under the threat of those weapons and knowing that some madman can push the button some place," he said. "My hope has been, and my dream, that we can get the Soviet Union to join us in starting verifiable reductions of the weapons. Once you start down that road, they've got to see how much better off we would both be if we got rid of them entirely." In his dealing with the Soviets, Reagan's two terms were almost those of two different presidents. Both the

hard-liner and the peacemaker were present throughout, but the balance shifted so decisively from one to the other as to create a discontinuity. The man who had denounced the nuclear freeze as Soviet propaganda was now suggesting not just reduction but elimination of all nuclear weapons.[31]

If the ultra-Conservative Ronald Reagan could overcome denialism and become a nuclear abolitionist, there is hope that a majority of Americans could become new abolitionists. Reagan's evolution is worth noting:

> What explains Reagan's remarkable transformation from Cold War hawk to nuclear peacemaker? His nuclear abolitionism had deep roots, going back to a flirtation with pacifism in the early 1930s. His antiwar side was connected to narratives and images that deeply affected him: seeing the British antiwar play Journey's End in 1929, being shown footage from the liberation of Auschwitz in 1945, and watching the ABC television movie The Day After in 1983. A projection that stuck with him was that at least 150 million Americans – two-thirds of the population in 1980 – would be killed in an all-out nuclear war, though he believed for some reason that Soviet losses would be limited to a much smaller percentage. Advisers who "tossed around macabre jargon about 'throw weights' and 'kill ratios' as if they were talking about baseball scores" appalled him. In his diary and to aides, Reagan even worried that the biblical prophecy of Armageddon was at hand.[32]

While Reagan's "conversion" is a sign of hope, it is misleading as a solution to the extinction crisis. Even if we were able to abolish nuclear weapons – in the spirit Reagan suggested – they would probably have been rebuilt without a larger shift in our politics away from the ruling system based on war and corporate expansion. We need a broader change to truly end the extinction threat, much as the 19th-century abolitionists needed a transformation in the entire economic and political system of the United States, including the North, to put a permanent and sustainable end to slavery, something yet not fully achieved in the institutionalized racism pervasive in prisons, housing, inequality, and geographic distribution of pollution.

The abolition of nuclear bombs and even carbon emissions is essential to preventing extinction. But to be a sustainable change, it cannot happen without deeper change. This challenge to change the larger system – particularly in a short period – seems an impossible agenda in light of the urgency of the extinction crisis.

But history has offered other examples where humans have mobilized to transform whole systems of destruction and death in relatively short periods, beyond just the anti-slavery abolitionist movement itself. One might think of the successful movement to eliminate apartheid in South Africa, which required transforming the entire political and cultural systems and power elites running the country for many decades. Or the successful change to end the British

Empire by Gandhi and the anti-colonial movement in India, along with many other former colonies rising to push out their rulers in the anti-colonial revolutions of the 1950s, 1960s, and 1970s.

In this book, we will use the example of the abolitionist movement that worked to do the impossible: abolish the institution of slavery that had existed thousands of years and was integral to the economic and political system not only of the South but the entire United States. Before the Civil War, the North had slave-owners and made some of its greatest profits off the slave trade and the sale of cotton produced by Southern slaves. Abolitionism undermined the immorality that sustained the South and enriched much of the North, fighting for what could only have been seen originally as a utopian and hopeless cause.

Nonetheless, abolitionism moved from a tiny movement of "dreamers" to a mass movement that created a new moral consciousness awakening millions to ultimately do the impossible: eliminate slavery. It did so by strategically undermining the "immoral morality" that gave slavery legitimacy and challenging the economic and political power of the tiny number of elite planters who dominated the slave South and owned the vast majority of slaves.[33]

Abolitionism achieved the unimaginable: helping to awaken an entire society to the death culture, wrapped in a culture of God and glory, at the center of the Confederacy. The abolitionists also awakened millions to the barbaric economic institutions that enriched slave holders and made clear that overthrowing the system was the greatest moral imperative of the age.

The abolitionist movement is just one of several transformative movements in US history that offer hope. In the 19th century, the populist movement, bred by a collapse in the farm economy and the rise of the Robber Barons, fought for popular control over the nation's financial system and broader economy.[34] Populism of that era could be seen as an anti-extinction movement waged by farmers to save the agrarian economy and US democracy. While the populists didn't succeed, it led to progressive movements culminating in the 20th century in the New Deal, which had its own elements of an anti-extinction movement.

In the Great Depression of the 1930s, the US economy collapsed and a long-term unraveling of the American experiment seemed possible. This can be seen as a type of national extinction threat – and FDR saw his New Deal as essential to saving the nation from collapse. His New Deal progressives, allying with a new fiery labor movement, advocates for the homeless and hungry and for old people without social security, including outright socialists and Communists, came together to stop the extinction threat of that era and ultimately succeeded in helping the nation survive. The New Deal showed that the abolitionists' emancipatory struggle had an enduring legacy, passed down from the abolitionists themselves to the 19th-century populists and then the early progressives and New Dealers of the 20th century.

The activist movements of the 1960s can be seen as another stage where the emancipatory torch of the abolitionists was seized by a new generation. The perpetuation of Jim Crow threatened to tear the nation apart, and the civil rights movement took up the abolitionist struggle to unite the nation again by abolishing segregation and creating a new America based on principles of racial equality. Likewise, in the shadow of the Cold War that threatened nuclear extinction, activists against the war in Vietnam challenged the morality of US militarism in the name of anti-Communism and tried to stop an unjust war while preserving the world from blowing itself up. Martin Luther King picked up the torch of abolitionism when he linked civil rights with struggles for peace and social justice, calling for a transformation in the ruling capitalist system as essential to racial justice and survival in the nuclear age. In fact, King equated the evils of capitalism with those of racism and militarism in his famous "Three Evils" speech, adding that,

> Capitalism was built on the exploitation and suffering of black slaves and continues to thrive on the exploitation of the poor – both black and white, both here and abroad.[35]

King became the most important leader of 20th-century anti-extinction struggles that called for visionary transformation of US race relations, war, and capitalism. King's legacy is being re-awakened through the rise of the massive anti-racist protests focusing not only on deaths caused by police brutality but on "systemic racism." Black Lives Matter (BLM), now supported by millions of whites as well as Blacks and other communities of color, is increasingly seeing and protesting the intertwined crises of racism, militarism, environmental destruction, and capitalism. COVID-19 helps expose the deadly deficits of public health and other public goods that are integral to US capitalism and threaten survival in the age of COVID-19 and climate change.

Today we face a new moral crisis of the ruling system and corporate elites of our era, which has created 21st-century full-blown threat of extinction. But while the system proclaims itself as the bastion of morality and liberty – something also claimed by the early Southern planter class – we have now a political and economic system hurtling toward the possibility of total human extinction, cloaked in a moralism of prosperity and freedom by our ruling corporate and capitalist system. Just as the abolitionists of the past united peoples and movements in a universal moral cause against the "morality" of slavery and the plantation system it served, so today, we need to embrace a new abolitionism that challenges the enslavement of our societies and most people in the world to corporate power and markets whose blindness and greed now lead inevitably toward climate or nuclear extinction.

The moral crisis of extinction, as of slavery, cannot be challenged and overturned without attacking the centers of power in the economy and state. While drawing on the history of the abolitionist movement and later movements to help inspire a movement to make the impossible possible, we need to recognize the limitations of all prior historical movements. No historical movement has ever had to confront today's totalistic threat of extinction of all life, since that threat has never existed before.

But history may still be our best guide, since there are earlier dire threats which movements have sought to meet. Movements that confronted enormous moral challenges – such as abolitionism – had to mobilize systemic change and offer solutions to intertwined crises of capitalism, environment, pandemics, and war. We hope to show that 21st-century abolitionism is already emerging and may yet unlock the secret to human survival.

Part I

The Hidden System
of Extinction

1 The Extinction Triangle

Capitalism, Environmental
Destruction, and Militarism

Human extinction is now a very real possibility with underlying causes rooted in the deepest systems of our society. However, while parts of the extinction crisis are in clear view, most people around the world have not put together a clear map of the "extinction system," which has been denied or obscured by many of the world's most powerful people and institutions, particularly in the United States.

In this chapter, we discuss the hidden triangle, a causal chain showing how the looming prospect of extinction is driven by three major intertwined threats to all life. The triangle is a global system, and imperils life across the entire world, with national triangles also existing in each country. It is largely invisible in most nations, and especially in the United States, a matter of overwhelming importance since the United States is the dominant global power and creates the most toxic triangle. Saving humanity, saving ourselves, cannot happen without exposing the triangle and overcoming it – in the United States and the entire world.

As discussed in the Introduction, we are not defining existential threats and extinction as only those leading to the total destruction of all humanity and life on the planet. Following Bostrom's analysis, we look at a range of catastrophic threats which, in Bostrom's definition, "would either annihilate earth-originating intelligent life or permanently and drastically curtail its potential."[1] The "bang" form involves sudden total destruction of all life, but the "crunch, shriek and whimper" threats are more prolonged and varied, allowing some survival but restricting life and human development to the point that they can be seen as a "softer" form of extinction.

The idea of a global extinction triangle linking capitalism, environmental destruction (including climate change, pandemics, and biodiversity collapse), and militarism (especially nuclear war) will be viewed in many nations, and especially the United States, as itself madness. It is so taboo that most analysts of climate crisis, pandemics such as COVID-19, and nuclear war – and indeed much of the climate and peace movements – avoid the subject of the capitalist system and the need for systemic transformation like the plague.

DOI: 10.4324/9781003401483-3

To take just climate, the notion that the capitalist system drives climate change is highlighted by only a few leading analysts, mainly on the Left. One is Naomi Klein, who argues that extinction arises from "the collision between capitalism and the planet" and that:

> We have not done the things that are necessary to lower emissions because those things fundamentally conflict with deregulated capitalism, the reigning ideology for the entire period we have been struggling to find a way out of this crisis. We are stuck because the actions that would give us the best chance of averting catastrophe – and would benefit the vast majority – are extremely threatening to an elite minority that has a stranglehold over our economy, our political process, and most of our major media outlets.[2]

Klein acknowledges that "autocratic industrial socialism" can also cause climate change, but argues that the ruling capitalist model is the major risk and we need to pursue a democratic "eco-socialism" to save the planet.

Joining Klein in the laser-like but lonely focus on the capitalist DNA driving extinction is the journalist, George Monbiot. He writes that:

> Ecologically, economically and politically, capitalism is failing as catastrophically as communism failed. Like state communism, it is beset by unacknowledged but fatal contradictions. It is inherently corrupt and corrupting. But its mesmerising power, and the vast infrastructure of thought that seeks to justify it, makes any challenge to the model almost impossible to contemplate. Even to acknowledge the emergencies it causes, let alone to act on them, feels like electoral suicide. As the famous saying goes: "It is easier to imagine the end of the world than to imagine the end of capitalism." Our urgent task is to turn this the other way round.[3]

Monbiot is not joking when he says our most important task is to "turn this the other way round." While this sounds daunting, imagining systemic change in the global capitalist economy has become essential to human survival. In a period when there is a new awakening about "systemic racism," we need now to expand our consciousness about our economy, recognizing that we are now living in a new stage of "extinction capitalism." Only systemic change in our political economy can save us.

Klein is Canadian and Monbiot is British. These are both societies where it has long been possible to offer critiques of capitalism without sounding like a crackpot. Both Britain and Canada have labor or socialist parties, and mainstreamed the idea that large parts of the society should be separated from profit-making and organized for the provision of public goods. These societies are less complicit than the United States in climate and military policies fueling extinction.

In the United States, mainstream socialist political parties do not exist, and "big government" and universal welfare programs are seen as enemies of liberty, with the exception of an enormous military. Klein and Monbiot have an audience in the United States, but their views that to survive means moving beyond capitalism and especially neoliberalism capitalism runs into huge hurdles, especially in American political discourse, even among liberals. However, we shall see that it is not an impossible dream, and that even a President as moderate as Joe Biden, pushed by people of color, young people, and social movements, has begun to break with neoliberalism and shift toward a public goods economy that could help save the planet.

Crossing the Threshold: Humanity Confronts Its Final Stage

Beginning in the mid-1940s, when the United States attacked Japan with nuclear weapons, we saw the emergence of the first period in human history – now known as the Anthropocene – in which capitalism began to threaten both nuclear and climate extinction. As Noam Chomsky writes:

> Review of the record reveals clearly that escape from catastrophe for seventy years has been a near miracle and such miracles cannot be trusted to perpetuate.
>
> On that grim day in August 1945, humanity entered into a new era, the nuclear age. It's one that's unlikely to last long, either we will bring it to an end or it's likely to bring us to an end. It was evident at once that any hope of containing the demon would require international corporation ....
>
> It was not understood at the time but a second and no less critical new era was beginning at the same time. A new geological epoch, by now, called the Anthropocene–an epoch defined by extreme human impact on the environment.
>
> The Anthropocene and the nuclear age coincide, a dual threat to the perpetuation of organized human life. Both threats are severe and imminent. It's widely recognized that we have entered the period of the sixth mass extinction.[4]

Extinction denialism has limited public awareness of the new stage that arose in the late 1940s but is rooted in the foundations of our economic system. Indeed, capitalism, even as it historically helped build new economic growth and innovation and pulled millions out of poverty, has always created war and environmental destruction. Its historical progress fueled "development" that catapulted the European and American world toward prosperity and material well-being for two centuries. But that huge leap forward also froze into society an unsustainable quest for unfettered growth threatening military and environmental catastrophe and externalized multiple costs onto the peoples of the Global South. The history of capitalist successes disguised latent crises now surfacing in the extinction stage. The historical benefits of capitalism have not disappeared, but their relative value has declined compared to the costs and risks – ultimately of extinction.

The Triangle of Extinction: Mad Money

To save humanity and all life on the planet, we need to understand the new extinction stage as rooted in a causal triangle of three intertwined threats. The only way that humanity will survive is if the world – including all states, peoples, and social movements – come together to dismantle the triangle and create a new circle of sustainable life systems.

Capitalism drives the triangle of extinction. Its very nature, as a system, foments militarism and drives environmental destruction. In Chapter 2, we argue that capitalism's constant need to expand both its resource base and its markets fosters a militarism to pry open markets and "protect" investments. Territorial expansion across national borders has a corollary in the capitalist dynamic to test and break ecological thresholds, producing the third corner of the triangle, environmental destruction.

However, these two corners – militarism and environmental destruction also feed back into, affect, and reinforce the logic of capitalism. Both create the disasters that leave communities and states turning to capitalists for solutions. The soil fertility depletion, for example, that capitalist agriculture produces, leaves us all more dependent on the petrochemical and agro-industrial corporations selling fertilizers and pesticides. Similarly, capitalism's inherent instability, particularly in the American case, produces a "military Keynesianism," using state spending to increase production and profits of military companies. This, in turn, compromises democracy, giving weapons contractors privileged access to the state, rendering the latter dependent on the "market" fortunes of these corporations (Figure 1.1).

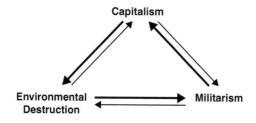

Figure 1.1 The Triangle of Extinction, Basic Version

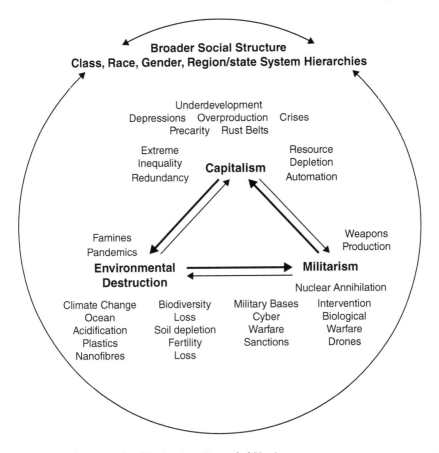

Figure 1.2 The Triangle of Extinction, Expanded Version

As we contemplate this triangle, we must recognize that its dynamics play out in social and historical structures that are profoundly intersectional, ones characterized at the global, regional, and national levels by evolving hierarchies including those of race, gender, class, and states. A more complete picture of the triangle therefore looks like this (Figure 1.2).

This second diagram spells out the variety of forms of environmental destruction and militarism that create existential and extinction threats, whether they be, in Bostrom's terms, forms of bang, crunch, shriek, or whimper risks. In both pictures, we are adhering to the idea that existential threats – and extinction itself – should not be defined exclusively as total annihilation.

The second picture shows that there are several major existential risks; among the risks in the environmental destruction corner are three well-known ones, climate change, pandemics, and biodiversity loss. But these interact with the others listed, as well as with the many other risks that are less well known. Similarly, militarism produces nuclear, biological/chemical, and cyberwar risks. All of these six varieties of existential risk are extremely important, and all are "systemic" in that they are partly caused and fueled by the United States and global capitalist system. All deserve urgent study leading to emergency transformative change because each of them could create devastating mass death from which humanity might not be able to recover. In addition to these six existential risks, the clusters around each corner of the second diagram also name other risks that may escalate into either existential risks or radically reduce the quality of life and pose civilizational risks.

In this book, mainly to keep the book shorter, we do not analyze biodiversity collapse, cyber war, or biological war, focusing instead on nuclear war, climate change, and pandemics. If we were to write a second volume, we would analyze with the same sense of urgency the other three incredibly dangerous threats; they are growing and increasingly intertwined with the threats we focus on here.

The arrows in the diagrams reflect causation. Capitalism itself creates a threat of extinction, independent of environmental death and war. But it also causes and fuels the environmental threats of climate change, pandemics, and loss of biodiversity, which multiply the extinction threat. And capitalism, especially the militarized hegemonic form modeled by US neoliberal capitalism, causes war, which further multiplies the extinction threat embedded in the possibility of nuclear war. Climate change, pandemics, and extreme war could arise from other systems than capitalism, but capitalism is a leading cause and accelerator of all these threats, which in turn intensify the extinction dangers of each other. Climate change is a major driver of war and war has become a leading cause of climate change. Scholarship on climate change and broader environmental matters typically recognize several major tipping points and environmental thresholds beyond which abrupt and catastrophic outcomes are to be expected. While we do explore these in depth, we consider these important aspects of the three corners of the triangle of extinction.[5]

The causal chains of capitalism here are not the only causes; religion, nationalism, racism, sexism, population growth, and technological change, among other factors, contribute to extinction as well. Race and racism play an especially important role – since the initial violence and death of the extinction system target people of color most powerfully. Much of the entire system is legitimated as a defense against non-white races who are portrayed to be threats to the nation in the West especially by right-wing authoritarian and neo-fascist movements.

The triangle of extinction is new but it grows out a long history of capitalism, which laid the foundations over several centuries of unfettered global growth and profit-seeking. It is easy to say that it is simply technological inventions – such as the creation of the nuclear bomb – that defines the new stage of extinction. But such technological determinism, while attractive in United

States and other capitalist nations, is far from a complete story. It neglects the historical choices and structural forces that led most recently to the neoliberal capitalist model in the United States that has made extinction a truly central systemic feature of both the United States and the global capitalist system it presides over.

The extinction stage – and the triangle of extinction that shows its intertwined perils – is wrapped up not only with all kinds of technological innovations, but also with a huge complex of economic, social, and cultural historical choices foreshadowing and entrenching the path toward unsustainable growth, climate change, global pandemics, and genocidal war. Technological determinism is a way of diverting attention from the dominant economic and political structures creating and ruling the extinction stage. Elites are eager to focus on technology as both the cause and the solution to our current predicaments, and many environmental theorists embracing the "environmental modernization theory," argue that new technologies will themselves liberate the world from dangers of extinction.[6] Similarly, many focus exclusively on eliminating nuclear weapons without looking at the same time as the need to eliminate the militarized state which can always rebuild nuclear weapons, the technological delusion we called earlier "weaponitis."[7] But those looking to sustain survival of humans and all life on the planet have to take a systemic perspective, focusing on the power structures and elites that benefit the most from the current extinction stage, even though it will ultimately kill them along with everyone else.

Caveats on Capitalism and Extinction

First, the emergence of capitalism as a global extinction system is, ironically, a measure of some of its historic successes. Capitalism is not the only economic system causing climate change or war, as we have already highlighted, but it has emerged as the most powerful driver of these threats. This reflects in part its rise as the dominant global economic system of the 20th and 21st centuries, a reflection in turn of its superior capacity to create productivity, growth, and technological innovation. These "virtues" not only had real positive effects on economic growth but also had shadow sides that evolved into existential threats themselves, even beyond their contributions to climate change and extreme war.

Second, market forces within capitalism, including its neoliberal system, can help begin to move energy production toward renewable energies. The price of oil was falling, even before COVID-19 reduced demand for carbon-driven transportation and products, and the costs of coal are rising sharply in relation to falling prices of wind and solar. Capitalist proponents argue that the market itself is driving Big Oil and Gas toward producing more green energy, the ultimate solution to climate change. But while these market factors are real and should be recognized as highly important, they do not create the scope and speed of change needed to prevent climate catastrophe. The oil and gas companies have too much profit "sunk" into the carbon infrastructure and the oil reserves they enjoy to jettison their short-term but vast returns; they will advertise themselves as "going green," even as they commit themselves to getting as much profit out of dirty carbon energy as possible before shifting to a sustainable energy system. In the short to medium term, while the corporations begin to shift toward major new green technologies such as electric cars, they will block the systemic change we need, pushing us in the name of green capitalism toward climate extinction.

Third, had capitalism not arisen, it is entirely possible that the extinction stage would have arisen from the development models of other industrializing models, including potentially authoritarian forms of socialism or communism. As capitalism flourished, it absorbed or subordinated nearly all other systems into the larger global capitalist order, making societies like China and Russia integrate with global capitalist markets that they could not control and had ideologically repudiated at various historical stages. But even had they not been exposed to capitalism, they could have fueled climate and nuclear extinction, probably over a longer period given their different values, growth capacities, and technological innovation rates. However, the extent to which many of the worst features of those societies arose out of a desire to catch-up or compete with capitalist and imperialist levels of consumption should not be underestimated.

The Intersectionality of Extinction

The triangle reflects an "intersectional" perspective of social and political analysis. Intersectional theorists and activists see that systems of power are organically intertwined. Economic systems are wound like strands of DNA around systems of military power and energy and environmental systems.

The triangle highlights the crucial interconnections between capitalism, environmental destruction, and militarism. Each point in the triangle can be analyzed separately, and each gives rise to extinction in ways that can be analyzed and fought solely on their own terms. This kind of analytical separation of the deep crises of capitalism, climate change, and extreme war has generally been embraced by theorists and activists alike who cannot imagine the end of capitalism or a viable alternative.

The triangle seeks to show that the extinction perils arise out of an interconnected set of systemic threats with deeply embedded roots in the ruling economic and political system. And it tries to show how the rise of each extinction peril is fueled by the other extinction crises in the triangle, and that they function together to create the most dangerous stage of history that humanity has ever experienced.

This means that social movements and political struggles to change society must themselves be intersectional.[8] There can be no effective movement to stop climate change without a laser-focused agenda on transforming our economic system and ending militarism. Likewise, there can be no successful peace movement that does not seek to end climate change and transform capitalism.

Forestalling and thwarting extinction requires, in other words, a universalizing resistance.[9] To universalize is to see the interconnection of major power structures, and to recognize the strength of power regimes is their intertwined roots, with the interconnections often invisible or hidden. In earlier work, we have argued that the weakness and failures of many progressive social change movements is their tendency to become "silo" movements – struggles that target one hierarchy of power and do not connect with other movements that are struggling against intersectionally connected power systems. In the age of extinction, humanity will not survive without connecting and universalizing the struggles against every intertwined extinction threat pictured in the triangle.

In recognizing the threat to all of humanity and the need to overcome the "silo-ization" of our movements, we do not wish to downplay the reality that the extinction risks are unevenly distributed, affecting some communities earlier and more intensely than others. That said, the accelerating threats will invariably encompass us all and the old labor movement adage, that "an injury to one is an injury to all" will become less a moral imperative than a literal, self-evident truth.

2 Is Capitalism Too Hot?

Corporate Capital, Power, and Climate Change

United Nations Secretary General, Antonio Guterres, didn't mince words when he talked about the catastrophic acceleration of environmental destruction as a clear and imminent extinction threat:

> The world is waging war on nature. This is suicidal. Nature always strikes back – and it is already doing so with growing force and fury. Biodiversity is collapsing. One million species are at risk of extinction. Ecosystems are disappearing before our eyes ... Human activities are at the root of our descent toward chaos. But that means human action can help to solve it.[1]

Journalist and climate author, Roy Scranton, backed the Secretary General's fear with a small sample of devastating recent examples of the extinction peril:

> It's easy to forget that 2020 gave us not just the pandemic, but also the West Coast's worst fire season, as well as the most active Atlantic hurricane season on record. And, while we were otherwise distracted, 2020 also offered up near-record lows in Arctic sea ice, possible evidence of significant methane release from Arctic permafrost and the Arctic Ocean, huge wildfires in both the Amazon and the Arctic, shattered heat records (2020 rivaled 2016 for the hottest year on record), bleached coral reefs, the collapse of the last fully intact ice shelf in the Canadian Arctic, and increasing odds that the global climate system has passed the point where feedback dynamics take over and the window of possibility for preventing catastrophe closes.[2]

Journalists Sarah Kaplan and Andrew Ba Tran observed in 2022, "More than 4 in 10 Americans live in a county that was struck by climate-related extreme weather."[3] Millions of Americans were also living in neighborhoods and towns where carbon infrastructure was being further expanded. In Derber's own town of Dedham, Massachusetts – a small suburb of Boston – a huge

DOI: 10.4324/9781003401483-4

Texan oil and gas pipeline company called Spectra began in 2015 to lay a big pipeline through a densely populated part of the town, filled with multi-unit dwellings, single family homes, senior centers, and schools. Believe it or not, a critical juncture of the pipeline was built at a Dedham quarry, where stone was being dynamited and the explosions could break parts of the pipe and create deadly methane leaks that could explode and kill or sicken hundreds of people.

A local movement of Dedhamites, most of whom had never been protesters or politically active, spontaneously began to talk and organize as they saw their streets dug up to put in these big pipelines. Stories circulated about health hazards from gas leaks in other communities, as well as about decline in property values. As people realized much of the gas was not for Dedham, or even Boston, but simply en route to markets in Europe, more residents wondered why their own community should be put at risk.

Local Dedhamites began protests against the pipeline, that brought some national attention when one of the town selectmen, a prominent small business man, personally stood in the way of the Caterpillar huge excavator digging up one of the town's major roads for the pipeline. He looked like the single protester standing against the tank in the famous Tiananmen Square crisis in China. As more communities faced similar crises around the country and looked at Dedham, with the Selectmen "facing the machine," the Dedham protests grew bigger and noisier.

But most interesting was the evolution of the consciousness and agenda of the protesters. They had started simply wanting to protect their kids' health and the property values of their homes. Most were not climate activists and had not thought much about extinction, let alone about the capitalist triangle that made human destruction a systemic nightmare.

But as they tried to stop the digging of the roads and even climbed into the trenches being built before pipe could be laid, a process of education took place. They came to realize that natural gas was not the clean renewable solution to the health problems they faced in Dedham or faced by a warming world. Moreover, when they tried to get government involvement to stop the pipeline, they came to realize that the decisions about pipelines in America rested in a small agency called FERC – the Federal Energy Regulatory Commission – that was controlled largely by the biggest US oil and gas and other fossil fuel energy companies. This was obviously a bit like the fox guarding the henhouse. Dedhamites learned that FERC would pay little heed to most communities seeking to stop dangerous pipelines being built.

The Dedhamites were suddenly forced to deal with power wielded by huge oil and gas pipeline corporations, with enormous political influence. No matter what they did, FERC seemed oblivious, dedicated rather to the interests of the giant fossil fuel and pipeline companies such as Spectra. The opponents of the pipeline suddenly began talking about the power of huge corporations – and how this power seemed to radiate through the agencies of the government and the energy system of the nation. And it also became obvious that profits were driving these companies, which didn't care at all about the health of the kids or old people in Dedham, or the dangers of the quarry explosions that could ignite leaking methane gas.

It didn't take a PhD to realize that money and profit trumped everything else. Dedham residents began not just to think about climate change, but some saw it in a broader economic picture. They were being impaled by the corners of the extinction triangle – and they were smart enough to realize the edges of this triangle were impaling them and Dedham. Posters of big greedy blood-sucking corporations began to pop up in the protests.

Dedham was just beginning to experience the same awakening as protesters fighting against the huge XL pipeline seeking to stop the flow of dirty slurry tar sands oil down new pipelines from Canada to Texas. Native Americans protesting these pipelines were joined by ranchers and veterans who had begun to think about climate change, extinction and big capitalist companies. The extinction of Native Americans seemed to be reappearing in the appetites for more Western land and water being swallowed up by some of the biggest and most profitable companies – timber, mining, gas, and other extractive firms – in the capitalist system.

But even as these new activists begin to see the faint outlines of the triangle of extinction, the shape of the triangle – and how capitalism causes climate change – is rarely discussed because of two forms of denialism. One is climate denialism, which is perpetrated most strongly by the Republican Party and exists among about 30% to 40% of the US population. The second is the failure of mainstream analysts and the media to discuss the capitalist system and possible systemic alternatives.

Both types of denialism are madness. They have contributed mightily to the US failure to bring the extinction crisis of climate change – almost certainly the greatest crisis in history – into a national emergency requiring our most urgent and highest policy priorities.

Even Americans who recognize the reality of climate change generally fail to see how capitalism is a central cause and needs to be transformed to prevent extinction. Even many climate activists and organizations fight climate change without seeking to deeply reform and then move beyond the US capitalist model, thus dooming their own aims.

Before analyzing how climate change is built into the DNA of the capitalist system, we need to reiterate a few key points. First, capitalism, whether the ruling US model or other varieties, is far from the only economic system that produces climate change and drives the world toward extinction. Russia and China produce vast amounts of carbon emissions. Middle East dictatorships and monarchies, such as Saudi Arabia, Iraq and Iran, produce much of the world's oil. Let us be clear: saving humanity will require massive transformations not just in capitalism but in almost all non-capitalist systems too.

We focus on capitalism in this book because, in one form or another, it has emerged as the dominant economic system in the world. Countries called communist, such as China, are actually mixed systems melding capitalist markets with autocratic state control; the same can be said of many other non-Western nations that are often not seen as capitalist but have embraced forms of capitalist markets and are deeply integrated into the world economy. As capitalism has globalized, there are few areas of the world, including China and Russia, which are not capitalist in some form or heavily influenced by powerful global capitalist companies and markets, and ones increasingly shaped by the United States.

The same is true in thinking about varieties of Western European capitalist models other than the United States. These offer reasons for hope, and a shift toward European capitalist or social democratic systems will slow the race toward extinction. But these nations are also heavily shaped by US influence, and are themselves integrated into and constrained by the global neo-liberal economic system dominated by the United States. Moreover, even if cut free from US influence, they retain elements of capitalism which must be transformed if we are to save humanity.

It is also key to recognize that reforming capitalism can help mitigate climate change. In the last section of this chapter, we look at capitalists who believe capitalism is going to solve the climate crisis. We show that capitalism is making reforms that are crucial to use as we rush toward our last chance at sustainability. But we also show that a truly sustainable "green capitalism" is an oxymoron – and simply cannot deliver the change that will save humanity.

The History Everyone Must Learn: How Capitalism Turned Development into an Extermination Agenda

Capitalism's long and many successes came at a heavy price. Capitalism has a history that is not in our high school history books but is ultimately the history of potential extinction. As capitalists built the modern world, on the backs of others, they produced a vision of "development" and laid down a fossil-fuel infrastructure that is a leading source of our current extinction crisis. Capitalists – and indeed all of us – are deeply tied to this infrastructure. Reversing the fateful investment priorities and infrastructure system capitalism has delivered over the last two centuries is essential to saving humanity – it's a history we can't afford to ignore any longer.

The rise of capitalism is so historically intertwined with the building of a fossil fuel infrastructure that it is hard to distinguish them. The intersection is so tight that is has led to books such as *Fossil Capital*, an important work by the environmental and economic historian Andreas Malm.[4] The title captures the theme of much of the historical literature documenting the long capitalist-climate death dance now threatening to extinguish all life.

Following an extended period of globalizing European power through slavery, land invasions, forced trade, and colonization, modern capitalism got its main start in Great Britain in the late 18th and early 19th centuries. In that period, British industrial and financial tycoons massively invested in coal to power the machines producing cotton textiles, the first major Western capitalist industry.[5] A century later, as the coal regime ran into labor and other socio-political problems, US capitalists turned to oil. So, while energy sources have historically changed within capitalism, a hopeful sign that some change is possible, even within capitalism, the dominant form has always been fossil-fuel.

In what follows, we describe the major energy transitions over capitalism's history in the British and American national contexts. After the move from human- and animal-power to water-powered mills in capitalism's earliest days, the pivotal transitions are the fossil fuel-driven ones: from water to steam and coal in the late 1700s to early 1800s, and then from coal to oil power in the late 1800s and well into the 1900s. The 20th century's two world wars radically accelerated the shift to oil. The much anticipated third transition, away from fossil fuels to renewable energy sources, is currently underway but it remains inadequate in scale and pace, a fact that we address in the final chapter.

The early British capitalist turn to coal makes clear that it was socio-economic and political factors that drove decisions about energy. The turn to coal did not reflect any definitive technological superiority of coal. In the late 18th century, as the British textile industry began, there were water-powered systems that were efficient and technologically on a par with coal-fueled machines.

In the early 18th century, as Malm shows, a British mill-owner named Robert Thom developed a hydraulic system of natural water flows that showed great technical promise and did not require the coal-fueled steam engine. The water was free and Thom's system demonstrated enough technical efficiency that the British Parliament looked into subsidizing water power on a broad regional basis, even as coal was already in early use. Imagine if they had made that choice, setting up an earlier industrial capitalism on a renewable energy system rather than fossil fuel.

But the mill-owners turned against this, as they feared they might lose control over water to the public. They also had fears about the system's workers. Thom's water system involved setting up mills in the country-side near natural water reservoirs, and drew on rural workers who would be housed in close-knit textile communities. Mill-owners worried that the rural workers lacked industrial discipline and that their close living quarters could lead to labor struggles that would reduce profits. That was a deal-breaker.

Meanwhile, the significant waves of enclosures of the commons (that is, the capitalist private taking of land held and used in common by ordinary villagers) in the mid-1750s — one of the earliest and important destruction of public goods brought on by capitalism — threw a huge number of people off the land and drove them into the cities. These "refugees" became desperate urban workers who were poor enough that they were ready to go into mining and work for low pay in dangerous conditions, exactly the kind of labor force that early capitalists were looking for.

By the mid-18th century, the use of coal as the main energy source had increased exponentially, along with the amount of carbon emissions. But in the latter third of the 19th century, deep problems in the coal regime began to emerge and capitalism itself began a great shift toward oil, an enormous change but one that left the marriage of capitalism and fossil fuels intact.

The emerging crisis in coal was heavily related to worker resistance. As early as 1842, an explosion of labor unrest in Britain known as the Plug Plot riots, rattled British industrialists. Coal workers pulled plugs out of coal-fired steam engines to allow water to escape, threatening production. They also moved into larger political action, joining with the pro-democracy Chartist movement to expand the franchise and the voting rights of the working public; later, they helped shape the modern union movement. This got the attention of the captains of industry, who always look to ways of keeping workers docile and loyal.[6]

By the late 19th century, several factors fueled a seismic shift to the new oil regime led by American capitalists. The most famous figure, oil titan John D. Rockefeller, was America's first billionaire and the iconic Robber Baron founder of a modern US capitalism that began to challenge the global capitalist hegemony of Britain. The rise of Rockefeller's Standard Oil highlighted the new US-dominated, petro-chemical global capitalist model that continues to this day and is at the root of climate change. Four historical factors stand out:

Looking first at transportation, the shift toward oil is historically linked to the rise of the automobile and trucks in the domestic economy – and of ships and tanks in Western militaries. Capitalism depends on profitable civilian and military transportation systems to get resources and deliver goods to markets. At the height of the coal regime of the mid-19th century, capitalism was turning, especially in the United States, to an intercontinental system of railroads that could unite markets across the entire country. Rockefeller bought up much of the US railway system in the late 19th century to control the competition, manage oil prices, and generate greater profitability. As Rockefeller's giant oil companies merged with Morgan banks as well as railroad and steel barons, and also bought coal companies, king coal was conquered by Rockefeller oil.

Coal did not die, and a variety of non-oil-based transport systems competed with oil well into the 20th century. Not only did coal and electricity keep trains running, but many late 19th-century and early 20th-century autos were powered either by electricity or by coal-fueled steam engines rather than internal combustion gas engines. The US orientation toward private rather than public goods led auto companies to use the state to help them eliminate public electric transport systems and to destroy their own early models of electric cars. In the 1920s, GM bought the electric public trolley system in Los Angeles and turned what could have been a green LA into a smog-filled model of urban climate disaster.

Returning to the coal regime, mass production of autos turned the United States into a mass private transport climate disaster in a crucial transition stage of the late 19th century. In the 1890s, the Stanley Brothers Steam Motor Company in the United States produced profitable steam engine cars powered by coal for affluent niche markets attracted by their high-quality artisanal production. But the virtues of a "craft" car – which might have reduced the enormous volume of cars and thus might have reduced the environmental cost of transportation despite reliance on coal – could not compete against the economies of the mass-produced, cheap, internal combustion car being developed by Henry Ford and others in Detroit.[7]

The fateful shift to oil and cars happened despite significant problems faced by oil producers. Unlike coal producers, oil companies had to refine their product – crude oil – in costly facilities requiring extensive research and development. They also had to expand their markets for new goods that used the enormous byproducts and waste of the refining process. Their international operations also expanded to secure plentiful reserves when domestic fields were depleted or when foreign firms might compete more efficiently with oil derived from the Gulf and Middle East or other geographic sources of incredibly abundant and easy-to-access fuel.

The turn to oil ultimately reflected the consolidation of power by the largest oil companies and their ability to get leading Western states to back oil, to ensure mass production of cars and other convenient consumer goods that legitimate capitalism itself as a prosperous wonderland for ordinary people as well as to ensure military victories securing global power and profits. The US government backed the oil shift most strongly – using tax breaks, subsidies, and other investments in highways and other carbon-friendly infrastructure – since the US system so fervently supported private profits while ignoring public costs and eroding the very concept of the public good. In European countries, where rising social democratic movements yielded a capitalism that was friendlier to public goods, much more investment poured into public transit and other environmentally friendly infrastructure. But because profit still was a major driver of European systems, European governments also invested in highways and other carbon infrastructure and oil technology. In addition, much of the government support – both in Europe as well as the United States – that locked in the shift to new oil regime had to do with military concerns and the desperate drive to win wars that dominated the first half of the 20th century.

Wars and the Turn to Oil

The importance of the military and wars in the shift to the oil regime is hard to over-estimate, one of the many early manifestations of the connection between militarism and climate change in the triangle of extinction. World

War I, taking place at a pivotal point in the transition from coal to oil, was a decisive event, as energy historian Bruce Podobnik observes:

> At first, oil-burning vehicles played only a limited role in military campaigns. As the war dragged on, though, military strategies turned to tanks and airplanes in efforts to break through the stalemate on the western front. Meanwhile, diesel-powered destroyers and submarines engaged in new forms of naval combat on the high seas. The result was a massive increase in the production of oil-burning vehicles, ships and airplanes.[8]

As British leader Lord Curzon famously observed, "The Allies floated to victory on an oil wave." And climate disaster is thus partly driven by the conclusion of capitalist Great Powers after the war that their system could survive and prosper only by building a massive oil infrastructure. But even before World War I, the perceived military benefits of oil in 20th-century colonial wars catalyzed a massive investment in an oil regime. As environmental and military historian, David Painter, argues:

> Oil became an important element in military power in the decade before World War I when the navies of the great powers, led by Great Britain and the United States, began to switch from coal to oil as their source of power. In addition, the major military innovations of World War I – the submarine, the airplane, the tank, and motorized transport – were all oil-powered.[9]

World War I propelled the most massive investment in carbon infrastructure ever seen. But this was just the beginning. The great capitalist powers doubled down on oil investment as civilization veered toward World War II, a war largely, as Podobnik argues, "determined by the oil resources that each coalition had at its disposal."[10] And after the war, global capitalism locked itself ever more deeply into an oil and gas infrastructure that set the stage for our current climate emergency. After World War I, the West, and especially the United States, committed to a militarized foreign policy to secure its political influence and rights to extract oil in the newly discovered oil wealth of the Middle East and the Gulf. After World War II, led by the United States, militarized global capitalism unleashed regime change wars to bring oil to the greatest capitalist powers and tie global capitalist profits to carbon-based commodities underlying our current extinction stage.

Commodification and Oil

Underpinning all this was the capitalist imperative to turn everything into a commodity – that is, as economist Bob Kuttner has put it, to make "everything for sale." The historian of capitalism, Harry Braverman, has shown how one of the great hurdles that capitalist had to overcome was the long human history of producing the necessities of life in their own gardens, work-shops, and communities rather than buying them on the market. As recently as the late 19th century, even New Yorkers in Manhattan tended common plots in the city to grow their own food. Likewise, they sewed most of their own clothes and constructed their own furniture.[11]

Capitalism required that people learn a whole new lifestyle, in which they bought what they needed and desired rather than producing for themselves. The culture of commodities had to take over, since capitalists make profit only by turning all sectors of life and subsistence into markets where consumers buy and keep buying. If social and economic exchange or provision remains outside the market, capitalism's first imperative is to colonize them within the market system.[12]

Western capitalism embarked full-scale on this social and cultural revolution in the late 19th and early 20th centuries, precisely in the historical era when the coal regime triumphed and then began to succumb to the new king: oil. Its conquest of king coal was closely tied to its development as a generalized commodity fuel. The big oil companies tied themselves not only to cars and the big auto companies but to new petro-chemical agricultural firms and major other corporate sectors, whether textiles and clothing, chemical and medical, or construction and homebuilding. The oil magnates' commercial strategies as well as the utility of oil itself in producing a huge range of petro-based commodities helped cement the shift to oil, locking in a "fossil capitalism" headed toward climate disaster.

By the 1920s, right after World War I, capitalists themselves, clearly recognized the virtues of oil as a master sword to help them conquer society and integrate autonomous or self-providing people into the market. As discussed by sociologist Stuart Ewen, in books like *Captains of Consciousness* and *Channels of Desire*, they began a full-scale campaign to make everything for sale.[13] In the postwar 1920s, when people from the victorious capitalist countries of the United States, the United Kingdom, and France wanted to enjoy life and celebrate, capitalists introduced the first major retail sales catalogues, such as the famous Sears catalogues, looking to create a new world of consumers who would lust after glamorized commodities. They would start purchasing their clothes and food, while learning to buy new commodities like toys or toothpaste or tables. The new industry of advertising and PR became capitalism's arch weapon of commodification gluing the population to an oil-based glut of goodies to buy and a future nightmare of climate change.

"Fossil capitalism" thus spread from cars and transportation to a complete commodification of life. Capitalists shifted to oil because it helped produce a super-profitable world of sellable goods in peace time after proving itself as essential to war victories. Oil had become central to military transport and then proved equally profitable in civilian transportation; after World War I, there was a similar evolution from oil-based military production to civilian economies. As historian David Painter observes about the entrenchment of oil in peacetime after World War I:

> Cheap and plentiful supplies of oil were a prerequisite for the automobile industry, which played a central role in the U.S. economy from the 1920s to the 1960s. Oil became the fuel of choice in land and sea transport as well as the only fuel for air transport, and challenged coal as the main source of energy for industry. Oil also played an important, if somewhat less crucial, role in heating and electricity generation, but oil-powered machinery became crucial to modern agriculture, and oil became an important feedstock for fertilizers and pesticides. Indeed, with the development of the petrochemical industry, oil reached into almost every area of modern life. Already almost one-fifth of U.S. energy consumption by 1925, oil accounted for around one-third of U.S. energy use by World War II.[14]

The military – especially in the run-up and fighting of World War I – thus set the stage for fossil-fuel based universalized commercial and commodity capitalism in peace as well as war. As the political economist and energy historian Andres Barreda shows, the effects of the Great War and then the build-up and fighting of World War II were pervasive – and profoundly significant for the rise of climate change:

> If the development of the petroleum material civilization is viewed from distance, World War I and World War II can be considered to be a single war, with an intermediate span of barely twenty years in which the different national powers were engaged in hastily exploring what different military advantages could be obtained from the intensive use of oil as a basis, not only of energy, but also of myriad new materials…there was a vertiginous development of all types of military vehicles and their respective engines (such as new planes, tanks, trucks, cars, motorcycles, ships, submarines, and trains), new types of fuels, new geological prospecting, new oil refining methods, as well as new material engineering derived from the petrochemical industry, new mining prospects, new media outlets, and so on.[15]

Barreda also shows that the political system helped create and consolidate the new fossil fuel civil economy by requiring that the state, scientists and industries engage with and spread the military lessons. President Wilson, he observes,

> forced the chemistry departments of American universities to obligatorily participate in the military design of all types of poisons and chemical explosives. Under this program, the United States prepared the chemical bombardment of the main German cities…A re-use of military waste, presented as the modern way to control the fearful agricultural pests

generated by large-scale American monocultures and, in doing so, sup-
posedly enabling the "fight against hunger." Another example of this
new policy of obtaining materials derived from the militarization of oil
was the development in the 1920s and 1930s of a new molecular hy-
drocarbon engineering focused on the production of various polymers,
mainly plastics. A discovery that DuPont triggers with its production of
a new, very resistant synthetic fabric that was to allow the creation of
parachutes. We're talking about nylon.[16]

Put simply, the wars stimulated a revolution by both political and economic elites
that turned oil into the foundation of the world capitalist system, creating a permanent marriage between fossil fuels and a globally commodified world destined
for climate disaster. Barreda summarizes a fossil fuel capitalism serving simultaneously military conquest and a universally commodified civilian system:

> With this decisive historical turn, the new national states transmuted in
> the image and likeness of oil, which suddenly became the main reason
> for their existence...This ultimately and integrally redefined capitalist
> democracy, as it progressively subordinated the general interest of the
> State to the specific interest of companies aligned with the oil lobby...
>
> The emergence of these new petroleum-based instruments was organ-
> ized as a system of instruments dedicated to the control of the sky, the sea,
> and the earth, which allowed for capitalist expansion and control of all
> territories, as well as the growth and worldwide export process of private
> capital throughout the world. A global capital expansion that, from then
> on, not only revolved geopolitically and strategically around control of
> oil sources of the totality of the means of production and subsistence.[17]

Working-Class Resistance and the Turn to Oil

A final part of the historical story involves issues of labor and prevention of
mass labor resistance. Starting in the late 1800s, historian Tim Mitchell shows
that coal workers were becoming a militant model of precisely the kind of
working-class resistance that capitalism feared. As Mitchell says,

> Coal miners played a leading role in contesting work regimes and the
> private powers of employers in the labour activism and political mobilisa-
> tion of the 1880s and onward. Between 1881 and 1905, coal miners in the
> United States went on strike at a rate of about three times the average for
> workers in all major industries, and at double the rate of the next-highest
> industry, tobacco manufacturing."[18]

The rise of coal workers as leaders of militant union organizing intensified throughout most of the 20th century in all the major Western capitalist

societies. In the United States, John L. Lewis, who founded the CIO in the New Deal era of FDR and was the most influential labor leader in the United States in the first half of the 20th century, rose as the head of the coal miners' union. He was an antiwar progressive, favoring more militant unions, higher wages and social welfare benefits, and he symbolized the leadership of coal workers in the broad struggle for social justice and public goods.

During and after World War II, convulsions of labor unrest in the United States were especially widespread in the coal industry, exceeding similar waves of labor militancy after World War I. Major coal strikes in the United States occurred in 1941, 1943, 1945, and 1946. Coal worker organizing was not restricted to the United States after World War II, spreading in multiple major coal strikes in the 1940s in Great Britain, France, Western Germany, Canada, and Australia.[19] These shook capitalist confidence in king coal and helped energize the shift to oil, making clear that political power and class struggles shaped energy choices as much as technical efficiency.

The labor militancy of coal miners throughout the world proved significantly higher than oil workers – and workers in general. The World Labor Group Database shows that worker unrest in coal far exceeded that of oil workers for the 100 years from 1890 to 1990, the century when capitalists shifted from coal to oil. This reflected the danger of mining, the close and difficult working conditions facilitating organizing in mines, low coal wages and benefits, and the history of strikes and unionization building a militant coal worker culture that was not found among oil workers, who were more dispersed, less organized, and better paid.[20]

To seek maximum profits, capitalists seek a compliant labor force. Workers in the energy sector may play a particularly important role, since they can impact and even shut down much of the economy. The history of the pre-extinction stage is a story of structural forces tilting capitalism toward a permanent and dangerous dalliance with fossil fuels, leading to the full-fledged climate change emergency we now face.

Going All the Way: Capitalism and Climate Extinction

As we move beyond the pre-extinction historical stage into the modern full stage of extinction, even the bastions of capitalist media are beginning to acknowledge that capitalism is destroying the environment. In *Forbes* magazine, a leading media outlet, contributor Drew Hansen writes that

> Corporate capitalism is committed to the relentless pursuit of growth, even if it ravages the planet and threatens human health.
>
> We need to build a new system: one that will balance economic growth with sustainability and human flourishing.[21]

Moreover, Hansen acknowledges that it is the major capitalist corporations that have helped create and fund climate denialism – with oil giants like Exxon and

Chevron ultimately prosecuted for their decades of lying about their knowledge that oil fueled climate change and threatened survival:

> Yale sociologist Justin Farrell studied 20 years of corporate funding and found that "corporations have used their wealth to amplify contrarian views [of climate change] and create an impression of greater scientific uncertainty than actually exists."[22]

The *Forbes* piece (and remember this is the big business journal expressing corporate perspectives at the highest level) argues that solutions will require rethinking capitalist essentials and moving toward an economy based on "employee ownership." This involves a fundamental shift in capitalist ownership towards a model something like the famous Mondragon, Spain's cooperative model.

This trend hearkens back to cooperatives where employees collectively owned the enterprise and participated in management decisions through their voting rights. Mondragon is the oft-cited example of a successful, modern worker cooperative. Mondragon's broad-based employee ownership is not the same as an Employee Stock Ownership Plan. With ownership comes a say – control – over the business. Their workers elect management, and management is responsible to the employees.[23]

Workers are less likely to want to poison their communities. What Mondragon is telling us is that the most basic institutions and rules of capitalism – for example, the idea that investors or capitalists rather than workers should control the corporations – are precisely the forces that need to be changed today.

The Bottom Line: Why Capitalism Is Too Hot

1. Profit Maximization

Capitalism enshrines profit as the central aim of the economy and society. US capitalism creates the ruling global neo-liberal model that most deeply entrenches profit as the central aim of society and that most deeply sacrifices people and nature to profit-maximization. This is partly the result of America's deep embrace of Adam Smith's "invisible hand," the idea that pursuit of self-interest is the best way to advance the common good. Smith wrote that the individual who:

> intends only his own gain is led by an invisible hand to promote ... the public interest.

Conservative novelist Ayn Rand became a folk hero because her basic philosophy updated Smith for the 20th and 21st centuries. It beautifully dovetailed with the ruling neo-liberal systems, captured in a book title: "*The Virtue of Selfishness.*" Rand wrote that the most virtuous person, whom she calls an "individualist," is

> a man who lives for his own sake and by his own mind; he neither sacrifices himself to others nor sacrifices others to himself. He is a trader ....[24]

This is a way of speaking about a model of capitalist society in which the main role of government is to protect a kind of human rights embodying "the virtue of selfishness":

> The only proper, moral purpose of a government is to protect man's rights, which means: to protect him from physical violence – to protect his right to his own life, to his own liberty, to his own property and to the pursuit of his own happiness. Without property rights, no other rights are possible.[25]

Rand's model of the good capitalist society is one that protects the individual's right to private property and to his/her own "rational" profit interests. Period! No notion of a common good here. Unless capitalist societies balance individualism with the community and subordinate profit to the public good, human survival becomes terrifyingly unlikely.

Speaking of rights, capitalism, especially the dominant neoliberal US model, not only champions Ayn Rand's right to "selfishness" but commits to "negative" rather than positive rights. Negative rights are the right of the individual to be protected from government control or dictate; government mandates limiting the individual are a form of "tyranny" – even when they just involve requiring people in the COVID-19 crisis to wear masks to protect others. But European capitalism offers some notion of "positive" rights inscribed in the UN 1948 Declaration of Human Rights – the rights to food, shelter and a living wage. When you accept positive rights, you can have a system of public goods, since goods and services that serve positive rights must be produced by governments even if they are not profitable and are eschewed by corporations.

Averting climate change requires a transformation in human rights theory. In the age of extinction, the right to survival of the species becomes the pre-eminent human right. The very idea of rights attached to humanity as a collective runs counter to capitalism's individualism. In the age of climate change, there is little prospect of survival until the community gains the same moral standing as the individual and the positive rights of the community itself are as strong as individual rights.

2. Blind Markets

To achieve profit maximization, capitalist markets discount or "externalize" social and environmental costs and benefits. US corporate charters and laws require that corporate directors subordinate social and environmental costs,

since profit maximization is their prime fiduciary obligation, explicitly cod-
ified in US corporate charters. European corporations have different charters, which permit more focus on benefits to workers or the environment.
But all forms of capitalism tend to put profit over social and environmental goals, since capital will flow faster to profitable "low road" companies
than to "high road" companies reducing profit to protect workers or the
environment.

True, governments in capitalist societies across the world can partly "internalize" social and environment costs – and can regulate pollution. In Europe
and some developing nations, states mandate a strong focus on the environment, reducing the nation's carbon footprint.

At this writing, many global corporations are branding themselves as "socially responsible" companies – and claim to be responsive to demands of
workers, consumers and the public to protect the environment. Even in the
United States, the Business Roundtable, a powerful association of the largest
US corporations, endorsed in 2020 "stakeholder capitalism" as preferable to
the classic US shareholder one, focused only on return to investors. Business schools in the United States and other developed capitalist nations offer idealistic students programs in "managing for social and environmental
impact."

But even as business leaders and teachers embrace these social values at a rhe-
torical plane, they continue to prioritize profit and oppose the urgent and massive environmental regulation, taxation and massive public investment required
to limit climate change. While governments in capitalist societies everywhere
permit a measure of taxation, regulation and corporate social responsibility that
"internalizes" some environmental costs, these efforts in all capitalist nations
are far from enough to minimize climate change before it is too late.

The underlying structural and political realities – including the costs of
abandoning the global fossil fuel-built infrastructure, the desperation to win
the competition in the global capital markets, and the flood of corporate
money into all the major capitalist political systems – prevent corporations
from making the drastic changes needed to rein in climate change at the pace
and scale needed. In the United States, the Wall Street banks and financial
markets which control much of the world's wealth – J. P. Morgan Chase,
Goldman Sachs, BlackRock, and their ilk – set the tone of "extinction finance," in the same predatory spirit that animates the thousands of finance
capitalists in London and Dubai or any number of other financial centers.
To put the environment over profits, would risk violating their charters and
send potential investors toward other "low road" competitors. That is why
Leonardo DiCaprio's *"The Wolf of Wall Street"* rang true for millions of the
film's global fans, who immediately recognized that predatory "wolves" run
rampant in Wall Street, London or Tokyo because our global financial system requires that they act "wolf-like." Whatever their rhetoric, they eagerly

finance oil pipelines, fracking, and other environmentally devastating projects that are highly profitable. This willful blindness and externalization of climate costs will not change around the world until global and national taxes and regulation internalize climate costs at a far higher level than seen in any capitalist nation today.

3. Elimination of Public Goods and the Commons

Capitalist markets and culture argue that all resources – land, labor, and capital itself – should be held privately and invested for profit. This idea became a kind of economic capitalist theology in 1968, when Garrett Hardin, a University of California professor who had earlier written a biology textbook arguing for the urgent need to control breeding of "genetically defective" people, wrote of the allegedly inevitable "tragedy of the commons" that occurs when you create or permit publicly shared land. Using the example of the typical 18th-century British village in which each person is allowed to use the commons for his own grazing, Hardin writes:

> The rational herdsman concludes that the only sensible course for him to pursue is to add another animal to his herd. And another; and another … But this is the conclusion reached by each and every rational herdsman sharing a commons. Therein is the tragedy. Each man is locked into a system that compels him to increase his herd without limit – in a world that is limited. Ruin is the destination toward which all men rush, each pursuing his own best interest in a society that believes in the freedom of the commons. Freedom in a commons brings ruin to all.[26]

In other words, publicly shared ownership means ecological "ruin to all." Capitalism seeks to eliminate the commons by privatizing any land, agriculture and industry that can generate profits. It has largely succeeded, creating the real "tragedy of the economists" now much discussed by environmental economists and social theorists. In the name of economic rationality, total privatization is pursued, thereby creating the very tragedy of the commons in the name of preventing such a tragedy.

The "tragedy of the commons" today is another name for climate change. The demonization of government and the privatization of as much land and national resources as possible have long been in the DNA of capitalism. In the 1980s, the "Reagan revolution" turned the privatization devils of capitalism into an extinction machine, seeking to make all land and resources around the United States and the world ripe for extraction and profit. Neoliberalism is fueling the most dangerous climate extinction forces ever seen. They are, at this writing, so deeply entrenched that even a president like Joe Biden, who has tried to resurrect government and invest in green jobs and other public goods is facing what the climate champion, Naomi Klein, described as capitalist anti-climate "pillars":

> Indeed the three policy pillars of the neoliberal age-privatization of the public sphere, deregulation of the corporate sector, and the lowering of income and corporate taxes, paid for with cuts to public spending-are each incompatible with many of the actions we must take to bring our emissions to safe levels.[27]

4. The Fetishism of Commodities

The "fetishism of commodities," is the title of a section of Karl Marx's first chapter in the first volume of his most important book, *Das Kapital*. He highlights that profit requires making everything for sale and ginning up the consumer's desire to buy. Mass consumption is integral to profit-driven capitalism, especially in Western developed capitalist societies but now spreading in Asian powers such as Japan and South Korea as well as in many developing countries. Fetishism hints that market exchange becomes erotic, even sexualized, as market transactions and "buying stuff" become the basic form of self-gratification.[28]

Capitalism aligns commodities with biology, even though the sexualization of commodities turns human desire into destruction of life and the earth. The eroticizing of buying stuff – essentially branding consumption as biological fulfillment – is consistent with the broader metaphysics of capitalism that identifies market exchange as "natural," a law of nature. We become our true selves only in activity that ultimately destroys the habitat that we need to survive.

People themselves accumulate commodities as a basis of happiness – in the capitalist culture of mass consumerism especially dominant in the United States – while also becoming themselves human commodities for sale on the labor market. Lifestyles and happiness itself become commodified. In her book, *Born to Buy*, sociologist Juliet Schor, a leading chronicler of mass consumerism, shows that this begins at the earliest stages of life.[29] It starts with mothers in maternity wards saturated with marketing for everything from diapers to strollers – the new mom walks out of the hospital loaded down with "stuff" for both herself and her new baby. Studies have shown that as these babies grow into teens, young people say that "shopping" and "buying stuff" make them happiest. Their social life is in the mall or online platforms where they talk about and show pictures of themselves with their latest "stuff."

Fetishism has an obsessive quality – when you fetishize something you can never get enough of it. Fetishizing consumption is thus a foundation of extinction, since every commodity that is consumed is extracted from finite natural resources. But if you are addicted, you will keep indulging your fetish, even if it leads you toward self-destruction or collective extinction.

5. The God of Growth

Capitalism is a dynamic system requiring constant expansion; it cannot survive as a static or steady state system without the growth of commodity production and profit. Capital keeps pouring into the engine that produces more stuff and profit, ending the survival prospects of companies and whole systems that don't keep generating more stuff and more profits. If the system is not speeding up, it is at risk of not just slowing but disintegrating. Growth without limits is absolutely incompatible with the preservation of the natural world. The planet is finite and cannot sustain infinite extraction and consumption of finite natural resources. But since capitalism depends on growth without limits, it would inevitably move into the final stage in which the contradictions between growth and survival pointed to the question of whether the survival of capitalism as we know it means the end of human survival.

As noted in the first section of this chapter, growth without limits is fatal to environmental prospects for two reasons. One is that infinite growth means in the current economic system growth of carbon emissions that will quickly produce extinction through climate. But, as Chira Dhara and Vandana Singh point out in their *Scientific American* article, "The Delusion of Infinite Economic Growth," unlimited growth will threaten environmental extinction even if we move toward the green technologies that come close to eliminating carbon emissions.[30] This is true because infinite material growth creates unsustainable material costs other than carbon emissions that imperial all life.

Dhara and Singh explain this vividly by showing how a world based on green technologies such as electric vehicles (EVs) will destroy the environment in a system without limits to growth:

> The electric vehicle (EV) has become one of the great modern symbols of a world awakened to the profound challenges of unsustainability and climate change ....
>
> Let us imagine the "perfect" EV: solar powered, efficient, reliable and affordable. But is it *sustainable*? EVs powered by renewable energy may help reduce the carbon footprint of transport. Yet, the measure of sustainability is not merely the carbon footprint but the material footprint: the aggregate quantity of biomass, metal ores, construction minerals and fossil fuels used during production and consumption of a product. The approximate metric tonne weight of an EV constitutes materials such as metals (including rare earths), plastics, glass and rubber. Therefore, a global spike in the demand for EVs would drive an increased demand for each of these materials.[31]

They go on to show that Capitalism's God of growth is thus fatal even assuming full embrace of green technology:

> Exponential growth swiftly, inevitably, swamps anything in finite supply. For a virus, that finite resource is the human population and in the context of the planet it is its physical resources. The inescapable inference is that it is essentially impossible to decouple material use from economic growth. And this is exactly what has transpired. Wiedmann et al.... did a careful accounting of the material footprint, including those embedded in international trade, for several nations. In the 1990–2008 period covered by the study, no country achieved a planned, deliberate economywide decoupling for a sustained length of time.[32]

Both neoclassical and Keynesian economists – the two mainstream economic schools which both embrace capitalism – are not seriously rethinking their views of growth in the age of extinction. They continue to see rapid and unrestricted growth as essential to economic health, prosperity and morality itself. The irony is that the economists are blinding the public from seeing that *not* ending GDP growth in the 21st century almost ensures ending both capitalism and all civilization.

GDP growth has undeniable great virtues. Historically, it has helped raise the standard of living for large sectors of the population. But capitalist growth has always had two fatal flaws. First, capitalists selected technologies – especially carbon based energy sources – that were most profitable, whatever their social and environmental costs. Second, the DNA of capitalism led, for obvious reasons, to a concept of growth that focused mainly on growth of material commodities for private profit.

How capitalism causes climate catastrophe is thus not accurately captured by highlighting the capitalist imperative of growth without limits. The capitalist commitment to growth became fatally intertwined with climate extinction by inventing and embracing an idea of growth that involved private rather than public goods – goods which are largely material. Public goods growth would not necessarily lead to environmental catastrophe.

In her book, *Eco-Mind*, Francis Moore Lappé argues that climate activists are in peril of losing the fight by opposing growth.[33] She shows that the problem is less growth per se, but the kind of growth created. While she does not explicitly advocate for growth in non-material public goods, she comes very close to the argument we are making: that an economy prioritizing such public goods can be a high-growth economy that does not threaten extinction. The reason is that public goods – whether education, transport by bicycles or walking, de-industrialized natural agriculture, sport and play, art, or simply social interaction in ordinary conversation for bonding and pleasure – are far more sustainable.

But What about the Green Capitalists' Solution?

Many reading this chapter may feel there is an easier solution than throwing away capitalism. Yes, capitalism is part of the problem. But, you think, realistically, the world is not going to invent anytime fast a visionary postcapitalist system. If we're going to be pragmatic, we should listen to the growing number of capitalist leaders and companies who are taking climate change seriously and proposing their own solution: green capitalism.

Capitalist companies are already responding to market incentives promoting green technologies that are important in slowing climate change. In fact, Big Tech leaders such as Bill Gates are beginning to focus on climate change, with Gates writing a 2021 book on how to transform the world to save the environment. But a closer look shows that Gates, like most corporate leaders in the United States and around the world, sees climate change as mainly a technological problem to be solved not by system change or politics but by innovative technologies. Gates starts off saying he is not a political guy but a tech expert. New technologies can get carbon emissions way down, without needing to distract ourselves with the giant and disagreeable task of changing our economic system. In fact, in his view, it is the Big Tech capitalist companies, as well as the smaller tech capitalist entrepreneurs that will solve climate change; capitalism is not the problem but the solution!

Gates's technological approach to the climate crisis typifies the "progressive" capitalist factions, including powerful capitalist groups in Europe and the developing world, willing to acknowledge a deep climate crisis. Technological innovation on a grand scale, subsidized by states when necessary, makes "green" capitalists like Gates, believe even more fervently in capitalism because they see it as the only system generating and rewarding technological leads of the kind necessary to stop climate change.

Moreover, because they see markets as rational and responsive to consumers, increasing public concern about flooding, drought, and extreme heat, are likely viewed as providing the "market signals" that will presumably increase the profitability of green investments. Twenty-first-century capitalist entrepreneurs – people like Elon Musk who have already made a fortune from electric cars – see this as the wave of the future. And even big corporations will end up on the global green capitalist wave. GM has announced it plans to stop producing gas engine cars by 2035 and go fully electric. Ford is building its electric F-150 Lightening trucks – one of the most popular vehicles in America – and plans to dramatically increase its electric truck and car fleet, President' Biden's 2023 executive order that half of all new US cars and trucks must be electric by 2030. Many other huge global companies are promising to drastically reduce their carbon emissions; Amazon has pledged to reach net-zero emissions by 2040 and Walmart promises to eliminate emissions by 2035. Their expectation is that the entire global capitalist system will follow – and save the planet.

This "capitalist solution" is seductive but deeply flawed. As we showed above, even "green" technology, such as wind turbines, solar panels, and electric cars, incurs grave environmental costs:

> Every stage of the life cycle of *any manufactured product* exacts environmental costs: habitat destruction, biodiversity loss and pollution (including carbon emissions) from extraction of raw materials, manufacturing/construction, through to disposal. Thus, it is the increasing global material footprint that is fundamentally the reason for the twin climate and ecological crises.[34]

As material or resource costs escalate, both climate change and material depletion imperil survival and the environment.

Since unlimited growth is in the DNA of capitalism, the shift to green technology is not enough to prevent environmental destruction. The tech-based vision, by focusing simply on technology, ignores all the other aspects of capitalism – from profit maximization to the public goods deficit to commodity fetishism as well as unlimited growth – that cause environmental destruction.

The green tech capitalist solution actually protects the wealth and power of Big Tech and other corporations, and is likely to accelerate environmental destruction by deflecting focus from the underlying systemic aspects of capitalism fueling climate change. But this doesn't mean we should ignore technology nor that capitalist innovation and reforms can't play a role. Technology obviously has a major role to play in solving climate and other environmental crises. Where capitalist corporations seek to invest massive amounts of capital into non-carbon energy sources, this may help with the larger economic, social, and political changes that will need to ultimately transcend the capitalist-driven forces that green capitalists such as Gates and Musk claim to champion. The greening that is possible within capitalism is hugely important, when not used as a substitute for crucial system change.

The key is to accelerate the green innovation possible within capitalism while making larger systemic changes where these technologies can truly prevent extinction. In the current corporate order, despite the importance of electric cars and other green products, the purely technological approach de-linked from systemic change will not create a sustainable world.

Green capitalists' reforms may be a step forward, but their claims of social responsibility should not be confused with actual solutions to the climate crisis. Even the biggest global corporate emission-spewers – Exxon, Royal Dutch Shell, BP, Chevron, and other large oil and gas companies – now advertise themselves as green companies, promoting a brand mixing renewables and fossil fuel together as the only road to prosperity and survival in a green capitalism. But these same companies used their money and political clout to prevent the necessary systemic changes that would solve the climate change crisis. In the United States, the American Petroleum Institute, the leading oil and gas lobbyist, put Exxon and Chevron's money to work opposing Biden-proposed climate policy changes. Nevertheless, these companies brand themselves as "green."

Green brands, according to extensive research, are most likely to create "green-washing" rather than sustainability.[35] Global auto manufacturers are talking aspirations rather than committed realities to electric cars; and the US auto firms, also talking a good green story like Big Oil, tried in 2021 to limit stricter carbon emission standards introduced by the Biden Administration. As one *Forbes* commentator noted, the greenwashing temptation is inherent to work of industry leaders, "The allure of greenwashing sustainability initiatives often taps into what CEOs are best at: projecting confidence, managing risk, and creating followership."[36] Again, this does not mean that we should not use all the reforms in capitalism that actually contribute to mitigation. But we should also not confuse those reforms with solutions that will save humanity.

3   Plague for Profit

Capitalism and Pandemics

Introduction: Systemic Disease

On May 25, 2020, George Floyd was killed in Minneapolis by a police officer, Derek Chauvin, who pressed his knee hard into Floyd's neck for about nine minutes as Floyd was held on the ground by several cops. The killing took the country by storm because it was caught on video. It showed officer Chauvin with an almost bored look, one hand in his pocket, as he cut off Floyd's oxygen. Officer Chauvin, who was later convicted of murdering Floyd, seemed nonchalant even as Floyd stopped breathing and lay dead, with his knee still on Floyd's neck.

The murder gave rise to a story by President Trump and leading Republicans that, yes, there are some "bad apples" among the police. There are rogue actors in every profession. The way to prevent more deaths like Floyd's is to look for these relatively few bad apples and get rid of them.

But too many African-Americans for too long had been killed like Floyd for the "bad apple" story to be convincing. Starting mainly with black and white young people, a huge protest movement erupted around the United States – and indeed around the world. Their focus was not on "bad apple" cops. They presented another story: systemic racism. The problem was not in the individual police officers but in the institutions of our "law and order" racist system and in the deeply embedded racism in US culture. To prevent more cop killings, it would take systemic change, not just in policing but in the entire social system.[1]

The relevance of this whole story to pandemics has not been widely discussed. Floyd's murder took place during the Spring 2020 surge of the Coronavirus. While Officer Chauvin was killing Floyd, the virus was metaphorically pressing its deadly knee against the faces of millions of Americans, infecting and killing hundreds of thousands. The parallels in the stories of the two events are instructive.

Many see COVID-19 as an inevitable bad apple in nature. This follows the view that it's impossible to prevent the rise of bad apple cops or people like Derek Chauvin because they have always existed, an inevitable and unfortunate element of human nature – or, one could say, inherent in nature itself. Likewise, the parallel view of COVID-19 is that pandemics are inevitable and an inherent feature of nature.

DOI: 10.4324/9781003401483-5

Pandemics do have roots in nature and in interactions across species. But the bad apple story is, nonetheless, deeply flawed when applied to COVID-19 and pandemics in general. It ignores the hidden essential truth: these are not just natural disasters but human-generated catastrophes arising from our most powerful social structures.

Much like racist cop killings, pandemics are systemic. COVID-19 and other pandemics are fueled by the most important institutional systems of the societies in which they arise. In fact, there is a strong connection between systemic COVID-19 and systemic racism. In modern times, these two systemic forces are intertwined. Systemic racism plays an important role in shaping how and where pandemics such as COVID-19 arise and kill masses of people. Systemic racism intersects with broader economic, political, and cultural systems that drive modern plagues and intensify their impact on the most vulnerable people of society. Moreover, because they are systemic, they can have catastrophic effects, including possibilities of one of several variants of extinction, including Bostrom's "bang" or "shriek" form.

In the last several hundred years, the most important system shaping society has been capitalism, as discussed in prior chapters. Capitalism is, of course, the dominant global economic system, but it also breeds political systems and shapes the culture of entire societies. It is accurate – though almost never acknowledged in the United States – to describe COVID-19 as a systemic capitalist disease, a type of environmental extinction like its closely linked cousin, climate change.

Seeing Floyd's death as systemic racism changes how we react to it. Likewise, understanding today's pandemics as systemic capitalist plagues changes everything about how we must respond. As capitalism evolves globally, its institutions and values will create ever more frequent and deadly pandemics. If we want to prevent a pandemic-filled dystopic future which is potentially a form of extinction, we need to change the system driving it. Since humans create these systems, we can transform them – and we must!

Pandemics through History: A Brief Tale

As noted above, pandemics have ravaged small tribes and large societies for many centuries. Pandemics such as the Justinian Plague, in the Dark Ages of the 6th century, killed millions of people and animals across several continents. There were three huge pandemics affecting much of the world before the 20th century, including the Justinian Plague in 541, the famous Black Death or Bubonic Plague of 1347 and the 1894 pandemic that started in Yunnan China. These might be seen as "crunch," "shriek," or "whimper" extinctions.

There have been many hundreds of significant plagues through history. Analyzing the long string of pandemics, Nicholas Le Pan notes:

> Disease and illnesses have plagued humanity since the earliest days, our mortal flaw. However, it was not until the marked shift to agrarian communities that the scale and spread of these diseases increased dramatically.

Widespread trade created new opportunities for human and animal interactions that sped up such epidemics. Malaria, tuberculosis, leprosy, influenza, smallpox, and others first appeared during these early years.

The more civilized humans became – with larger cities, more exotic trade routes, and increased contact with different populations of people, animals, and ecosystems – the more likely pandemics would occur.[2]

A key observation here is that since early history, humans have helped create pandemics as they changed their behavior, built agricultural villages and then increasingly crowded cities, and expanded their economies through trade. As the economic systems developed into bigger production and trade routes globally, pandemics grew accordingly. The spread and globalization of economies and empires spurred greater pandemics, giving us a hint of the systemic character of pandemics, reflecting new kinds of societies and global economic systems, including ultimately today's global capitalism.

It is noteworthy, though, that many of the early pandemics erupted long before the rise of capitalism. This makes clear that capitalism is not the only system that can cause pandemics. Pre-capitalist, early economies and political elites had some of the expansionary and predatory elements that are also found in capitalism, and contribute to deadly plagues. Some of these like the Justinian Plague might be seen, in Bostrom's terms, as "shriek" or "whimper" extinctions because they killed 30–50 million people and held back the development of vibrant civilizations.

Our argument is, thus, not that capitalism is the only system causing or fueling pandemics. Rather, we are proposing first, that it has been an important systemic cause since the early rise of capitalism in the 14th century; second, that it became the major systemic cause or pandemics as capitalism developed from the 14th to the late 20th century; and third, that capitalism has evolved since around 1980 into a hyper-globalized system that is creating and fueling more frequent and widespread pandemics. While these are not necessarily more deadly than earlier pandemics, partly because of advances in technology, public health, and health care, they hint at the possibility of a new capitalist world ravaged by endless plagues such as COVID-19 – or worse – that could spin out of control and lead to new extinction threats.

Institutionalizing Disease: How the Capitalist System Generates Pandemics

It has been rare during the COVID-19 era that people, pundits or politicians connect pandemics to capitalism. This partly reflects the dominant US and Western view that capitalism has increased the resources, skills and knowledge needed to control disease. Rather than fueling plagues, capitalism is seen as the antidote, a view that has some credibility since capitalism has created many scientific, health and technological advances, and the death rate from specific pandemics has tended, at least until COVID-19, to decline rather than grow. One *Wall Street Journal* writer triumphantly proclaims that "Capitalism Is What Will Defeat

Covid," adding, "The vaccine revolution didn't happen on its own, it's a product of decades of planning and investment."[3] Moreover, socialism and other non-capitalist systems are widely viewed, especially in the United States, as either under-developed or evil, crucibles of all manner of social problems and diseases.

And capitalism has escaped blame partly because it discourages any type of systemic analysis, tending to view individuals rather than institutions or systems as the root causes of social problems. This is especially true in the United States, where capitalism breeds a culture of extreme individualism. Corrupt or diseased institutions or systems are simply reflective of individual pathology.

Consider the dates of major pandemics relative to the rise of capitalism, as well as the frequency and amount of death created by these plagues.[4]

Name	Time Period	Type/Pre-human Host	Death Toll
Antonine Plague	165–180	Believed to be either smallpox or measles	5 M
Japanese Smallpox epidemic	735–737	Variola major virus	1 M
Plague of Justinian	541–542	Yersinia pestis bacteria/rats, fleas	30–50 M
Black Death	1347–1351	Yersinia pestis bacteria/rats, fleas	200 M
New World Smallpox Outbreak	1520– onwards	Variola major virus	56 M
Great Plague of London	1665	Yersinia pestis bacteria/rats, fleas	100,000
Italian Plague	1629–1631	Yersinia pestis bacteria/rats, fleas	1 M
Cholera Pandemics 1–6	1817–1923	*V. cholerae* bacteria	1 M+
Third Plague	1885	Yersinia pestis bacteria/rats, fleas	12 M (China and India)
Yellow Fever	Late 1800s	Virus/mosquitoes	100,000–150,000 (United States)
Russian Flu	1889–1890	Believed to be H2N2 (avian origin)	1 M
Spanish Flu	1918–1919	H1N1 virus/pigs	40–50 M
Asian Flu	1957–1958	H2N2 virus	1.1 M
Hong Kong Flu	1968–1970	H3N2 virus	1 M
HIV/AIDS	1981–present	Virus/chimpanzees	25–35 M
Swine Flu	2009–2010	H1N1 virus/pigs	200,000
SARS	2002–2003	Coronavirus/bats, civets	770
Ebola	2014–2016	Ebola virus/wild animals	11,000
MERS	2015–present	Coronavirus/bats, camels	850
COVID-19	2019–present	Coronavirus – unknown (possibly pangolins)	>5.76 M[5]

The chronology shows, as noted earlier, that many very destructive pandemics preceded the rise of capitalism, and led to huge numbers of deaths, such as the Antonine Plague of 165–180 AD that killed 5 million, the Japanese Smallpox Plague of 735 AD killing 1 million, and the Justinian Plague killing 30–50 million. It is estimated to have killed somewhere between a quarter to a half of the world's population.

But as we move chronologically down the chart, into the early stage of capitalism, we find another one of the most deadly plagues of all times, the 14th-century Bubonic or Black Plague – a "crunch" extinction that killed an astonishing 200 million people, with some estimating that the deaths may have represented 40% or more of a world population numbering around 450 million at the time. This took root in crucial areas of the earliest stages of capitalism in Europe, in trade centers such as Venice in Italy and around the Mediterranean that were the crucible of the development of capitalism. Here, we see the rise of the confluence of multiple trade routes that both helped build European capitalism and cause the Black Plague. Then, half of all Europeans may have died during the 14th century and more during multiple European plagues through the 18th century.

The chart suggests the increasing frequency of pandemics as capitalism developed. Four systemic drivers of pandemics lie at the heart of capitalism and these, become more entrenched and toxic as the capitalist system expanded. They will be familiar because they are also drivers of climate change and of militarism.

1. Profit over People

Adam Smith argued that "an invisible hand" ensured that unfettered pursuit of profit – the defining feature of capitalism – resulted in the common good. History proves this false. Early capitalist critics such as Karl Marx, and especially his life-long collaborator, Frederick Engels,[6] focused on how capitalists pursuing profit exploited workers and their communities, creating long and debilitating hours of labor in dirty and dangerous factory conditions. They paid low wages, largely insufficient for safe and healthy shelter, and created congested slums filled with infectious agents, raw sewage, and other health-threatening conditions.

The profit-driven exploitation of labor and industrialized urban life during the 19th-century industrial revolution was an obvious driver of disease. Clearly, impoverished workers subjected to exhausting hours and toxic working environments inside and outside the factory are more likely to get sick. While social struggles during industrial capitalism in the 19th century improved living conditions and health for sectors of the working classes, as well as creating important medical and health advances, a reality Marx recognized but failed to discuss adequately, capitalism took a brutal toll on the health of a huge sector of workers, since the bosses kept wages and working conditions low to drive profits higher. This became the subject of great novelists like Charles Dickens, who wrote about the greed of capitalist Scrooges and the misery and illness of Tiny Tim workers and their poverty-stricken neighborhoods in 19th-century London.

Dickens's novels painted a picture of developing capitalism as a profit-driven disease engine – and hinted that it fueled pandemics. This is not only because of the health vulnerability of workers but the breeding of systemic environmental factors – in factories, industrial slums, and congested cities – that made pandemics more likely. Here is where the priority of profit over people as a systemic breeder of plagues became obvious, as elites were not willing to raise wages or tax profits and invest in cleaning up hazardous workhouses, factories, and slums. The result was a tsunami of pandemics in the center of rising capitalism: Dickens's 19th-century London and other rising British industrial urban centers. As one report titled "Public Health in the Industrial Revolution" notes:

> Plagues and other diseases regularly killed huge numbers... A rising population coupled with poor housing and long working hours, led to conditions in urban areas becoming atrocious. Slums quickly grew as cities bore the weight of the rapid increase in people. Diseases wreaked havoc.[7]

Among the most common and deadly diseases and plagues were the following:

- *Typhoid*: Between 1830 and 1836, there were four major British typhoid epidemics. Typhoid was carried by contaminated water and food in dirty conditions.
- *Cholera*: Cholera pandemics erupted so frequently that the disease became known as "King Cholera." In 1831 alone, cholera in Britain killed over 50,000. In 1848, another cholera pandemic killed 70,000.... Between 1817 and 1923, cholera epidemics globally killed more than a million people.
- *Tuberculosis*: TB was the deadliest British pandemic as capitalism developed through the 19th and early 20th century. A pulmonary variant was most prevalent; it hit mainly teenagers and young adults who were malnourished, overworked and exhausted. These included young workers like Tiny Tim in Dickens's Christmas Carol, who suffered from TB according to scientists analyzing Dickens's descriptions of one of this most famous of working-class literary characters. In the early 19th century, TB killed over a quarter of the British population and around 1900 accounted for one-eighth of all deaths. As capitalism developed, it was the largest single killer of adults.[8]

No wonder that the acclaimed historian of plagues, Kyle Harper, calls our attention to the negative health impacts "generated by industrialization and the rise of global capitalism":

> For several decades in the mid-nineteenth century, progress stalled, even in western Europe where early gains had been achieved ... the emergence of new diseases, and the recrudescence of old ones, proved devastating

around the globe. To understand the interplay of health, wealth, and power in the formation of the modern world, we need to see this story in full planetary perspective.

Harper adds:

> The narrative is not one of unbroken progress, but one of countervailing pressures between the negative health feedbacks of growth and humanity's rapidly expanding but highly unequal capacities to control the threats to our health.[9]

As these plagues ravaged the center of rising global capitalism in England, they began to make clear the systemic character of pandemics, While the search for profit over people in the system was the obvious systemic driver, other systemic aspects of capitalism were creating pandemics around the world, as capitalism spread its wings and began to dominate the planet. Following the era of colonialism, the neo-colonial era spread its own deadly diseases. Led by the United States after World War II, profit became the central global imperative, and profiteering – by big AG, big Pharma, big Oil, and big Banks – has played a major role in promoting today's pandemics, including COVID-19.

2. The Public Goods Deficit: The Hidden Heart of the Matter

Charles Dickens and others shocked by the eruption of disease and pandemics as the industrial revolution took off in the 19th century bemoaned the state of public health in Britain, then the most developed capitalist country in the world. Numerous commissions to improve health were formed, but they never had the economic resources or political clout to prevent the endless rise of pandemics of cholera, TB, typhoid, and other diseases.

Almost two centuries later, the eruption of COVID-19 – and the failure to prevent millions from getting it and hundreds of thousands from dying of it in even many affluent countries around the world – would again have shocked Dickens. Pandemics such as COVID-19 in advanced capitalist societies reveal systemic, institutionalized deficits of public health, public housing, public transit, and larger public goods systems. Pandemics are closely related to both environmental destruction and militarism, and highlight public health as one of the most important public goods along with environmental protection and building peace.

Dr. Michael Mina, a Harvard physician and professor of epidemiology and public health has made the provocative distinction between "medicine," a profitable system to heal individuals by doctors, and "public health," offered by non-profit clinics or governments to protect community health. Many capitalist societies, most notably the United States, are big on "medicine," and small on public health. This poverty of public health is not characteristic of all capitalist societies, but it is not surprising in an economic system organized to produce private commodities rather than public goods. Capitalism is systemically tending to be deficient in public goods, as noted in earlier chapters, because capitalists view the market as the only true source of wealth and value, investing mainly in profitable commodities for sale on the market.

As Derber and June Sekera have written elsewhere, societies cannot function efficiently or compassionately without adequate public goods, an argument that capitalist societies tend to ignore:

> The history of civilization," wrote Martin Wolf of the *Financial Times* in 2012, "is a history of public goods." Public goods are what governments produce on behalf of their citizens: clean air and water, safe food and drugs, libraries and parks, highways and bridges, and scores of other services that citizens rely on every day.
>
> Public goods are funded collectively by citizens through their taxes. The government produces them because the market does not or because a society decides that all citizens should have access because the societal benefits are so important.[10]

But capitalism systemically hides its own necessary public goods and public health deficits, creating "an invisible crisis." It is hidden for many reasons, as Derber and Sekera make clear in their discussion of capitalist interests and the prevailing market ideology:

> [The] hidden deficit remains hidden by design, a deliberate strategy developed by conservative elites with enormous power over the public discourse. Cornell political scientist Suzanne Mettler has argued that influential, monied groups do not want people to know how much they are getting from government. If people recognized how many personal and social benefits come from government spending, it would threaten the conservative anti-government position, a stance long at the center of right-wing ideology. In 2008, Mettler showed that of all who deny ever receiving benefits from US government programs, over 90 percent had participated in at least one such program. As Mettler writes, the state's role – and thus the existence of public goods – has been intentionally submerged and shrouded, "making it largely invisible to ordinary citizens."[11]

Capitalism even deprives its workers of the vocabulary to think of public goods, to even imagine their existence:

> [We] lack the language to discuss the hidden deficit. You cannot see what you lack the words to describe. Neo-classical economists and conservative corporate interests have taught that only private businesses can

produce lasting and true wealth, and that government is inherently un-productive since it displaces private enterprise and is only useful as a tem-porary corrective to transitory "market failures." Such ruling orthodoxy undermines the very possibility of a "public good" produced by govern-ment, and helps explain why people heavily reliant on public goods claim they get no government benefits.[12]

Catastrophes like COVID-19 and other pandemics begin to expose the sys-temic public health and public goods crisis. They are simply too overwhelming in the lives of workers and all citizens to ignore. They make clear that public health – health provided by government or communities for the general popu-lation and especially vulnerable working-class groups – is inadequate. Yet, as seen in COVID-19, the discussion of the public health and public goods crisis as a systemic capitalist creation remains largely ignored.

3. Expansion: Capitalism's Historic War on Nature

A third capitalist driver of pandemics is the system's inherent tendency to ex-pand. Almost 200 years ago, early capitalist critics such as Marx and Engels marveled at the dynamism of the rising system, leading to globalization and colonization, and ensuring the triumph of capitalism across the world through war as well as trade. They realized it would bring growth and benefits, es-pecially for tycoons and the captains of industry, but that it would also bring militarism, disease and global exploitation, including global health disasters.

Expansion has always happened within nations as well as across them. Inside advanced capitalist countries such as the United States, miners and big agricul-tural companies expanded constantly into more wilderness and public lands, destroying nature and putting more people and companies into pandemic-fueling contact with new germs and animals traditionally sheltered from hu-man invasion. And capitalism has always relentlessly expanded abroad, includ-ing not just through increased trade and outsourced production and globalized consumption, but production of a highly profitable travel, tourist and airline capitalist sector, all of which, as we shall see, spreads disease and fuels pandem-ics that can become shriek or whimper extinctions around the globe.

In this brief section, we look at a few deadly highlights of the history of such expansion; in a later section, we focus on today's expansion crisis related to health. Nearly every pandemic has historically been associated with the movement of people, warriors, goods, and trade into new areas. The huge his-toric plagues we discussed earlier all took this form, although the earliest dis-eases were spread by pre-capitalist traders and fighters. The Plague of Justinian, 541–750 AD, was brought to Italy by soldiers returning from the Mideast.[13] The Bubonic plague or Black Death started in Asia and reached Europe and the Mediterranean probably through Italian merchants fleeing war in the Crimea.

The "Third Pandemic" of the mid to late 19th century started in China but then spread through population movement and trade to India, where it killed 10 million people and by 1900, spread into the United States through travel and trade.

Capitalism's pandemics in history are perhaps most evident in colonialism. In the era of mercantilism, colonialism became the classic historical capitalist model of expansion across the world. It has been associated with millions on millions of deaths brought through disease by the "Christopher Columbuses" of the world: traders, merchants, and soldiers in search of gold, profit, and power. They typically have been recruited and funded by capitalist colonizing countries and corporations. This helps explain the rise of movements today tearing down the statutes of Columbus and his colonizing ilk, as the scale of the disease and pandemics they brought is now being taught in schools and is almost too much to bear:

> Encounters between European explorers and populations in the rest of the world often introduced local epidemics of extraordinary virulence. Disease killed the entire native (Guanches) population of the Canary Islands in the 16th century. Half the native population of Hispaniola in 1518 was killed by smallpox. Smallpox also ravaged Mexico in the 1520s, killing 150,000 in Tenochtitlán alone, including the emperor, and Peru in the 1530s, aiding the European conquerors. Measles killed a further two million Mexican natives in the 1600s. In 1618–1619, smallpox wiped out 90% of the Massachusetts Bay Native Americans. During the 1770s, smallpox killed at least 30% of the Pacific Northwest Native Americans. Smallpox epidemics in 1780–1782 and 1837–1838 brought devastation and drastic depopulation among the Plains Indians. Some believe that the death of up to 95% of the Native American population of the New World was caused by Old World diseases such as smallpox, measles, and influenza.[14]

By the late 19th century, as capitalism matured, public health systems emerged out of working class and social reformers struggles in Europe. But capitalism remained lethal in the colonies. Mike Davis, late historian and political economist, describes the interaction of droughts, famines, and disease:

> Hugely destructive epidemics of malaria, bubonic plague, dysentery, smallpox and cholera culled millions of victims from the ranks of the famine-weakened. The European empires, together with Japan and the United States, rapaciously exploited the opportunity to wrest new colonies, expropriate communal lands, and tap novel sources of plantation and mine labor. What seemed from a metropolitan perspective the nineteenth century's final blaze of imperial glory was, from an Asian or African viewpoint, only the hideous light of a giant funeral pyre.[15]

In the "late Victorian" period that Davis studied, these famines and diseases took between 31.7 and 61.3 million lives across India, China, and Brazil.[16] The relative underdevelopment of the Global South, Davis believes, finds its explanation is this period and these facts.

Today, in the postcolonial world, intense globalizing forces continue to spread disease across continents, even as expansion of capitalist agriculture, mining, logging, and other industries break down the nation's own protected public lands and wildlife. We save this discussion for later in the chapter, when we look at late stage capitalism, which has intensified the plunder of nature and the forced interaction of people and companies with sheltered animals in former wildness or forests such as the Brazilian Amazon. These invasions by profiteering hordes of people and companies have generated many of the viral pandemics that are plaguing us today.

4. Class Structure

A defining feature of capitalism is a class structure separating small elites of the wealthy capitalist and managerial or professional classes from the stagnant or declining working classes. Derber, with Yale Magrass, has discussed the architecture of the "capitalist house" as an upstairs downstairs house, with each floor housing a different social class.[17] As inequality and class divisions have grown more severe in most advanced capitalist societies, many have the extreme architecture that we find in the United States.

What does the US capitalist house look like? It has a lavish upstairs where … the 1% live luxuriously and can push buttons that control the societal house. The top 0.01% – 16,000 households led by CEOs, hedge fund managers and multi-millions with minimum wealth over $100 million – are the true capitalist aristocrats, living at the very top of the house, led in 2018 by over 400 billionaires.[18] There is a mezzanine of the house, where perhaps 20% of the population lives comfortably, with many relatively affluent. These are doctors, lawyers, and upper middle managers, in what sociologist Alvin Gouldner has dubbed the "professional-managerial" or "new" class. But the majority of the population lives below the top floor and mezzanine in the first floor and basement:

> the house has a huge downstairs, with many different rooms and partitions on the first floor, where the working class (which includes blue-collar, pink-collar and white-collar employees) live under a wide degree of economically insecure, indebted and declining conditions …. Many of these people live in the downstairs basement.[19]

The COVID-19 economic meltdown has greatly expanded the number of basement dwellers in most capitalist nations. Millions of workers lost their jobs and were driven into the poverty and debt that plagues the basement. Many were locked in poverty before the pandemic – and remain with low prospects of moving up.

Those who almost never catch up live in a dark dirt-floor basement, where millions of unemployed and poor people have a miserable life, often hungry and sick. They are disproportionately people of color and undocumented immigrants, though the majority in the basement are native whites and rural.[20] As the basement population expands and the first floor gets dirtier and more congested, it is easy to see why the capitalist house is a systemic breeding ground for pandemics. The majority of people, as discussed by Dickens 200 years ago, are stuck in untenable, insecure, dirty, and diseased parts of the house. The lower working classes are chronically prevented by their impoverished conditions and widespread basement diseases from developing their humanity and full potential. Using Bostrom's terminology, such workers are chronically subjected to a "whimper extinction" even before an epidemic such as COVID-19 emerges.

Neoliberal Global Capitalism: Fueling COVID-19 and Risking Extinction

In the 1980s, President Reagan and UK Prime Minister Margaret Thatcher inaugurated a rising capitalist model highly conducive to illness and pandemics. What Reagan and Thatcher really did was inaugurate a new stage of "late capitalism," which, as discussed in earlier chapters is generally referred to as Neoliberalism. It spread rapidly around the world and has become a dominant form of the global capitalist system. It took root most strongly in the United States and the United Kingdom, and in many poorer nations such as Chile and Brazil, where the United States exercised strong control. It also has penetrated some nations in continental Europe, weakening but not yet replacing Europe's historical social democracy and social welfare system.

Global neoliberalism does not change the capitalist fundamentals but rather take them to new extremes. Here, we look briefly at three neoliberal systemic developments and show how they gave rise to recent pandemics, including COVID-19.

1. Anti-government: The Erosion of Public Health and Other Public Goods

Neoliberalism is most famously associated with the demonization of government. Anti-government rhetoric has long been a staple of capitalist ideology, with government defined as coercive and the enemy of liberty. If government is the enemy, then public goods, including public health, become enemies too, because they depend on and are provided by government. They come to be seen as threats to freedom.

The structural deficits of capitalist public health and other public goods give rise to today's pandemics. The public health deficit fueling is intensified in neoliberalism, representing systemic failures rather than simply mis-management by leaders like Trump in the United States or Jair Bolsonaro in Brazil. As a team of epidemiologists and political economists, including Rob Wallace, write about COVID-19 failures in capitalist societies:

> The failures were actually programmed decades ago as the shared commons of public health were simultaneously neglected and monetized. A country captured by a regimen of individualized, just-in-time epidemiology – an utter contradiction – with barely enough hospital beds and equipment for normal operations, is by definition unable to marshal the resources necessary to pursue a China brand of suppression.[21]

Wallace and his co-authors are making explicit that the problem is systemic, with neoliberal capitalism eviscerating the public goods and public health system that could have prevented the turning of COVID-19 into a pandemic.

2. The War on Nature Today: Neoliberal Capitalist Expansion and COVID-19

At a 2017 Aspen Ideas Festival in Colorado, a number of moderate policy analysts, some associated with Joe Biden and the Democratic party, summarized their session, well before COVID-19 but after Ebola, with the following observation:

> Often overshadowed by terrorism, nuclear weapons, and cybercrime in the public imagination, pandemics may actually be the more existential threat to human civilization. And most experts agree: We're woefully unprepared, and crucial funding for basic research, foreign aid, and preparedness is on the chopping block.[22]

The policy analyst Nancy Sullivan, who also spoke on the panel with President Biden's then future chief of staff, Ron Klain, hints at the acceleration of expansive forces that are bringing humans into more intrusive interactions with nature and wildlife, breeding ever more pandemics in the neoliberal capitalist era:

> They seem to be happening with increasing frequency, and it may have something to do with the increasing frequency with which humans are interacting with nature, and pushing into areas where these viruses are harbored in other animal species. And so we have what's called a zoonotic crossover. So, more than 70 percent of these viruses that occur in humans come from animals. And so as we move into where they live, I think that the risk of exposure gets higher, and we've seen that now over the last years with MERS, and SARS, and Ebola, and Zika ....[23]

While nailing the core problem of expansion involving humans invading all nature, with mushrooming human, animal and other species interactions giving rise to "a zoonotic crossover" causing pandemics, Sullivan does not specify that these are systemic capitalist forces. None of the speakers at this Aspen panel identified these as systemic, making no reference to capitalism or neoliberalism. Some scientists and a growing number of political economists are now beginning to expose the systemic roots of the problem. In September 2020, a group of scientists reported to the UN about the extreme dangers of rampant new pandemics if the current rate of deforestation continues or accelerates. They also warn of dangerous expansion of farming and mining, pointing implicitly at Big Ag's new assault on nature and the capture and sale of animals and land for profit, despite the high risks of causing pandemics:

> Rampant deforestation, uncontrolled expansion of farming and the building of mines in remote regions – as well as the exploitation of wild animals as sources of food, traditional medicines and exotic pets – are creating a "perfect storm" for the spillover of diseases from wildlife to people...
> Almost a third of all emerging diseases have originated through the process of land use change, it is claimed. As a result, five or six new epidemics a year could soon affect Earth's population.[24]

The scientists are not political economists, but their work takes them deep into the capitalist system. They are effectively telling us that capitalism's central commitment to profit requires the commodification of everything, including all land on the planet. The scientists' work leads them unwittingly into revealing the new invasive production and consumption practices of globalized neoliberal capitalist agriculture:

> There are now a whole raft of activities – illegal logging, clearing and mining – with associated international trades in bushmeat and exotic pets that have created this crisis .... In the case of COVID-19, it has cost the world trillions of dollars and already killed almost a million people, so clearly urgent action is needed.[25]

It is estimated that tens of millions of hectares of rainforest and other wild environments are being bulldozed every year to cultivate palm trees, farm cattle, extract oil, and provide access to mines and mineral deposits. This leads to the widespread destruction of vegetation and wildlife that are hosts to countless species of viruses and bacteria, most unknown to science. Those microbes can then accidentally infect new hosts, such as humans and domestic livestock.[26]

The neoliberal assault on nature for profit shows no sign of relenting. Their analysis was confirmed by the many huge fires laying waste in 2020 to the

Amazon forest in Brazil, the world's most important absorber of carbon emissions. The Amazon destruction is tied to a right-wing neoliberal dictatorship under Jair Bolsonaro, who opened the Amazon to loggers, miners, and animal-hunters for Big Ag and many other profitable corporate interests. These companies are happy to get rich even as they threaten extinction by intensifying climate change and COVID-19; Brazil in 2021 descended into one of the world's worst COVID-19 hotspots, threatening Bolsonaro's hold on power.

For the global neoliberal capitalist system, the planet as a whole – and all land and animals are plants – are simply market commodities. This destroys biodiversity and undermines the protective barriers between humans and sheltered ecologies such as the Amazon forest; it represents a systemic capitalist assault on life itself. The biodiversity crisis is a "bang" extinction, much like climate change, and both are intertwined with the Big Ag circuits of capital that are invading all sectors of the earth and privatizing them, while turning the animals, plants and invading human profiteers into a brew of toxic pandemics that is a major extinction threat.

A growing number of scholars are developing a more explicit analysis of COVID-19 and other pandemics as capitalist systemic disease. As Wallace and his co-authors write:

> If by its global expansion alone, commodity agriculture serves as both propulsion for and nexus through which pathogens of diverse origins migrate from the most remote reservoirs to the most international of population centers.... However unintended, the entirety of the production line is organized around practices that accelerate the evolution of pathogen virulence and subsequent transmission. Growing genetic monocultures – food animals and plants with nearly identical genomes – removes immune firebreaks that in more diverse populations slow down transmission.... Meanwhile, crowded conditions depress immune response. Larger farm animal population sizes and densities of factory farms facilitate greater transmission and recurrent infection. ... Housing a lot of animals together rewards those strains that can burn through them best ....[27]

They have a colorful way of summarizing their argument:

> That is, capital's alienation is parsing out in pathogens' favor. While the public interest is filtered out at the farm and food factory gate, pathogens bleed past the biosecurity that industry is willing to pay for and back out to the public. Everyday production represents a lucrative moral hazard eating through our shared health commons.[28] The explicit conclusion that COVID and other pandemics is systemic capitalist disease

bred by neoliberal Big Ag expanding through and plundering nature is well summarized by political economists John Bellamy Foster and In-tan Suwandi: "SARS-CoV-2, like other dangerous pathogens that have emerged or reemerged in recent years, is closely related to a complex set of factors including: (1) the development of global agribusiness with its expanding genetic monocultures that increase susceptibility to the contraction of zoonotic diseases from wild to domestic animals to humans; (2) destruction of wild habitats and disruption of the activities of wild species; and (3) human beings living in closer proximity. There is little doubt that global commodity chains and the kinds of connectivity that they have produced have become vectors for the rapid transmission of disease, throwing this whole globally exploitative pattern of development into question".[29]

As Mike Davis argues, 21st-century capitalism points to "a permanent triage of humanity ... dooming part of the human race to eventual extinction."[30]

3. Pandemics and Class Structure in the Neoliberal Capitalist House

Inequality is the systemic reality that capitalism, a class-based system, can never eliminate or reduce to a humane level. We have already described above the upstairs/downstairs capitalist architecture long breeding disease in the basement and first floor.

But if deep class inequality has always defined the upstairs/downstairs capitalist house, neoliberal capitalism has created a revolution: a level of extreme inequality never seen before. Inequality expert Thomas Piketty argues that a transformation of the system is emerging – and, in some ways, is surprisingly like the feudalism from which capitalism emerged. The billionaire "lords" of plutocratic capitalism are like the blue-blood nobles of medieval feudalism, inheriting astonishing fortunes while the new working classes are permanently impoverished feudal serfs. The misery of workers' wages and their health creates a systemic vulnerability to disease and pandemics leading toward crunch or shriek extinctions, a threat also often faced by feudal peasants.

Piketty sees this extreme inequality skyrocketing in the future. The bottom line is that the bottom half of the population seems doomed to suffer in ways that could give new fuel to pandemics such as COVID-19 that could lead to crunch, shriek or whimper extinctions.

Studies of COVID-19's impact on the population prove the point over and over again. In the first year of COVID-19, from March 2020 to March 2021, the world's billionaires gained an astonishing $1.2 trillion in wealth. By early 2022, Oxfam could report that the "wealth of the world's 10 richest men has doubled since the pandemic began. The incomes of 99% of humanity are worse off because of COVID-19."[31] Indeed, poor and working people lost wages and sunk deeper in debts to pay for rent, food and health care. A summary of these studies concludes:

> As the coronavirus spreads across the globe, it appears to be setting off a devastating feedback loop with another of the gravest forces of our time: economic inequality.
>
> In societies where the virus hits, it is deepening the consequences of inequality, pushing many of the burdens onto the losers of today's polarized economies and labor markets. Research suggests that those in lower economic strata are likelier to catch the disease.

They are also likelier to die from it. And, even for those who remain healthy, they are likelier to suffer loss of income or health care as a result of quarantines and other measures, potentially on a sweeping scale.[32] Poorer countries are least able to survive the onslaught of pandemics, not just because of the vaccine inequalities that we will discuss in Chapter 7, but for related reasons summarized by Foster and Suwandi, namely that the countries of the Global North "take the poverty of the populations of the Global South ... as the justification for a Malthusian or social Darwinist approach, in which millions would die in order to "keep the global economy growing". Moreover, within the North *and* South, they note the "extraordinarily exploitative and destructive nature of the system is evident in the fact that blue-collar workers everywhere ... are expected to carry out production mostly without protective gear while the more privileged and dispensable classes socially distance themselves." Adding that

> [It] is precisely because of the class nature of social distancing, as well as access to income, housing, resources, and medical care, that morbidity and mortality from COVID-19 in the United States is falling primarily on populations of color, where conditions of economic and environmental injustice are most severe.[33]

Poor countries lacking wealth for public health systems were unable to afford the COVID-19 vaccines and were likely to suffer mass death or whimper extinctions before vaccines ever became available to them. In 2021, this became a terrifying reality, marked by the explosion of COVID-19 in nations such as India, Brazil and South Africa. As 2022 drew to a close, still other strains of the disease and even novel viruses continue to wreak havoc with public health systems that must be significantly strengthened to meet the continuing challenges.

4 Bloody Money

Capitalism, War, and the Doomsday Machine

Derber still remembers the Cuban missile crisis of 1963. He was a college student at Yale, and like all his classmates, he was panicking about what to do to survive. He had seen the folly of "duck-and-cover" under his desk in grammar school as the juvenile plan for survival in a classroom during a nuclear war. But now the only thing that passed through the students' minds was to escape into the forests of Canada, an equally crazy notion of how to survive.

At some level, we knew this. We were living in a new era, where for the first time our leaders had ordered and succeeded in creating a military system that could destroy us all – and where there was and remains no possible way to survive inevitable coming conflict. The reasons are different than publicly described, and have little to do with deterring strikes from other countries. Instead, these reflect a mad willingness to pursue global profit and power with force, even at the risk of extinction of all life on the planet.

This mad system remains today. It is even more dangerous than during the Cold War. But while during the Cuban missile crisis, it was widely seen as a threat of extinction that would likely destroy all life on the planet, today prospects of general nuclear war are out of the headlines and largely out of our minds – even with 2022s and 2023s dangerous escalation focused on Ukraine.

Until Russia's invasion of Ukraine, recent wars seemed to many to be less likely to become global nuclear war, and more limited or survivable conflicts – whether battles with smaller "jihadist" groups, trade wars, immigration battles and culture wars internal to nations. With terrorism rather than a nuclear Soviet Empire at the core of the Western security narrative, the argument has been that current threats – while very dangerous – can likely be managed without a massive nuclear conflagration.

This is a form of denialism by inattention and repressed fear, as well as elite-managed propaganda to help keep the public calm. It ignores the dangers posed by Western and non-Western development of their nuclear arsenals, the breakdown of conventional and nuclear arms control treaties, perpetual US wars to protect global power and profit, and the rise of a New Cold War era, centered around direct or proxy conflicts with Russia and China, that can escalate over time into nuclear war.

DOI: 10.4324/9781003401483-6

Regarding the need to focus anew on the extinction threat of nuclear war, famed Vietnam war whistleblower and former high-level nuclear planner, Daniel Ellsberg made clear in his 2017 work, *The Doomsday Machine*, that extinction by nuclear war is as great and probable a threat as during the Cold War between the United States and the Soviet Union, when the world was much more focused on it:

> The hidden realty ... is that for over fifty years, all-out thermonuclear war – an irreversible, unprecedented and almost unimaginable calamity for civilization and most life on earth ... [was and remains] a catastrophe waiting to happen.[1]

Ellsberg, at this writing just diagnosed with terminal cancer at age 92, has been one of the most persistent and important critics of nuclear militarism and the never-ending "danger of near-term extinction." Despite fading attention, "the problem remains still true today," as it was when students and the whole world focused on the possible end of life during the Cuban missile crisis. This ongoing crisis, Ellsberg writes, is the greatest moral crisis humanity has ever faced, one created by our own invention and policies:

> No policies in human history have more deserved to be recognized as immoral. Or insane. The story of how this calamitous predicament came about and how and why it has persisted for over half a century is a chronicle of human madness.[2]

The New Cold Wars and Extinction

The madness Ellsberg describes has not gone away. Two extinction threats arising from war exist and are growing today – and both are subject to continuing denial. This is, itself, madness, since denying the threats undercuts the ability to respond to them.

The first major threat is the view that the end of the Cold War and collapse of the Soviet Union in 1990 – has greatly reduced the chance of a global nuclear war destroying life on the planet. This is an illusion partly because the Cold War has not disappeared. In fact, the rivalry and tensions between the United States and Russia are evolving now into a New Cold War, arguably more dangerous than the old one. And, indeed, the growing competition and hostility between the United States and China is seen by a number of observers as eerily parallel to the old Cold War with United States and Russia.

The New Cold War can be seen in both geo-political rivalries and the breakdown or weakening of nuclear arms agreements that could quickly escalate political and military tensions in US–Russia relations, as well as potentially between the United States and China. The US media and national security apparatus focus increasingly on the "China threat," a major security theme of the Trump and Biden Administration. This could bring the United States into conflict with both Russia and China around east Asian as well as global economic and military security matters. In 2021, the Biden administration hit both Russia and China with sanctions for cyber-hacking that signaled a hardening of conflicts with both these nuclear rivals, both of which could escalate into extremely perilous military conflicts. We look here at the New Cold War with Russia, and take up the risks of a new Cold War with China later in this chapter and again in Chapter 8.

A multitude of other conflicts pit the United States against other Russian allies that could inflame the US–Russian relationship, including Iran, Syria, Venezuela, Crimea, Cuba, and Syria. Moreover, border disputes between Eastern European and Baltic nations with Russia, disputes over the existence and aims of NATO, and conflict over international trade all are dangerous issues that pit Russia and the United States against each other. Any one of these issues could escalate into a more serious crisis and war.

The view of Russia as the primary enemy is an enduring legacy in a New Cold War. It presents itself as an unspoken but nonetheless central threat to US national security and survival. It is an operational premise of US foreign policy elites in the State Department and Pentagon as well as both the Republican and Democratic Parties, as documented authoritatively by the late Princeton political scientist, Stephen Cohen, in his 2019 book, *War with Russia*.[3]

The depth of New Cold War thinking became evident, ironically, when the Democratic Party and many liberal media elites, including progressive MSNBC cable hosts such as Rachel Maddow, continuously attacked President Trump for "going soft" on Russia. The larger hidden story told by even liberal outlets is that Russia is a hostile, aggressive and expansionary enemy of the United States and the "free world." Defining Russia in this way appeared to be the way that anti-Trumpists of all partisan persuasions felt they could get legitimacy, because it was the foreign policy bedrock view of the national security apparatus and the public.[4]

The extinction threat invisibly grows as both political parties embrace the story of Russia's antagonism and dangerousness. Nuclear crises could obviously escalate in the South China sea and east Asia, where China and Russia tend to be allied in opposing US military and economic dominance. But the dangers of escalation and war with Russia could quickly emerge in places like Iran where Russia (and nuclear China) both support the Iranians and may resist military provocations by the United States. Perhaps an even greater nuclear threat lies on the Russia border, where Cold War tensions and NATO expansion have always been tinder for a major firestorm between the United States and Russia. This began with the US breaking its 1988 promise to Russian president Mikhail Gorbachev to not advance NATO "one inch closer" to the Russian border. This pledge was made in return for Gorbachev's acceptance of a unified Germany, one aligned with the United States and Western Europe.[5] The nuclear extinction threat is particularly dangerous here, and growing as the United States seeks to deploy new nuclear and anti-ballistic forces near that border, partly in the name of a growing threat of Russian border expansion in Ukraine.

Between 2016 and 2019, as discussed in Chapter 8, the Trump Administration essentially tore up the major nuclear arms agreements that appeared to be stabilizing the Russian–American nuclear relationship. Biden upped the ante by approving and funding further new "small" tactical or battlefield nukes most likely to trigger a nuclear exchange on the Russian Border. President Biden has taken a far more adversarial stance toward Russia than Trump did, especially on issues from Russian expansion to cyber ransomware attacks to Russian gas and other trade deals with the Europeans.

But beyond the New Cold War, other factors have made the existential nuclear threat ever larger. One is the proliferation of nuclearized nations that are growing their nuclear arsenals, such as North Korea, Israel, Pakistan, India, and China, as well as other non-nuclear countries, such as Iran, that may be moving to create a nuclear force. These are all in volatile regions where military conflict is frequent and often suck in both the United States and Russia.[6] They are also nations, along with Iran and North Korea, where long-standing conflicts about nuclear proliferation could blow up. The denial of nuclear extinction rests partly on the view that any conflicts between such countries, while dangerous, will not likely to lead to the global nuclear war resulting in the extinction of humanity. While conflicts involving nuclear exchanges between these countries could remain limited, there also is the real possibility that they could go global. As noted earlier, the escalation from conventional to nuclear war is by far the most likely way nuclear war will break out. Many other countries are also in volatile, unstable regions where a "limited" conflict could quickly escalate into a bigger one, drawing in the United States and Russia. This happened in the 1973 conflict between Israel and the Arab nations that sucked in both the United States and Russia. It is now regarded as the war that came closest to destroying the world, second only to the 1963 Cuban missile crisis.[7]

Iran and North Korea today are two other volatile zones in which conflicts over nuclear weapons could trigger a regional or global nuclear war, potentially pulling in Russia, China, and the United States. The same can be said about conflict between India and Pakistan, both nuclear states long at odds over Kashmir and now inflamed by India's 2019 nationalist move to annex the occupied Kashmiri territory.[8] Any war between India and Pakistan could trigger huge nuclear destruction, even if it didn't draw in China, Russia, or the United States, which it obviously might. A group of scientists, mostly based at the University of Colorado, simulated the outcome of a nuclear exchange between India and Pakistan; their terse description of such a "limited" event is bone chilling:

> [Fatalities] could reach 50 to 125 million people, and nuclear-ignited fires could release 16 to 36 Tg of black carbon in smoke, depending on yield. The smoke will rise into the upper troposphere, be self-lofted into the stratosphere, and spread globally within weeks. Surface sunlight will decline by 20 to 35%, cooling the global surface by 2° to 5°C and reducing precipitation by 15 to 30%, with larger regional impacts. Recovery takes more than 10 years. Net primary productivity declines 15 to 30% on land and 5 to 15% in oceans threatening mass starvation and additional worldwide collateral fatalities.[9]

These catastrophic outcomes assume that the conflict does not involve the two states' allied nuclear superpowers.

The downplaying of nuclear danger at the end of the old Cold War also reflects two important misperceptions. One is that the reduction in the overall size of the world's nuclear arsenals significantly reduces the risk of nuclear war and extinction. Reduction in the size of arsenals is welcome for many reasons, but to believe that it massively lowers the risk of either nuclear war or extinction is wrong. It reflects what we have called "weaponitis,"[10] ignoring not only the risk of escalation from conventional to nuclear war in any conflict involving a nuclear nation, but also the reality that it takes only a small nuclear exchange, perhaps involving as few as a hundred hydrogen nuclear bombs dropped on ten cities, that could create what astro-physicist Carl Sagan called "nuclear winter," that could destroy human civilization. Sagan and his colleagues wrote soberly of the existential threat:

> When combined with the prompt destruction from nuclear blast fires, and fallout and the later enhancement of solar ultraviolet radiation due to ozone depletion, long-term exposure to cold, dark, and radioactivity could pose a serious threat to human survivors and to other species ... The possibility of the extinction of *Homo sapiens* cannot be excluded.[11]

The extreme power of nuclear weapons makes their numbers far less decisive in survival; even a small number of nukes create the capacity and probability of a nuclear holocaust.

The other misperception is that nuclear annihilation is less likely today because countries, including nuclear powers, do not want to commit suicide and are rational enough to engage only in wars with conventional weapons. The assumption of rationality is problematic. War itself has always been cloaked in irrationalities of glory and power that make assumption of rational military decisions historically unfounded.[12]

Moreover, even if such rationality existed and led countries to only start or enter wars with conventional weapons, the dangers of nuclear annihilation would persist; the escalation of conventional conflicts and wars – perhaps increasingly involving trade and cyber hacking as well as conventional military provocation – is the primary route to nuclear wars.[13] The nuking of Hiroshima and Nagasaki in World War II, the only actual nuclear war, represented an escalation of a very large conventional conflict to a nuclear war. This came close to happening in the 1973 war between Israel and the Arab states.

Profit and War: Capitalism, Militarism, and Extinction

Capitalism is often viewed by its advocates as systemically peaceful. The idea is that capitalist democracies don't tend to fight each other, preferring trade to war. This view prevails in the United States, where dominant neo-conservative and realist thinkers in the State Department and Pentagon tie the threat of wars to the alleged aggressiveness of non-capitalist states such as Russia, Iran, China, Cuba, or Venezuela, which are seen as non-capitalist aspiring leaders of war blocs.

Capitalist theorists and think tanks have been explicit in denying any inherent war-like disposition in capitalist systems and about the connection between capitalism and peace. The Mises Institute, the Cato Institute, the Hoover Institute, and other influential capitalist think tanks churn out tracts explicitly denying that capitalism is war-like or systemically inclined toward imperialism:

> Of all the false charges leveled against capitalism, the indictment of promoting or requiring imperialism and warfare is most certainly the least deserved .... Capitalism neither requires nor promotes imperialist expansion. Capitalism did not create imperialism or warfare. Warlike societies predate societies with secure private property. The idea that inequity or underspending gives rise to militarism lacks any rational basis. Imperialistic tendencies exist due to ethnic and nationalistic bigotries, and the want for power. Prosperity depends upon our ability to prevent destructive acts. The dogma of destructive creation fails as a silver lining to the cloud of warfare. Destructive acts entail real costs that diminish available opportunities.[14]

In this spirit, capitalist elites and their political allies who run foreign policies of top Western states celebrate what they see as a Western capitalist and US exceptionalism breeding a more peaceful world than pre-capitalist societies could ever imagine. This view is used by elites to blind the public to the history and systemic DNA of capitalism that breeds chronic militarism and now threatens global survival.

We consider below five core DNA strands of capitalism that breed violence and war. They play a central role through the history of Western capitalist societies into the present.

In the 18th and 19th centuries, European capitalist countries built huge militaries to ensure their own empires, which required economies oriented toward global military expansion and control. Since the end of World War II, the United States has emerged as the military goliath, promising to maintain global security against Communism and terrorism. While justified as the only way to secure global freedom and democracy, President Eisenhower's warning about the growing power of the military-industrial complex (MIC) offers a better framework for understanding US militarism, and the Cold War, and current extinction threats. For underneath all the national security ideology about protecting freedom and democracy lie the imperatives of a militarized capitalist system, which depends on expansion and military power to secure profits both at home and abroad. In a nuclear age, this is a recipe for a permanent extinction threat.

Military-Backed Expansion

Capitalism is systemically intertwined with militarism to expand and ensure profit through global military dominance. This is not just a Marxist shibboleth. *New York Times* journalist Thomas Friedman, hardly a Marxist of any flavor, has wryly observed that:

> The hidden hand of the market will never work without a hidden fist. ...
> ... Indeed, McDonald's cannot flourish without McDonnell Douglas, the designer of the U.S. Air Force F-15. And the hidden fist that keeps the world safe for Silicon Valley's technologies to flourish is called the U.S. Army, Air Force, Navy and Marine Corps.[15]

Britain's expansion from a small island to an empire stretching from "sea to shining sea" is the iconic historic model of capitalism expansion, which led to globalization. America's McDonnell Douglas, a giant of the US military industrial-complex whose very existence depends on US military expansion, is the American heir of the European military companies that made European colonial globalism possible and underwrote the profitability of both civilian and military European corporations. America's militarized capitalism in the current era reflects the destruction of European economies in two World Wars, and the rise of the United States itself as the military guarantor of expansion essential to both US and European corporate profitability.

Karl Marx claimed more than 170 years ago in *The Communist Manifesto* that capitalism is inherently expansionist and had already evolved by the mid-19th century into a global system.

> The need of a constantly expanding market for its products chases the bourgeoisie over the entire surface of the globe. It must nestle everywhere, settle everywhere, establish connexions everywhere. ...
>
> ... It [capitalism] compels all nations, on pain of extinction, to adopt the bourgeois mode of production; it compels them to introduce what it calls civilization into their midst, i.e., to become bourgeois themselves. In one word, it creates a world after its own image.[16]

Influential 20th-century social scientists and theorists, such as US sociologist Immanuel Wallerstein and European economic historian Fernand Braudel, argue that capitalism is a "world-system," in which capitalist nations carves up as large a part of the world as they conquer and divide it into a "core" and a "periphery." The core is the imperial heartland of Western powers that sucks blood from the periphery to secure oil and other profitable resources, as well as cheap labor and global markets.[17]

History offers considerable support for this way of thinking – as almost all Western capitalist nations – Great Britain, France, Germany, Spain, and even little Belgium and the Netherlands expanded their reach to build empires for exactly these purposes. US expansion became fully globalized in 1945, after World War II, seeking control of the areas conquered by most of the European powers over the prior two centuries. Today, it still seeks to control nearly every part of the world in the name of freedom and national security – but actually to secure maximum resources and markets, and to gain in its competition with European nations or China.[18]

Military expansion is almost as old as civilization itself, but European colonial capitalism organized it into a far more vast and deadly agenda than did precapitalist civilizations. For our purposes, the key new reality is that after World War II, military expansion, for the first time in history, threatened to blow up the whole world. The invention of nuclear weapons changed not the motive for systemic military expansion but the potential consequences. Never before was extinction a potential result of an age-old drive to conquer for money.

Militarized Hegemony

The idea of hegemony builds on the idea of expansion; it describes the kind of power that the expansion is intended to achieve. Hegemony is a system of enduring control – ultimately based on military power – over a large area. As just noted, in Western capitalist nations over the last few centuries, it historically has taken the form of the world-system project, achieved first through colonialism and then the neo-colonialism still favored by the United States, and documented most thoroughly in the numerous historical analyses of US hegemony analyzed by Noam Chomsky, including in his *Hegemony or Survival* and *Who Rules the World?*[19]

The pursuit of global hegemony is endemic to global capitalism and organizes the world system around one or more competing hegemons. This systemic economic and military infrastructure of hegemony is parallel to the fossil-fuel infrastructure built over centuries. The two infrastructures are intertwined, and both are breeding grounds for the contemporary extinction stage.

The fierceness and endless hegemonic wars of empires before capitalism makes clear that hegemons arise in many different economic orders. But pre-capitalism hegemons do not enshrine profit as essential to their system's survival, even if they do reflect a willingness to slaughter others for booty or glory.

Wallerstein and Arrighi argue that virtually all major Western capitalist societies expanded and developed as hegemonic powers.[20] European nations could not have built and consolidated their capitalist systems without hegemonic militarism.[21] The competition for dominance among the British, French, German, and other European capitalist nations was fierce and led to endless European wars as well as massive investment in colonial conquest, since those refraining from such investments and violence would ultimately lose power to more militarily successful rivals and could see their markets and profits shrink or disappear. Competition among colonizing hegemonic powers, especially Britain and Germany, helped fuel both World War I and World War II. But it bears repetition that never before the current era has the struggle for hegemony meant taking the risk of blowing up the world, a kind of madness that Ellsberg views as systemic insanity.

Arrighi has written about the prospects of a dangerous hegemonic conflict between the United States and China,[22] a theme raised by many other scholars, including the political scientist, Graham Allison. The thread underlying both their analyses is that a world organized around hegemonic principles become particularly dangerous in a period of hegemonic transition. Many analysts now see China as a rising hegemonic power challenging the declining hegemonic power of the United States. Looking historically at the relation between Athens and Sparta, Allison notes that tensions become explosive when a hegemon in decline sees a new hegemon rising and threatening its power. He calls this the "Thucydides Trap," based on the ancient historian, Thucydides, who described the rise of Athens as a structural threat to Spartan hegemony that led to war. As Allison writes:

Thucydides identified two key drivers of this dynamic: the rising power's growing entitlement, sense of its importance, and demand for greater say and sway, on the one hand, and the fear, insecurity, and determination to defend the status quo this engenders in the established power, on the other.[23]

In his best-selling book, *Destined for War*,[24] Allison argues that the rapid rise of China as a regional and potential global hegemon, is leading to a new Thucydides Trap. Analyzing 16 cases over the last several centuries of a hegemonic transition, Allison argues that 12 led to war – including those between leading competing colonial powers such as Britain and France and Britain and Germany. Allison argues that there is now need for urgent diplomacy to avoid a US–China war. When the rising power, in this case China, is expanding its economic and diplomatic or military power at great speed, and the established hegemon, in the case, the United States responds with fear, antagonism, and resolve to remain number one, history suggests a serious possibility of war, either by miscalculation or design. As we show in Chapter 8, many areas of contention suggest a New Cold War with China is already underway and is a serious extinction risk.

War Stimulus

The United States pulled out of the long Great Depression only after World War II. During the four years of that war, the US government spent more money than in all the prior years combined since the beginning of the nation. It didn't take genius to realize that opening the floodgates of money spent on war might prove to be the most powerful way of pulling capitalist societies out of their recurrent deep recessions and depressions.

This was not an accidental discovery. The great British economist, John Maynard Keynes, a leading advisor to the United States, the United Kingdom, and other powerful capitalist nations that nearly collapsed in the Great Depression, argued that capitalism was inherently vulnerable to serious downturns, linked to insufficient demand by consumers. The only solution to such inherent capitalist "demand-side" crises, Keynes argued, was for the government to pour vast amounts of money into the economy, a kind of pump-priming or economic stimulus that would kick-start the economy out of Depression.

During the 1930s, Keynes advised President Roosevelt to spend massively on jobs and social programs as the way to solve the demand-side crisis and move the United States out of its Depression. Roosevelt did not immediately become a Keynesian but by 1936 he had begun to craft major spending programs on public works, highways, forest reclamation, and other job-creation programs.[25] Along with his investment in new social programs like Social Security, this vast government spending became the core of the New Deal, organized to jump-start demand. It would put people back to work and the capitalist economy would be humming again.

But while the civilian spending helped, the US economy did not pull out entirely from the Depression. It wasn't until the United States began investing vast amounts in war preparations after the German invasion of Poland in 1939 that the economy began to grow more rapidly. When the United States invested massively in munitions, ships and planes as it prepared for war, demand for goods put millions of US workers back on the payroll. As the United States formally entered the war after the Japanese bombed Pearl Harbor in 1941, millions of women gained wages that could be spent on their households, with the money ricocheting through the economy and kick-starting massive new and broad-based economic growth.

By the end of the war, the United States had spent in the four years of wartime far more than FDR had invested in the civilian programs of the New Deal – indeed, as noted above, more than all prior spending by the US government. This proved to be an astonishing powerful stimulus to put the economy back on a roaring path to growth. The spending on war to revitalize the economy has come to be known as "military Keynsianism."[26]

Military Keynsianism was not new, since European capitalist countries had long been using military spending to boost their economies and expand growth and profit at home and in their colonies. It has now become a standard fiscal policy and economic stimulus by which the government of many capitalist countries, and especially the United States, use to keep their economies growing. Such spending is costly, and a delicate balance by policymakers is required to ensure enough spending in bust cycles to revive the economy but not so much in boom times that it causes inflation or unsustainable debt.

Nonetheless, war stimulus is a central way that capitalist economies have sought to manage recurrent capitalist recessions and other down-turns. Since most capitalists were not prepared to boost worker wages, seeing labor costs as a major drain on profit, capitalism is recurrently faced with "demand-side" crises in which wages are too low to create demand for the products that employers are churning. Capitalists don't want high government spending on New Deal-style, civilian job-creation or social programs. So, they are looking toward military spending as a better, double-barreled solution. On the one hand, it pumps up aggregate demand and primes the capitalist pump in down-turns. On the other hand, it also creates the military infrastructure enabling the chronic wars that pay for expansion abroad and underwrite hegemonic war. This became part of Establishment thinking after World War II:

Theories of Military Keynesianism and the Military-Industrial Complex became popular after the Second World War, and perhaps for a good reason. The prospect of military demobilization, particularly in the United States, seemed alarming. The U.S. elite remembered vividly how soaring military spending had pulled the world out of the Great Depression, and it feared that falling military budgets would reverse this process. If that were to happen, the expectation was that business would tumble, unemployment would soar, and the legitimacy of free-market capitalism would again be called into question.

Seeking to avert this prospect, in 1950 the U.S. National Security Council drafted a top-secret document, NSC-68. The document, which was declassified only in 1977, all but explicitly called on the government to use higher military spending as a way of preventing such an outcome.[27]

Both Keynesian and Marxist analysis suggest that capitalism is systemically dependent on a MIC. The MIC carries out essential economic functions, including capacity for guaranteeing global markets, access to global resources and cheap labor. Simultaneously, it serves as the essential backstop to prevent collapse of capitalist domestic economies into demand-side crises, recessions and depressions.

The corollary of this is that wars and military spending do not simply enrich the Lockheed-Martins, Raytheons and other giants of the complex. The MIC depends for its very existence on military spending and war. But civilian companies are themselves dependent on military spending and war to ward off the demand-side recessions that their own low wages help create. Military spending allows the economy to keep going robustly even with low wages – with the government putting the pedal to the military metal to compensate for the demand crisis built into low-wage capitalism.

In other words, militarism is essential to the profits of both the military industrial complex and the entire civilian sector in modern capitalism. Military and civilian companies are mutually dependent on militarism, and tend to become promoters of "national security" and sponsors of war. Before the nuclear age, this led to colonial empires and mass warfare but not the prospect of extinction. But, today, as capitalism remains ever more dependent on militarism to secure global profits, the cost has become incalculable. The MIC since 1945 – which Eisenhower warned us about – is the first in history that poses a real and present danger of extinction. As capitalism becomes more dependent on a nuclearized MIC, it is unlike any prior system of economic stimulus because it inextricably ties profit and prosperity to a willingness to destroy all life.

Legitimation: Enemies, Security, and Glory

The capitalist nation is like an upstairs/downstairs house we described in the last chapter. Capitalists themselves live in luxury upstairs. Working people live downstairs in plain quarters or in the basement in dark poverty.

As monopoly capitalism evolves out of earlier competitive capitalism, the inequalities between the upstairs and the downstairs get worse. The upstairs becomes a capitalist aristocracy and the downstairs a kind of modern servant quarters. This is perhaps why television shows like *Upstairs/Downstairs* or *Downton Abbey* became so popular.

This creates what the Italian theorist, Antonio Gramsci, called a chronic "legitimation crisis" in capitalism.[28] A big difference between upstairs and downstairs raises questions about the fairness of the system. Capitalists try to quell such questioning and unrest downstairs by pointing to the stairways in the house. People who are hard-working and smart can climb to the upstairs. The only people condemned to stay in the downstairs or basement are lazy or unworthy. This is how capitalists have often tried to show the legitimacy of their system. They tell the story of meritocracy. The differences between upstairs and downstairs simply reflect the differences between those with merit and those without it. The meritocratic system is fair because it sorts out these natural differences and rewards the deserving.

But over time, the inequalities between upstairs and downstairs not only increase but the stairways narrow. This throws the meritocracy story into question. If narrow stairways prevent people with the true opportunity to move up, merit is no longer being rewarded and the house seems designed simply to reward people born upstairs.

Workers downstairs could begin to look around at other houses in the neighborhood. The danger is that they might begin to identify with the people living downstairs in other houses rather than with the people living upstairs in their own house. That is the deep crisis that capitalists seek to avoid at all cost.

When the meritocracy story loses credibility, capitalists have to find another story – and it is deeply connected with enemies, glory and war. One version could be called the "security story," which Derber fleshed out with Yale Magrass in *Moving Beyond Fear: Upending the Security Story In Capitalism, Fascism and Democracy*.[29] The security story tells people downstairs that the other houses in the neighborhood are enemies of "our house." Downstairs workers in the house need to unite with their own upstairs housemates, who have the money and desire to protect them. If other houses (nations) attack, in fact, the lives of the downstairs workers are in grave danger. A nationalist renaissance uniting the upstairs with the downstairs is the only way to guarantee survival and security against a dangerous neighborhood of hostile houses.[30]

The security story requires preparation for war. Each capitalist nation needs to be ready to defend itself against enemy houses. This means investing large amounts in the military and in actual wars when the house is attacked – or needs to pre-emptively attack enemies to ensure security. It's an old story but only today is it an existential threat. Constantly fighting enemies means a permanent risk of human destruction.

Another way of characterizing the security story is a story about glory, as discussed in Derber and Magrass's book, *Glorious Causes*.[31] As the capitalist house, whether in Europe or the United States, took up arms and went to war, it needed a deep cultural and visceral idea of what the house was fighting for and who were the true enemies. This led to a story about the glory of the house and its civilization threatened by its enemies, as well as a story about the glory of war itself.

Today, the capitalist glory story has gained its greatest strength and legitimacy in the United States, where, as just noted, extreme inequality between upstairs and downstairs has grown greater than in the European capitalist countries. The Reagan revolution led a military struggle of glory to defeat the "evil empire" of Soviet Communism. George W. Bush would lead a glorious war against "radical Islamic terrorism." Donald Trump would "make America great again," by promising to restore the glory of traditional American power. Trump's nationalism was a glory crusade, playing on the fears of "evil Muslims," criminal immigrants, fanatic terrorists, and resentments of a "forgotten" US downstairs.[32]

Trump would restore the honorable culture of deserving white downstairs workers in the American house, by fighting for their religion and traditional family values. Dividing the downstairs in the house by race, Trump resorted to one of the most successful chapters in the glory story, arguing the security and honor of the white downstairs was being eroded by lazy moochers, "those people" who liberals try to unfairly subsidize with welfare. The "deplorables" needed defense,[33] and Trump's story of security and honor would put them back at the center of the world's greatest nation, symbolized by the red hats of MAGA.

Trump, like Reagan, Churchill and all the Western capitalist champions of Western power and nationalism, recognized the glory of war itself.[34] This again goes all the way back to feudalism, before capitalism, where the blue-blooded knights and aristocrats fought in God's name to bring glory to their people. Capitalism would save itself by returning to the glory story of the earlier ancient aristocratic systems it replaced. War and civilizational glory would prove that capitalism was a divinely inspired force for Christianity and the West, the world's greatest religion and civilization. But, once again, the old glory story has completely new consequences. Never before in history have glorified wars threatened total extinction of life. This is the uniqueness and madness of capitalist glory today.

Irrational Rationality and Wars of Extinction

The bottom line of this chapter: while war has been a staple of civilization for millennia, capitalism is the first system that fuels wars threatening the total extinction of life. Ironically, this is a reflection, in some ways, of the "successes" of capitalism. It is also a product of the system's "irrational rationality."[35]

Capitalism reflected the emergence of the 18th-century Enlightenment's commitment to reason over religion. Religion and faith had dominated the Middle Ages and much of the pre-capitalist world. But the European Enlightenment of Locke, Voltaire, and Diderot would celebrate the rise of a new capitalist order that was based on science, rationality and technological advancement. Capitalism promised a future of individual freedom and prosperity, that would unlock both economic prosperity based on efficient scientific technologies and personal freedom and fulfillment unshackled by traditional religious rules and constraints.

Capitalism delivered on its economic and technological commitments to materialistic advance, based on scientific rationality and organizational and technological efficiency. It was the first system promising that scientific rationality could be harnessed to generate economic productivity and technological advancements on a scale never seen in history. Marx himself celebrated this achievement, writing in *The Communist Manifesto* that capitalism had unleashed a revolution of technical advances and an explosion of productivity:

> The bourgeoisie, during its rule of scarce one hundred years, has created more massive and more colossal productive forces than have all preceding generations together. Subjection of Nature's forces to man, machinery, application of chemistry to industry and agriculture, steam-navigation, railways, electric telegraphs, clearing of whole continents for cultivation, canalisation of rivers, whole populations conjured out of the ground – what earlier century had even a presentiment that such productive forces slumbered in the lap of social labour?[36]

But capitalism's rationality and productivity was also tied inextricably to the irrationality of greed and violence, equally inbred parts of the capitalist order. Capitalism sought expansion and profit at the expense of needed public goods and the well-being of workers and the environment. For all the reasons discussed above, this led to expansion and control, ultimately guaranteed by military force. Any capitalist society seeking to beat the competition has to ensure that its state produces the most rational and technologically advanced military, one that could defeat any rival.

Capitalism sought an all-powerful military with the rationally sophisticated organizational capacity and military technology. But since war is a system of violence and destruction, the more rational the means, the more irrational the ends. As the military is rationalized, it creates the demand and capacity for more and more death and extreme war, something that is inevitably irrational in its scale of destructiveness.

This was most profoundly proved by the development of nuclear weapons and their use in World War II. It is hard to imagine a more "irrational rationality." The most sophisticated scientists had brought into the world the technology that could destroy it. In the extinction stage after World War II, the most powerful nations, especially capitalist nations but all others that could copy or create nuclear technology, built their militaries into mass instruments of extermination that could turn war into nuclear holocausts of extinction.

The irrational rationality of militarized capitalism became clear with the rise of European empires over the last few centuries, well before the current extinction stage of the nuclear era. In the pre-extinction stage, European capitalist powers applied their scientific and technical rationality not only to progressive economic innovation but to increasingly lethal military technology and capacity. The quest for colonial empires of the great European states incentivized more and more capable militaries that could conquer and create imperial empires, using weapons causing death on a scale that pre-capitalist societies could not achieve. Capitalist wars became more and more destructive, using technologically advanced weapons and organizational discipline not seen before.

This irrational rationality reached its apogee in World War I and World War II. Over 20 million people died in World War I, a senseless war among capitalist European powers to competing for more colonies and greater imperial control. In World War II, the same players with different leaders fought an even more destructive war, leading to the death of 60–70 million people. The rationality that capitalist powers created virtually destroyed Europe and Russia – not to mention its actual destructiveness across many proxy wars – producing the height of irrationality involving a kind of collective suicide. And the two world wars led to the ultimate irrational rationality: the technology of nuclear weapons that was used by the "winners" and could exterminate all life on the planet, inaugurating the extinction stage beginning in 1945.

In a sense, this reflected the successes of capitalism. Over a few hundred years, it had harnessed science and rationality to create systems of both the production and violence that it needed. But its successes translated into the irrational rationality of the extinction stage, which can only be seen as the product of the greatest scientific rationality in history and also the most evil and extreme irrationality that put the future of all life on the planet in jeopardy. The dangers in the current era are now magnifying even further in the United States, as it intensifies hegemonic militarism in the nuclear age, one in which militarized capitalism for the first time in history becomes a leading threat of total extinction of life through nuclear war. This Americanized extinction threat is fleshed out in Chapter 8.

Part II
The United States and Extinction

5 America's "Extinction Exceptionalism"

A growing number of Americans are "preppers" – more specifically "dooms-day preppers." In the past, this term evoked images of wild-eyed cultists, fringe libertarians, or survivalists with gun arsenals, mainly in rural areas of the West or South. But the term now includes much broader sectors of the population who worry about and prepare for possible extreme disaster, including global annihilation. Religious and non-religious, urban and rural, college educated or high school drop-outs, preppers are increasingly part of mainstream America.

A survey report by Finder.com showed that the number of preppers mush-roomed during the first year of the COVID-19 pandemic. But there were mil-lions anxious about and preparing for the end of the world even *before* the pandemic – and even after the majority of Americans were vaccinated in the United States. A survey by Finder.com reported in 2021:

> Until recently you may have heard the term "doomsday preppers" and pictured a squirrely, Kaczynski-esque, person preparing for the end of days. But in the wake of a global pandemic, a time where even the sim-plest of items like toilet paper were conspicuously absent from the shelves, having a house stocked with sundries and staples seems logical. Perhaps that's why the number of people prepping for doomsday more than dou-bled from the beginning of 2020 to the beginning of 2021 ….
>
> In the last 12 months, roughly 45% of Americans – or about 115.6 mil-lion people – say they spent money preparing or spent money on survival materials. This is way up when compared to the previous year, which saw 20% of Americans (52 million people) spending money on survival materials.
>
> How many Americans are prepared for survival?
>
> In addition to the roughly 45% that bought survival supplies in the last year, with a further 27% of American adults (69 million) say they didn't need to hit the stores because their homes already included survival items at the ready for an emergency.

DOI: 10.4324/9781003401483-8

Adding up the numbers, that's roughly 72% of American adults (184.6 million adults) who are prepping for the end times, a dramatic increase from only 55% of American adults at the start of 2020.[1]

Preppers exist around the world, but may have the most visibility in the developed world in the United States, and for good reasons. One may be the unique role as a country that the United States plays in fueling the extinction threat. The stark truth is that there is no other nation that is as important as the United States in contributing to climate change, nor one more likely to unleash nuclear war. This horrendous reality has a silver lining for Americans: they live in the country with more power than any other nation to help stop extinction. If Americans can change their own country, they might just help save the planet.

During the 2016 Presidential campaign, Noam Chomsky wrote that:

> The two most important issues in all of human history, on which the fate of species depends, are virtually missing from the extensive commentary on the choice of leader for the most powerful country in the world history and from the electoral extravaganza itself. It's not easy to find words to capture the enormity of this extraordinary blindness.[2]

Chomsky was referring, of course, to the two issues of climate change and nuclear war. His analysis leads toward the conclusion that the United States is now the most dangerous nation in the history of the world, essential fueling global extinction. In this chapter, and in all of Part II, we show why this is true – and why it opens up certain possibilities and responsibilities for the United States to play a unique role in saving humanity.

Ultimately, the only solutions to extinction are global. Any "nation-centric" critique or solution could obscure what is obvious. Extinction is a global crisis and requires global action, international solidarity and world-governance and agreements focused on sustaining life on the planet.[3] But America is the world's leading "extinction nation," and still creates and enforces the world's rules more powerfully than any other nation. That could be an asset rather than a liability if the United States were enforcing a survival-friendly set of global values and policies. But the opposite is true.

The United States has created the developed world's most existentially perilous model of capitalism.[4] The US neoliberal model, ushered in by the Reagan revolution in 1980, has catapulted the United States to the role of the nation fueling extinction most powerfully. Neoliberal capitalism promoted by the United States helped create by far the worst climate policy among the economically developed nations and the most dangerous military policies, while also spreading a neoliberalism extinction crisis at home, imperiling economic survival among millions of America's own workers. In other words, America's "exceptionalism" lies now in its policies both at home and abroad leading the world toward extinction.

By virtue of its global hegemonic position, it is imposing and enforcing the triangle of extinction as the rulebook for other nations and the entire world system.

The pace of extinction – and the possibility of stopping it – depends on the toxicity of the triangle that the current hegemon promotes. There are different forms of capitalism, which lead to different rates and forms of growth, expansion, consumerism, and military or environmental destruction. And the culture of the hegemonic elites also varies, in terms of how much they are prepared to sacrifice the common good and survival itself to advance short-term greed and profits. In this Part of our book, we focus on the United States and show why and how it functions as the lead "extinction nation."

Europe vs. United States: Who Leads the Extinction Race?

While all developed nations promote policies leading toward extinction, the US neoliberal capitalist model is far more dangerous to prospects of survival, partly because of its own size, dynamism and successes. American hegemony is a legendary story of the history of US economic power and growth, which has translated into rising standards of living and consumer comforts for many years along with military power, environmental devastation, and global control. America has long celebrated its global economic power, but now resists understanding how its capitalist model and success threaten survival.

A key to understanding American "extinction exceptionalism" is to compare the United States with European nations. In referring to Europe and European nations in this chapter, I will be referring primarily not only to the "Viking" economic and social models of Sweden, Denmark, and other Scandinavian nations, but also considering other major European countries such as Germany and France. While viewed by some as socialist, most European countries represent a more inclusive and socially protective form of capitalism than US neoliberalism. The European systems remain capitalist and even neoliberal in key ways; they are still market economies and have private ownership of big companies and banks, which are profit-driven and create substantial inequality. European wealthy classes, while less oligarchic and powerful than the 1% in the United States, have greater political influence over their societies than is consistent with a fully democratic society; their ability to sustain great power rests on the ancient history of feudalism, monarchy, and bureaucratic history bred deep in the soil of Europe. In the last three decades, the Europeans have incorporated significant features of the neoliberal US model into their own systems. While noting that Europe has a less toxic extinction system today than the United States, we are not romanticizing Europe, which has a long history of imperial power, racism, destructive colonizing hegemony and, notwithstanding social democratic aspirations, class warfare.

Indeed, Europe and the EU continue to have toxic economic and social policies, including its attack on immigrants and its embrace of neoliberalism, especially the fiscal neoliberalism imposed by major financial institutions, such as the German Central Bank. These ruling institutions have embraced neo-liberal policies that undermine distribution of wealth, perpetuate poverty, weaken the most robust environmental initiatives and promote European participation in US military adventures. Europe is often described as a "social democracy," but its long history of feudalism, class hierarchy, and colonizing bureaucracies have led to existential dangers directed toward immigrants and their own working classes. The current European war against Middle Eastern and African immigrants, which is fueling the rise of Far Right and neo-Nazi parties, make clear that Europe is far from a model of a system assuring survival of its own population, let alone the rest of the world.

As shown in Chapter 2, European nations, including Sweden and other "social democratic" capitalist countries, are still fueling extinction, as all capitalist systems do. But the Europeans have taken significant sectors of their economies outside the market and distribute public goods – such as education, health care, and green jobs – to a far wider section of their populations than does the United States.[5] Until the radical changes wrought by the 2022 Russian invasion of Ukraine, countries such as Sweden and Germany have also baked a European form of a partial Green New Deal into their capitalism, have reduced militarism and nuclear arsenals, and have embedded significant human rights into their economies and foreign policies. All this has slowed the race to extinction in Europe, with Sweden, Portugal, and the Netherlands among the leaders on climate reforms.[6]

The European system is not going to end the threat of extinction. They are wealthy nations with high levels of consumption and still high per capita carbon emissions. As one cautionary note on Europe warns:

> The ranking shows that all EU countries are off target: they are failing to increase their climate action in line with the Paris Agreement goal. No single EU country is performing sufficiently in both ambition and progress in reducing carbon emissions.[7]

But European capitalism moves Europeans and the world a step away from the direct dive off the cliff, the direction in which the United States is currently driving the world. If the world moved toward European rather than American capitalism, we might buy time to make the deeper changes that are required to sustain life on the planet.

The difference between the position of the United States and Europe in the extinction race shows that history, economics, politics, and culture all matter. The uniquely dangerous model of US capitalism arises from special features of

America as a nation, including the exceptional power of its monied elites who are committed to both military dominance abroad and corporpate dominance at home. They undermined class politics within the United States as "Un-American" and greatly weakened the countervailing powers of labor that developed in Europe. Europe has had powerful labor unions for more than a century and ruling labor parties through much of the 20th century, with more than 70% of Swedes unionized; in contrast, less than 6% of US private sector workers were in a union in 2019, and the United States has never had a true labor party.[8]

All this translated into an American abandonment of millions of its lower-income workers generating low wages, homelessness, hunger, and poverty not known in most of the social welfare societies of Western and Northern Europe where universal public goods and services protected people. *The abandonment of workers in America normalized a culture of economic triage and extinction of life prospects for millions of working people, a culture that would make it easier to de-sensitize US elites to broader extinction of all social life and the environment fueled by climate change and war.*

What's the Matter with America?

The first step in stopping the race to extinction is an unsentimental education about American capitalism. Such education should be a core requirement of for every US citizen, for survival of life depends on whether Americans understand what is at stake. That "survival education" is the topic of the final chapter of this book. In the current chapter, we briefly note the unique US dangers, introducing five key ways in which the United States has clearly become the world's most dangerous extinction regime.

The five ways are all integral to the US neoliberal capitalist model. They arose in less extreme forms before Reagan's neoliberal revolution. But Reagan's "regime change at home" intensified and fueled all five as extinction forces baked into the US neoliberal system. In this chapter, we briefly introduce these systemic forces, fleshed out in the following chapters.

1. The United States as Hegemon

The US position as global hegemon or super-power helps explain its uniquely militarized capitalism and threat to human survival. European nations played the hegemonic role for several centuries before the United States took over in the 20th century. But since the end of two World Wars, which destroyed much of Europe, and even with the still unfolding consequences of the Ukraine invasion, today's European nations have abandoned the drive to dominate the world militarily, letting the United States assume that role. Europe not only pays a price in power but also benefits by escaping the burden of the massive military spending that a global hegemon must assume. But whether you focus on the price or the benefits, there is no question that it makes the United States unlike all other nations, and is the foundation of the extinction threat the United States now poses to the world, in the name of defending it.

The United States became the world's unquestioned hegemonic power only after World War II, and its position as a globally dominant nation became more and more important since 1945. In the Reagan revolution, the drive toward hegemony mushroomed, a symptom of the globalization inherent in neoliberalism. Neoliberal appetites for profit on a global scale intensified the US hegemonic imperative since 1980 to secure control of global markets and resources.

US history is a long story of hegemony – and of the development of the most militarized capitalism in the world.[9] In Chapter 4, we discussed US hegemony since World War II in some detail, showing how it makes America unique militarized and uniquely threatening to human survival. Here, we just briefly highlight the long history of this claim to global "leadership," and how US hegemonic aspirations lie at the root of the existential threats it now poses to survival.

From the very beginning, America has seen itself as a "beacon on the hill," inspired by God to guide the world.[10]

But American hegemony today is ill-timed in the long arc of history. In other eras, no hegemon could end human civilization and kill off all life species. Hegemons have always been dangerous, but the United States is the first global hegemon in the age of extinction, giving it extinction powers never matched in history.

Even if the outcome is potential extinction, US elites have always assumed that the world prospers only when it follows American values and dictates. American rules must save the world and America itself, even, perhaps, if it requires destroying it.

2. The Exceptionalist American Oligarchy: Wealth and Extinction

Every year in Sun Valley, Utah, there is a festive gathering of the nation's billionaires, who mingle together with top politicians, media moguls and other United States and global leading corporate tycoons.[11] This is the playground of today's neoliberal billionaires, whose wealth and power have become unprecedented – and a threat to democracy. In 2021, US billionaires owned 31% of the total wealth of the nation, amounting to about 1.2 trillion dollars. In the same year, the bottom 50% of Americans owned about 2% of the nation's wealth. Sun Valley is the playground of creators and rulers of neoliberal capitalism, the current US oligarchy, and they are pushing the pedal to the metal in the race to United States and global extinction.

In all capitalist nations, including partially in Europe, large corporations, banks and wealthy individuals – the capitalist class – tend to rule the country and constitute a ruling oligarchy. Europeans may have their own Sun Valleys, but the power of their oligarchs is far more strictly limited by their commitment to social democratic and social welfare systems. These have permitted workers and labor parties to exercise substantial power throughout the last century, a power that has allowed popular concern about climate change and military extinction to cool the heat of the US oligarchic race to power and extinction.

The modern history of the United States, since the rise of the 1890s original US Robber Barons, has been an oil and military driven capitalist oligarchy at war with democracy, a war increasingly tied now to the fate of the planet. In our new Gilded Age, the oligarchy has used the courts to cement a "pay to play" racket that enshrines unprecedented corporate funding and control of politics in the name of free speech, while driving the policies of fossil fuel growth and militarism creating our 21st-century extinction nightmare. The Supreme Court's decision in 2010 of *Citizens United* gave corporations (and other private entities) the constitutional right, in the name of free speech, to spend virtually unlimited funds on candidates running for office, a constitutional tragedy unleashing billions of increased corporate dollars intensifying the capitalist politics of extinction.

As capitalism evolved toward a neoliberal global system, the US oligarchy created a growing chasm between itself and the mass of US workers, essentially a crisis in economic democracy with implications for extinction. When the oligarchy succeeds in keeping most workers stuck in the downstairs or basement, disenfranchised both economically and politically, they are carrying out a kind of extinction of life prospects at home for economic and human development. This has made it easier for the US oligarchy to deny or desensitize themselves to a routinized, if unconscious, acceptance of broader extinction of the population caused by climate change of war.

3. The American Public Goods Desert

European capitalist societies create a vast range of public goods, ranging from universal health care to free higher education to well-funded public transportation systems (including bicycles-to-share and bicycle lanes) to national public programs of child and elder care. In the age of extinction, their most important public goods are ambitious environmental protection programs and far-reaching policies to fight climate change, as well as reduce militarism, and protect comprehensive public health systems, that underlie hopes of controlling COVID-19 and future pandemics.[12]

In the last several decades, when the Reagan revolution took his neoliberal sledgehammer to welfare and to the health care and environmental protections that help ward off extinction perils. President Biden's health care, child care and climate agendas challenged Reagan's neoliberalism, but Biden faced enormous Republican obstruction. The economist J. K. Galbraith offered a colorful picture of the US public goods desert even before Reagan, a picture that is still recognizable today:

> In one of the best-known passages in *The Affluent Society*, Galbraith described an American family going out for a camping trip in a top-of-the-line "mauve and cerise" automobile, cruising along on a badly paved highway, past a countryside whose natural beauty had been blotted out with billboards, dining on a picnic of packaged foods beside a polluted stream. "Just before dozing off on an air mattress, beneath a nylon tent, amid the stench of decaying refuse, they may reflect vaguely on the curious unevenness of their blessings. Is this, indeed, the American genius?[13]

The United States remains exceptional in its denial or discrediting of the very idea of public goods, even in the age of extinction when public goods are essential to any prospect of human survival. To some degree, that denial is what the idea of capitalism is built around. Nonetheless, European capitalist nations have come to their senses, seeing that a society will die without public goods. They understand that public goods protect their citizens not only against the harsh economic perils faced by US workers, but also are the foundation of climate and environmental programs that are now central to survival.

4. America's Hatred of Government

> Government is not the solution to our problem; government is the problem.
> (Ronald Reagan, 1981)[14]

President Ronald Reagan spoke those exceptional words in his 1981 inaugural address to the country. In a society that devalues public goods, it is hardly surprising that there is hatred of government. Government is the main source of funding for public goods, and the huge US public goods deficit, clearly arises today from the neoliberalism that the Reagan revolution enshrined. The neoliberal breeds a systemic hostility to government as a form of tyranny.

Cornell political scientist Suzanne Mettler, who studies public attitudes toward government, notes that US hostility to government has long been higher than in all other developed nations. She notes that US working people who need government support and depend on it the most have been taught to hate government, equating it with hand-outs and welfare queens[15]:

> Every group throughout the middle class had very unfavorable views toward welfare. Even African Americans, if they were middle-class, were more resentful of welfare than African Americans who were low-income or high-income.

So we've got these parallel patterns going on at once. There's the racial bias, as you mentioned, and then there are the views of middle-income people. The past several decades have been particularly rough for the middle class. Productivity is very high, people are working more hours than ever, and incomes are stagnant. Many of these people feel like they're trapped between the poor, who receive lots of benefits, and the rich, who don't need any help.[16]

The US exceptionalist pattern of hatred is evident when contrasted with European nations. European capitalists and their political allies have been willing to support substantial levels of government spending on the needs of the public and the environment, and have supported massive government investments in social welfare and green transportation and broader green infrastructure. Such public acceptance of activist government is why the Europeans are fueling extinction far less rapidly than the United States. Whether Bidenism can be pushed by a growing majority of Americans to create a public goods rather than neoliberal system is critical to whether humanity will survive.

5. The American Culture of Me, Me, Me

Culture and economics are intertwined, with huge and perilous consequences in the age of extinction. American individualism – leading to the American Dream of pursing one's own star or fortune at the cost of everything else – has long been the master cultural script of US capitalism. When US elites embraced neoliberalism and rejected the New Deal, the culture of individualism became even more extreme, since neoliberals regard all value as coming from prizing above all else individual self-interest in the market.

This individualistic dream has now become a recipe for extinction, since, in the spirit of neoliberalism, it defines success and happiness largely around the frenzied accumulation of wealth and freedom to buy anything I want – a big car, a big home, a long air travel trip – that imperils survival. How many Americans would follow the example of European "green teen" Greta Thunberg, who took a small solar-powered yacht on an uncomfortable two-week sail across the Atlantic in August 2019, to come to a UN climate conference rather than risking the carbon emissions of a plane or big steam ship?[17]

A cultural script of "me, me, me" is no longer part of an abstract academic debate about the merits of capitalism individualism or social democratic collectivism. It is a death knell for society in the age of extinction. Survival now requires that corporations limit their own super-profits, whose growth mercilessly requires and produces more expansion, extraction, and carbon emissions, while ginning up the individual's desires for fantastic wealth and a life of endless consumerism. And survival also requires that ordinary people curb their personal consumerism and materialist ambitions for the sake of survival of the planet.

6   Molecules of Freedom?
America's Climate of Exceptionalism

In 1972, before most Americans had ever heard of climate change, comedian George Carlin rewrote "American the Beautiful," foreseeing the early signs of environmental death in the US:

> O beautiful for smoggy skies
> Insecticided grain
> For strip-mined mountain's majesty
> Above the asphalt plain
> America, America
> Man sheds his waste on thee
> And hides the pines with billboard signs
> From sea to oily sea.
> (George Carlin, Comedian,
> February 28, 1972)[1]

Fifty years after Carlin's rewrite, as the Coronavirus was subsiding and people were celebrating a return to normal, journalist and climate author Roy Scranton reminded Americans what normal means now:

> I remember last March, in the first throes of the pandemic, when normal was upended. Everything shut down. We hoarded toilet paper and pasta. Fear gripped the nation.
>
> Going back to normal now means returning to a course that will destabilize the conditions for all human life, everywhere on earth. Normal means more fires, more category 5 hurricanes, more flooding, more drought, millions upon millions more migrants fleeing famine and civil war, more crop failures, more storms, more extinctions, more record-breaking heat. Normal means the increasing likelihood of civil unrest and state collapse, of widespread agricultural failure and collapsing fisheries, of millions of people dying from thirst and hunger, of new diseases, old diseases spreading to new places and the havoc of war. Normal could well mean the end of global civilization as we know it.
> (Roy Scranton, January 25, 2021)[2]

DOI: 10.4324/9781003401483-9

In his 2019 book, *Internationalism or Extinction*, Noam Chomsky writes about how extinction was being politically locked in by the Republican Party:

> When you consider the stakes, it's a fair question whether there has ever been a more dangerous organization in human history than today's Republican Party.[3]

Chomsky notes that in the 2016 Republican primary presidential debates, "every single GOP candidate denied the facts about climate change." This denialism and extinction position of the GOP intensified under President Trump – and was loudly promoted by the GOP long after Trump was defeated in 2020. Even as mega wildfires burned out of control in California, Oregon, and Washington, sending soot all the way over to cloud the skies over Boston, the Republicans claimed this was caused by bad forest management.[4] The GOP mantra continues that man-made climate change remained a huge hoax while scientists showed that rising temperatures were a primary cause of the fires. Even though the forest fires combined with massive hurricanes, melting of the Arctic ice sheets, sea rise, and extreme heat – with the decade of 2010 to 2020 the hottest United States and global decade in recorded history – the majority of Republicans continued to deny that climate change was real and man-made, proposing more subsidies for oil and gas drilling and fracking.

While focusing on the Republican Party, Chomsky notes the GOP is reflecting broader "amazing blindness as the lemmings march to the precipice," with the mass media and millions of Americans failing to hold the Republicans accountable. President Biden began to change the game, a source of great promise for the future. But Republicans kept obstructing and, despite growing numbers of young US climate activists, the public as a whole is not sounding the emergency alarm needed to prevent the accelerating climate disaster.

The problem clearly goes beyond the Republican Party to the nation itself. True, the Republican Party has been far more complicit in climate denial than the Democratic Party. When President Biden was elected in 2020, he made stopping climate change among his top priorities, promising to halve US carbon emissions by 2030. In 2021, he promoted a massive climate and infrastructure bill costing $3.5 trillion. Millions of ordinary US citizens supported and cheered this "generational" transformation.

But many mainstream businesses, unions, and millions of ordinary voters do not put climate disaster at the top of their list. Biden's immensely important climate initiatives are still far from enough. It is useful again to contrast Europe with the United States. The comparison highlights again America's extinction exceptionalism. In 2021, the EU adopted a major climate initiative for the 27 European countries that would cut carbon emissions by 55% by 2030 from its 1990 level. Biden's plan is more modest, cutting emissions by 40% to 43%

by 2030 from a 1990 level far higher than that of the EU. The Biden Administration is making important progress, but it is far from enough and lags Europe, which is, itself, not ambitious enough to meet the extinction threat. The United States needs to lead the way beyond the EU if we want to save the planet. But even with the Biden climate agenda, the United States, which leads the world in both cumulative carbon emissions and current emissions, is entrenched in a carbonized infrastructure and has not been able to jettison its history of neoliberal policies leading the entire world toward climate catastrophe.

American Gas: The World Can't Breathe

We can begin with some global metrics and comparisons about the American climate of exceptionalism, as shown in Figure 6.1.

China emits more carbon dioxide than the United States, but it emits less per person.[5]

In 2015, China created 28% of the world's total carbon emissions from fuel combustion, the United States created 15%, and the entire rest of the world 21%. India creates 6%, Russia 5%, and Japan 4%. China and the United States continue to lead the world.

The emissions of European nations, which are among the world's wealthiest and thus would predictably be among the top emission producers, are different. The highest emitter is Germany with 2%. The United Kingdom, France, and Italy each contribute just 1%, lower or equal to South Korea, Mexico, and Indonesia.

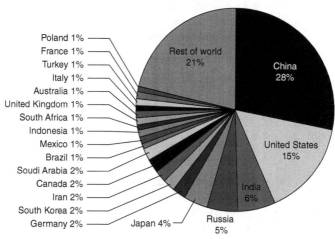

Share of global carbon dioxide emissions from fuel combustion (2015)

Figure 6.1 Share of Carbon Dioxide Emissions From Fuel Combustion (2015). Data: IEA; Image: Union of Concerned Scientists.

If we consider carbon emissions per person, or per capita, the picture looks much worse for the United States. In 2015, the United States emitted 15.53 metric tons of carbon per capita compared to China's 6.59 metric tons per person. India's per capita production is even lower, at 1.58 metric tons per capita.

The current level of carbon emissions shows the share each country has produced over the entire period of industrialization, reaching back to 1750. This is important because the climate crisis is a cumulative one reflecting the total amount of emissions created over a long period of time. Much of the carbon in the atmosphere now endangering the world was produced many years ago. If we consider the historical record of complicity, consider the following picture:

Top Ten CO_2 Emitters, Cumulative 1750–2020

Ranking,[6] 1750–2020:

Rank	Country	Metric Tons (Billions)
1	United States	416.72
2	China	235.56
3	Russia	115.34
4	Germany	92.64
5	United Kingdom	78.16
6	Japan	65.63
7	India	54.42
8	France	38.73
9	Canada	33.58
10	Ukraine	30.56

American exceptionalism is captured in one sentence by Carbon Brief, which compiles this data (see below Figure 6.2):

> What's abundantly clear is that the United States of America is the all-time biggest, baddest greenhouse gas emitter on the planet.[7]

The data are unequivocal. The US cumulative contribution to the climate disaster is by far the greatest – and it continues in this role today. President Biden's strong climate agenda showed the United States can go beyond climate denialism. But for now, for all the reasons detailed below, the United States remains locked into its position as the world's worst fossil fuel regime, leading the race to climate extinction.

Ending the New Deal: The Reagan in Trump and Today's GOP

The Reagan revolution begun in 1980 aimed to kill the New Deal. Indeed, the Reagan revolution has remained busy since Reagan himself died, with presidents of both parties undoing much of the crucial regulation and the public goods that

Cumulative Emissions, 1750–2020

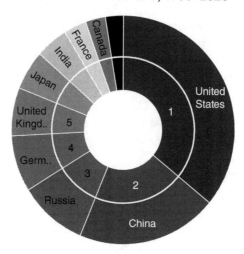

Figure 6.2 Cumulative Emissions, 1750–2020 (Table compiled from: Robbie M. Andrew, "A Comparison of Estimates of Global Carbon Dioxide Emissions from Fossil Carbon Sources," Earth System Science Data 12, no. 2 (June 29, 2020): 1437–1465, https://doi.org/10.5194/essd-12-1437-2020.)

the New Deal created. Democratic Presidents, including Clinton, Obama, and Biden, all embraced Reagan's neoliberal corporate globalization and his massive investment in the military. Only Biden made a surprising and critically important effort to restore a New Deal belief in government and public goods, with the ultimate outcome uncertain at this writing, because of Republican obstruction and the entrenchment of decades of neoliberal policy. The United States remains behind European nations in trying to slow or stop climate extinction.

With the election of Donald Trump in 2016, the US climate agenda embraced policies entirely consistent with the neoliberalism that is Reagan's main legacy. But Trump was more nakedly shameless and extreme about it. While the election of Biden changed US climate policy significantly, we need to briefly review Trump's extreme anti-climate policies, because they hardened the climate denialism that remains fervent in the Republican Party after Trump's defeat, and is still obstructing President Biden's new climate policies. In fact, even with Trump out of office, the forces that he represents remain uncowed, fighting against government at every level and perpetuating climate denialism among millions of Americans.

Trump not only rejected the very idea of climate change but made his efforts to re-invigorate coal and expand oil and gas a kind of moral and cultural crusade. By executive order, in 2017, Trump ordered that the words "climate change" be struck from every federal government document, including scientific research dealing with sea rise or fires, and not be used again. Trump himself, tweeted that carbon fuels were "molecules of freedom." And he describes natural gas as "freedom gas." Moreover, *Forbes* notes this has become more than a random one-time presidential tweet:

> The United States Department of Energy (DOE) has apparently started referring to fossil fuels as "molecules of freedom" and specifically natural gas as "freedom gas", according to its latest press release.[8]

This Orwellian assault on language and truth was accompanied by appointment of cabinet and administrative agency personnel who were climate-deniers tasked with eliminating policies designed to mitigate climate change and, instead, create a more "fossilized" America. Most of the relevant Trump appointees came from the coal and oil industries, or were fossil fuel industry-funded scientists, think tanks or legislative lobbies designed to promote fossil fuels and dismantle environmental regulation.

Trump appointed prominent climate denialists to head the EPA, the Department of Energy, the Department of the Interior, as well as climate skeptics to Secretary of State and Defense. All pursued horrific policies that drastically weakened climate and environmental protection. The most notable example was Oklahoman Scott Pruitt, who Trump appointed as his EPA leader in 2016. Pruitt was arguably the most prominent climate change denier in the United States, other than Trump himself, with a long record of opposing climate and environmental protection. Pruitt, with tight links to oil and gas firms, led the successful effort to withdraw from the Paris Climate Agreement, arguing that its emission targets would negatively impact the US economy and reduce fossil fuel production and use.[9] Pruitt sued his own agency and approved at least 24 regulatory rollbacks at the EPA, and cut his own EPA budget by 30%.[10]

Whether the Biden Administration is able to overturn Trump's disastrous climate legacy is perhaps the most important question of his presidency. Biden rejected the comprehensive Green New Deal proposed by progressives Senator Ed Markey and Rep. Alexandria Ocasio-Cortez in the Democratic Party but he has prioritized climate change, entered back into the Paris agreements in his first day of office, reversed many of Trump's executive orders to deregulate Big Oil and Big Gas, and appointed climate advocates including Al Gore and John Kerry to champion his climate agenda. His 2021 signature $3.5 trillion infrastructure deal did not go as far as the Green New Deal, but placed strong emphasis on creating green infrastructure and cutting carbon emissions. He allocated major funding for electric cars and charging stations, more billions for wind and solar construction, and has sought to create millions of union-based well-paid green jobs in housing construction, public transit and other areas. But Republicans continue to try to obstruct every one of these policies. Moreover, major structural forces, including Big Oil and

US militarism, are blocking the comprehensive, transformative change in climate policy we desperately need – and climate activists show that Biden's proposals omit many of the most urgent deadlines and don't sufficiently tax and shut down the coal, oil, and gas power plants fueling extinction.

War and Climate Change: How US Militarism Drives Climate Disaster

We showed earlier that the United States as hegemon is by far the most militarized nation, locked into endless wars in the Middle East, Southwest Asia, and Central and Latin America. Moreover, the United States is moving toward more aggressive policies and potential militarized conflict with Russia and China. This raises the risk of nuclear extinction but US military policy also fuels climate change, a matter little discussed by the military itself, nor by politicians, the mass media or even by climate protesters or peace activists. Let's be clear: the United States is the greatest climate threat partly because it is the center of the war system and central to the global war system driving climate change.

A quick look at the extinction triangle of Chapter 1 shows that war is a major cause of climate change and that climate change is a major cause of war. The Pentagon has acknowledged as much, stating in its annual reports on major threats that climate change is a major threat to United States and other countries' national security.[11] This is not just because US naval bases in places like Norfolk, Virginia, have been repeatedly flooded by storms and sea rise there. It's a recognition that climate change creates floods and droughts and fires that drive millions of people off their land, seeking shelter where people are already facing Malthusian struggles for survival.[12] Land and food shortages caused by extreme climate-driven heat waves are now widely understood to have been major factors leading to devastating wars in Rwanda, Darfur, and Syria.

What the US military has not acknowledged is the reciprocal way in which the military and its wars drive climate change. It has never, to our knowledge, issued a report about how war fuels climate change. And it has certainly never acknowledged how the scale of US militarism creates one of the greatest threats of climate disaster, far greater than that posed by the militaries of other major capitalist nations, particularly by those in Europe.

The most obvious way that war and militarism cause climate change have to do with the technology of modern war. In the nuclear age, this would seem to be related most of all to the danger of nuclear war; it would destroy not only millions or billions of people but much of the environment capable of supporting life. Radiation in a large thermo-nuclear war would kill other animal species and many of the plants in and out of water that support life. Ironically, nuclear war would create climate change leading to extreme cooling and potential "nuclear winter," where smoke and debris of targeted urban areas would block sunlight and rapidly kill off people, plants and animals.[13]

The greatest high-probability extinction dangers are those connected with preparations for both conventional and nuclear war. Keep in mind that escalation from conventional war is the most likely path to nuclear war.[14] The nations with the greatest threat of climate disasters are the ones already creating massive carbon emissions from their conventional military infrastructure and war training. When European empires were hegemonic, European militaries and wars created the most emissions, especially in the 19th century. But after two world wars in the 20th century, European empires had disappeared and the Europeans abandoned national hegemonic projects. The United States had already stepped in and successfully claimed the role of the world's hegemonic power.

The US military is so much larger than that of any other country that it is hard to imagine how any other nation could create the same scale or frequency of military-driven climate change. We can start with the simple recognition that the annual carbon emissions of the Pentagon are astonishing. The Pentagon has consumed 77% to 80% of total US government energy since 2001. Analyst Neta Crawford notes that "I have studied war and peace for four decades. But I only focused on the scale of US military greenhouse emissions when I began co-teaching a course on climate change and focused on the Pentagon's response to global war." In a Brown University study, she reports that:

> In 2017 the Pentagon's greenhouse gas emissions totaled over 59 million metric tons of carbon dioxide equivalent. If it were a country, it would have been the world's 55th largest greenhouse gas emitter, with emissions larger than Portugal, Sweden or Denmark.
>
> The largest sources of military greenhouse gas emissions are buildings and fuel. The Defense Department maintains over 560,000 buildings at approximately 500 domestic and overseas military installations, which account for about 40% of its greenhouse gas emissions.
>
> The rest comes from operations. In fiscal year 2016, for instance, the Defense Department consumed about 86 million barrels of fuel for operational purposes.[15]

Much of this has to do with the carbon-intensity of US warfare. This can be seen most obviously in transportation. Air planes are at the heart not just of the Air Force but also of the Navy and some parts of the Army. US military airplanes are among the most carbon-intensive forms of transport in the world. Military training – and wars themselves – require large number of planes and pilots flying multiple hourly or daily missions, often involving long carbon-burning flights of many hundreds of miles. As Crawford reports:

> Military weapons and equipment use so much fuel that the relevant measure for defense planners is frequently gallons per mile.

Aircraft are particularly thirsty. For example, the B-2 stealth bomber, which holds more than 25,600 gallons of jet fuel, burns 4.28 gallons per mile and emits more than 250 metric tons of greenhouse gas over a 6,000 nautical mile range. The KC-135R aerial refueling tanker consumes about 4.9 gallons per mile.

A single mission consumes enormous quantities of fuel. In January 2017, two B-2B bombers and 15 aerial refueling tankers traveled more than 12,000 miles from Whiteman Air Force Base to bomb ISIS targets in Libya, killing about 80 suspected ISIS militants. Not counting the tankers' emissions, the B-2s emitted about 1,000 metric tons of greenhouse gases.[16]

Beyond airplanes, hundreds of thousands of US military tanks, ships, and other armored vehicles are fueled by oil. Many have engines which were built a long time ago and are hardly fuel-efficient. US naval carriers are among the largest mobile and carbon-intensive military fighting machines, deployed all over the world, carrying planes and troops capable of getting to any hot spot quick. But the size of the ships and the global scale of their deployment are an exceptionalist climate threat.

Beyond the transport systems is the carbon price of simply feeding, supplying, and training the two million soldiers in the US military, as well as maintaining the approximately 800 military US bases around the world. This requires a huge oil-based agricultural production, as well as massive subsidies to the military firms – whether Lockheed-Martin, Boeing, Raytheon, McDonnell Douglas, Northrup-Grumman, or other military suppliers – that produce guns, bombs, uniforms, and military hardware of all kinds. Most military production in this military-industrial complex (MIC) is oil-based and the scale required to sustain US forces is hard to imagine. Moreover, the approximately 800 military bases are "carbon purchasers and emitters" on a grand scale. Military bases are carbon-based cities and it's hard to think of any parallels, either military or civilian, that churn out so much carbon emissions. The United States has so many more military bases than any other country that it is the obvious militarized king of climate disaster.

Beyond this military infrastructure is the actual costs in money and carbon emissions of the wars themselves. Nobel economist Joseph Stiglitz has written a book about Iraq as a "3 trillion dollar" war. That vast sum did *not* include the carbon costs of the war – the emissions created by all the military bomber and surveillance planes, the emissions of all the tanks and other armored vehicles, the naval ships bringing US troops into the Kuwaiti desert to oust Iraqi troops, the supply planes flying all the munitions and troops from the United States to Iraq, and the demolition and reconstruction of buildings all over the country, with construction projects always one of the biggest source of carbon emissions. In quantifying Pentagon carbon emissions, Crawford gives numbers:

> The Department of Energy publishes data on DOD energy production and fuel consumption, including for vehicles and equipment. Using fuel consumption data, I estimate that from 2001 through 2017, the DOD, including all service branches, emitted 1.2 billion metric tons of greenhouse gases. That is the rough equivalent of driving of 255 million passenger vehicles over a year.
>
> Of that total, I estimated that war-related emissions between 2001 and 2017, including "overseas contingency operations" in Afghanistan, Pakistan, Iraq and Syria, generated over 400 million metric tons of CO2 equivalent – roughly equivalent to the greenhouse emissions of almost 85 million cars in one year.[17]

None of this speaks to an even greater military contribution to climate disaster: the purpose for which US wars are fought. Since World War II, the United States has been dependent on Europeans as among the greatest consumers of American goods. That requires that Europeans have jobs and can buy US goods. But Europe lacks its own oil supplies, and the United States has wanted to get control of nations such as Iraq, Saudi Arabia, the UAE, and Iran, supplying oil both to the United States and to Europe, to ensure high levels of both US and European consumption.

US wars thus underwrite the major capitalist nations' consumption of oil-based production. Without access to foreign oil, Europe might have turned to renewable sources faster, but America could keep oil cheap enough to ensure its use. As the United States turns to gas for its own energy production; it also seeks to export US gas to Europe and ward off total control by Russia of the European gas market, with the war in Ukraine ending most European import of Russian oil and now replaced by US liquified natural gas. Gas is promoted in both the United States and Europe as "clean" or "natural," but it is neither; it is loaded with methane and creates pipelines that are "leaky" and that poison underground water supplies.

The US military opens the world's oil-production and other resources to massive extraction and use at home and abroad. As Michael Klare writes in his book, *Blood and Oil*, securing oil is undoubtedly the most important aim of modern US wars.[18] The European Empires fought for oil and other resources but could develop many of them in their colonies. The US extracts and ships oil back to the "core" of its world system, where it refines much of the oil and then exports it back to Europe or other oil-consuming nations. All of this is basically a huge military investment in keeping the fossilized infrastructure of US and world production intact and profitable.

Of course, it is not just oil that the US military helps secure. It is other resources such as land, minerals (including "rare minerals"), and cotton, which the US fossilized capitalism requires for all forms of production, from textiles to computers. The military is the ultimate guarantee that global supplies will be secured and global demand met, in order to keep our fossilized regime running.

The American Dream and Your Carbon Footprint: Individualism, Consumerism, and Climate Disaster

In the last chapter, we discussed the role of culture in driving extinction. Here, we want to highlight again how US individualism plays an exceptional role in fueling America's leading role in climate-driven extinction, particularly because of the uniquely powerful individualism at the heart of American society. It is a central reason why US capitalism is so climate exceptionalist. This becomes especially clear in contrasting European and US culture, as we began to do at the end of the last chapter.

The American Dream helps make this clear. The idea of focusing on oneself and the moral virtue of getting ahead of others as essential to happiness, in this world and the next, goes back to the Puritans of the 17th century.

The American Dream shifted the Puritan story from heaven to earth. Whether or not you believed in God, the measure of your virtue and worth was the size of your assets. The American Dream glued people to accumulation of money or capital, making clear why it is the master US cultural script of American capitalism.[19]

The American Dream is essentially the reflection of the culture of individualism, which is central to the United States as a nation. Individualism puts the highest value on the self and one's own needs. This is entirely consistent with US capitalism, that starts with the right to private property and the capacity to use it and accumulate wealth as your birthright in America. British philosophers like John Locke and Scottish economist and moral philosopher, Adam Smith, developed these ideas. But they were most deeply enshrined in the American soul, and one can credibly argue that the United States may be the most individualistic country in the world.

Derber has shown that sociopathic societies arise when the culture teaches and normalizes anti-social behavior.[20] When individualism is extreme, people focus on themselves at the expense of all others – and lose the crucial empathy essential to creating solidarity and community.[21] This is catastrophic in issues such as climate change, where millions of folks will tune it out as long as they believe they are unlikely to be affected personally.

When combined with neoliberal capitalism, extreme individualism fuels catastrophic climate threats. Individual freedom and the American Dream both focus people on themselves, especially their money and material success, whatever the cost to others. Happiness comes from accumulating as much private property and wealth as possible. For many, it means buying a big house, often in the suburbs with big lawns and gas-guzzling commuter cars and perhaps a big motor boats. It means stuffing your closet with expensive and fashionable clothes.

The competition to "live big" is a cultural recipe for irreversible climate change.

Extreme inequality combines with individualism to fuel climate disaster. Billionaires and multi-millionaires can buy anything they need to "live it up," and thus set models of glamorous and opulent lifestyles that become fantasy dreams for millions of other Americans. As neoliberal inequalities have accelerated since the Reagan revolution, the mass of working people can less and less afford to emulate the rich and "live big." But such loss of purchasing power does not extinguish the dream. For many Americans, drenched in super-materialistic and individualistic versions of the American Dream, they fight even more tenaciously to get ahead, accumulate astonishing wealth, and consume since the example set by mega-billionaires such as Jeff Bezos and Elon Musk, worth $150 billion or more at this writing, is simply too magnetic and glamorized to be abandoned.

Extreme inequality compounds the individualistic underpinnings of the climate crisis in another crucial way. Billionaires like Bezos and Musk can literally buy themselves years of personal protection from the costs that most of the rest of the population will suffer from climate change. Bezos can buy mansions on the highest and most beautiful land while the seas rise and threaten to drown black and brown communities in places like Miami Beach and many of the poorest parts of South Florida and most of the rest of the country living on the coast.

Meanwhile, the intersection of extreme inequality and individualism has a very different effect on the poor, who have the greatest environmental risk exposure – in their work and neighborhoods – and the least resources to escape it. The growing awareness that pollution has been increasingly exported to poor neighborhoods and poor countries has led to the transformation of the very name of the climate movement into the movement for "climate justice."

Since capitalism is, by definition, a class system of unequal wealth, the crisis of "climate justice" is endemic in a capitalist system. Where inequality is systemically reduced as in European capitalism, the harms of climate are more likely to be shared widely. In tandem with the lower individualism and greater community in European capitalism, this can help explain the far lower carbon emissions in Europe compared to the United States.

Returning to the issue of the entrenched individualistic culture of mass culture, it is clear for most of the working population, the carbonized infrastructure of the United States doesn't permit easy lifestyle alternatives. When GM bought up public transit systems and dismantled them, in cities like Los Angeles in the 1920s, it made Angelinos dependent on congested highways to get around.[22] In Boston, in 2019, the "T" or subway system was so underfunded that delays became unbearable – and more people began to shift to cars. The design of the heating and cooling systems of large homes and offices made it unaffordable for many to shift over to green energy sources. Lack of good public transit led people to fly rather than take trains on job assignments or vacations because public transit options often are not available. And because jobs require getting back and forth quickly, time constraints keep people on planes, the fastest way to increase your carbon footprint.

The European lifestyle is far lighter on the planet, reflecting both the culture of community and the availability of all kinds of public transit and other public goods not provided in the United States.[23] The European Dream says that people will be happier if they live in urban spaces where they can hang out with friends in parks or public gardens to grow their own vegetables or socialize in museums or sidewalk cafes. Since community is the path to fulfillment, there is a psychological pull toward the urban rather than suburban, toward public rather than private space. And there is little yearning for huge houses or cars because they can isolate you from neighbors and workmates who can be socialized within public spaces, plentiful in European cities at all hours.[24] Instead, Europeans are drawn to "urban villages" such as the Barbican in central London, which houses 3,000 people who walk outside their apartment buildings and are immediately in beautiful parks with lakes. It takes three minutes for a Barbican resident to walk to a Barbican art gallery, auditorium for speakers and comedians, restaurants, film and play theater, with most spaces open not just to Barbican residents but the general public.

Europeans choose relatively low-carbon lifestyles relative to Americans, because their culture and political structure have created a society and living spaces with far more public goods. Their urban public transit systems and European-wide trains allow Europeans to forgo cars. European cities are full of public space – parks, gardens, libraries, and museums, pedestrian areas where cars are prohibited, public outdoor theater, benches to sit on along rivers spanning the city, grassy or paved areas outside of buildings which people can use to read, eat or chat – all open for socializing throughout the day and night. In contrast, US big cities, with the one exception of New York City, become ghost-towns at night since corporate offices which crowd city space are shut down and their employees have driven back to suburban homes after work. Derber remembers one US book tour in 2014 where even in "public" cities like Seattle, most of the downtown became empty after 6 PM, with little public transit or life on the streets. There was nothing moving other than the escalator on the ground floor of a locked bank.

Europeans like to travel and buy good food or nice furniture for their apartments, but the availability of public goods and the place of work allow people to avoid the pressure of mass consumerism and over-stuffed closets. If a good life can be lived without daily high consumption, your carbon footprint will be far lower. Even Americans who don't like over-stuffed closets or don't want cars will find it hard to choose climate-friendly alternatives because America's fossil capitalism hasn't created the public goods infrastructure and the kind of work-environment that will allow it.

The Carbon-Industrial Complex and Corporate Power: Fueling America's Climate Exceptionalism

We mentioned earlier the huge military companies – Lockheed-Martin, Raytheon, Northrup Grumman, McDonnell-Douglas, and Boeing – at the center of "the Military-Industrial Complex." Along with their thousands of contractor and supplier companies, and their major buyer, the Pentagon itself, they are a massive source of carbon emissions. The irony is rarely noted: all this emission production is done in the name of national security, even though carbon emissions are one of America's biggest national security threats.

The MIC is immensely influential politically. It circulates its corporate elites through Congress, the executive branch and K Street, the center of DC lobbying. War preparations and war itself are promoted by the US MIC, the most powerful constellation of military firms in the world. Columbia University political economist Seymour Melman, who spent his life studying America's "permanent war economy" became convinced that even though that war is bad for the economy, it will always be massively funded because of the overwhelming political influence of the MIC. If you want to end war, you have to get rid of the military-industrial complex.[25]

Parallel to and intertwined with the MIC is the CIC, or the Carbon-Industrial Complex, sometimes also called "the fossil fuels lobby." On a global level, based on a history of market capitalization, the biggest oil and gas giants are shown below[26]:

Rank	Company	Country	Highest Market Cap Ever (Historical) (USD Billions)
1	Exxon Mobil Corporation	United States	519.3 (Oct 2007)
2	Royal Dutch Shell	Netherlands United Kingdom	458.6 (Jan 2013)
3	Chevron Corporation	United States	256.1 (Jul 2014)
4	Total S.A.	France	201.1 (May 2008)
5	BP	United Kingdom	263.3 (May 2006)
6	PetroChina	China	472.1 (Oct 2007)
7	Sinopec	China	131.2 (Oct 2007)
8	Schlumberger	Netherlands	153.4 (Jun 2014)
9	Enterprise Products	United States	77.2 (May 2008)
10	Eni	Italy	152.4 (May 2008)
11	ConocoPhillips	United States	112.6 (Jun 2008)

In 2017, two US companies, Exxon and Chevron, ranked first and third in the world in terms of market capitalization, with a third US giant, Conoco-Phillips ranked eleventh. Exxon capitalized at its peak at about half a trillion dollars. Moreover, unlike giants such as Saudi Aramco and the Chinese giant oil companies, Sinpec and China National Petroleum, the US companies are private corporations and constitute a profit-driven complex that leverages private wealth to influence all aspects of public energy policy and consumption.

The biggest coal companies in the United States are Peabody Energy Corporation and Arch Coal Inc., that, together, produced in 2017 about one-third of US coal. Coal remains big in the US energy mix, powering 27% of US electricity in 2018 and employing 50,000 miners in 25 states.[27] Nonetheless, US coal is in decline, with both Peabody Energy and Arch Coal filing for bankruptcy in 2016 but exiting bankruptcy in 2018.

The oil and gas companies at the center of the US CIC are very much alive, rapidly taking the place of coal in electricity and other energy production. The discovery of huge new shale fields, such as the Permian Basin, in Texas, are leading Exxon, Chevron, and Conoco to massively expand not just their oil production but all aspects of natural gas production, including the hydraulics of extraction and pumping, known as "fracking," and the huge expansion of high-speed gas pipelines across the country.[28] Despite the growing controversy and protest against fracking, and rising protests about the pipelines themselves, the amount of fracking and of pipeline development is mushrooming. New gas pipeline companies have been sprouting up quickly since 2018, including Alaskan Natural Gas Pipeline, Atlanta Coast Pipeline, Bluegrass Pipeline, while big older pipeline companies such as Trans-Mountain build new pipelines bringing Canadian oil into the United States and Texas-based Spectra are rushing into New England and build new pipelines through New York, Pennsylvania and Massachusetts, with much of the gas for export to Europe.[29]

Gas is growing more rapidly than any other US energy source and will, along with oil, dominate the US CIC for decades to come. The big oil companies, such as Exxon and Chevron, have the capital and technological skills to rapidly spread the entire infrastructure of gas. This includes massively increasing capacity for fracking – the process of hydraulic drilling deep into shale rock and using super-explosive water force and chemicals – to get to oil and gas previously inaccessible. The giant oil and gas companies will take over much of the rising gas market, which made the United States the biggest national producer of oil and gas by 2017, larger even than Saudi Arabia. As the American Petroleum Institute, the huge oil and gas lobbying group that has enormous influence over US energy policy, reported in 2018:

> Because of shale and fracking, the United States is leading the world in natural gas and oil production. The U.S. Energy Information Administration (EIA) projects domestic crude production will average

12.4 million barrels per day (mb/d) this year and 13.2 mb/d next year. Simply put, fracking is the engine in the U.S. energy revolution.[30]

The American Petroleum Institute embodies the overwhelming political influence and lobby of Big Oil and Gas. It is regarded as one of the most powerful forces in Washington. In 2021, it geared up to work with Republicans on sabotaging as much of the Biden climate change and green infrastructure proposals as possible.

While the enormous new investment in fracking gas and in oil is driven by the huge profits it creates for globally dominant fossil fuel companies, gas is being marketed aggressively in the United States as climate-friendly, since it is "natural." The industry's television ads show beautiful, pristine countryside with the pipelines underneath and invisible, making CIC oil and gas companies look like champions of clean energy.

While gas is much more clean-burning than oil, the notion that gas is climate-friendly is a lie. It is a fossil fuel that threatens continuing massive environmental destruction. Getting the gas out of the shale fields through fracking involves chemical and water extraction processes that are toxic. Moreover, the growth of new gas pipelines is literally "explosive," since they are leaky and produce high amounts of super-toxic methane in US pipeline leaks and explosions that have become common.[31] Sold to Americans as the only way to make United States make "energy independent" because of the nation's huge domestic gas shale fields, it will only lock in further a fossilized infrastructure that will not, according to the Union of Concerned Scientists (UCS), likely reduce overall US fossil fuel emissions. The Infographic below produced by the UCS shows that shifting toward natural-gas dominated energy by 2050 barely nudges total US fossil fuel emissions while a shift toward renewables using "current available renewable sources" would drastically cut US fossil fuel emissions in the same period (Figure 6.3).[32]

Natural gas, thus, is diverting us from a climate solution by 2050, which the UCS shows as realistic and cost-competitive based on clean energy sources available now.[33] Why, then, isn't the United States moving even more ambitiously than Biden's climate agenda to save the planet? The answer is political. The CIC includes some of the United States' most politically influential companies, notably Exxon, Chevron, Koch Industries, and other giant oil and gas companies. Like the US MIC, the US CIC is far larger and more politically powerful than in any other country. This is hardly surprising because just as the United States has by far the biggest military and MIC in the world, the United States now produces more oil and gas than any other country, reflecting the biggest national CIC. Because of US subsidies and the massive new investment in fracking and shale oil and gas fields, this dominance of American oil and gas in global fossil fuel production will only increase.

US Electricity Generation
Natural Gas, a Fossil Fuel, and Coal Pose Similar Climate Risks*

Energy Sources for Electricity

	2008	2012	2021	2050 (projections)
Coal	48%	37%	22%	19%
Natural gas	22%	31%	38%	56%
Nuclear	20%	19%	19%	1%
Renewables	9%	12%	20%	24%

Projected Natural Gas CO_2 Contributions Would Continue Global Heating, Climate Breakdown

	2012	2050 (projections)
Total emissions from Electricity Production[+]	2,036	1,972
Coal	1,512	780
Natural gas	493	1,180
Others	31	12

[+]Data in million metric tons of CO_2 emitted
*Adapted from a Union of Concerned Scientists data sheet published in 2014. Since that time, our dependence on natural gas has only increased and climate risks have not diminished in the intervening years. Data for 2021 from the US Energy Information Administration.

Figure 6.3 The Climate Risks of Natural Gas

The International Energy Agency (IEA) released its annual World Energy Outlook today, with the report showing the United States poised to lead in the effort to fill the growing global energy demands. Forecasting global energy production and consumption through 2040, the IEA projects the United States will account for nearly 75% of global oil growth, and 40% of natural gas growth through 2025.

Shale development across the country – "relentless Shale development is escalating across the country to record levels, and has allowed the United States to emerge as the world's leader in both natural gas and crude oil production.... The shale revolution continues to shake up oil and gas supply, enabling the United States to pull away from the rest of the field as the world's largest oil and gas producer. By 2025, nearly every fifth barrel of oil and every fourth cubic meter of gas in the world come from the United States."[34]

Five of the world's seven largest oil companies – the "seven sisters" – are American and at the center of the American CIC. In no other country do fossil fuel companies exert such enormous political power. That power is used to ensure that our "fossilized capitalism" will survive the green transition beginning to emerge in Europe, the United States and other developed nations.

In addition to the huge lobbying firm, the American Petroleum Institute, the political influence of the Koch Brothers makes clear the huge political power of US oil and gas producers and of the US CIC. The Kochs sponsor Washington think tanks and policy institutes devoted to deregulation, and craft new laws for expanding drilling and exploitation of public lands. They are among the most influential lobbyists in Washington – and a central funder of the Republican Party. They are the de facto heads of the US CIC – coordinating companies, fundraising, and lobbying on behalf of all fossil fuel companies. In fact, in a recent book, "Kochland," Christopher Leonard argues they have transformed the world of political lobbying and become the most important corporate lobby in the nation:

> What drew me to this corporation was the realization that the story of Koch Industries over the last 50 years really is a history of American capitalism during that time. You can explore our entire economy by telling the story of this one corporation…This is a massive company whose annual revenues are larger than that of Facebook, Goldman Sachs and U.S. Steel combined….
>
> And finally, you're talking about one of the largest corporate lobbying operations in the United States … and shines a light on this fact that corporations have this level of influence over our public policy and our laws that they haven't had in 100 years.[35]

The US CIC lobbies to increase the already enormous subsidies – about $18 billion annually – that the government gives oil and gas companies. The CIC power has long ensured that oil and gas executives rise to power in Washington and in the White House. Dick Cheney, Bush's Vice-President, was CEO of Halliburton, ensuring that Bush's invasion of Iraq would turn to Halliburton as the first US oil company to get access to Iraqi oil fields. It is hardly surprising that Donald Trump appointed Rex Tillerson, the CEO of Exxon, as his first Secretary of State. Ironically, Tillerson claims to believe in climate change but has insisted that the market will not price in enough renewables to replace oil and gas as the principal energy engine of the US economy. The Koch Brothers succeed in placing many of their own people in high and mid-level positions in federal executive agencies dealing with energy policy.[36]

The big oil and gas companies are not all-powerful, as grassroots groups and state attorney generals are beginning powerful protests and lawsuits against them. On October 22, 2019, the New York Attorney General opened a lawsuit against Exxon, charging them with lying to shareholders about the true climate costs that will drive down corporate profits over time, while also lying to the public about the health and climate effects of their pollution.[37] This is reminiscent of the criminal suits against Big Tobacco for lying for decades about their knowledge that smoking causes cancer. A rising tide of such suits and broader popular protests against Big Oil and Gas will be part of the broader politics to abolish the CIC discussed in the "new abolitionism" movements we chronicle in the final chapters.

The huge political influence of the CIC and the MIC is partly because their own interests coincide with those of the larger corporate world, which requires the energy and military exceptionalism of the United States. Most US corporations in every sector depend heavily on oil and gas or coal; shortages of any of these fuels will increase general corporate costs and reduce overall corporate profits. Virtually all US corporations are on the fossil fuel grid, sucking electricity or oil or gas fuel to produce and transport their goods and services, heat and cool their offices, and market their products at home and abroad. Wall Street is heavily invested in CIC companies. The success of the CIC and the MIC is essential to the overall growth and profitability of the entire US corporate economy.[38]

Moreover, aggregate corporate power in the United States is greater than in other nations. This reflects the relative weakness of countervailing labor and popular forces in the United States, and helps explain the US neoliberalism fueling climate disaster more than any other capitalist model. Thus, labor unions are far weaker in the United States than in Europe, with only about 10% of the entire US labor force unionized.[39] In Sweden, 70% are in unions. Labor parties have ruled Europe for much of the 20th century,[40] while the United States has never had a real labor party at all.

This leaves Wall Street and the giant corporations as the overwhelming US political force, far greater than in other capitalist countries that have not adopted the neoliberal model. European nations have been run since the early 20th century by a tri-partite coalition of labor, corporations, and government itself. Corporations have to bargain with labor and government leaders to pass laws, requiring compromises and accommodation to the social welfare and social democracy long popular in Europe.[41] But in the United States, corporations do not have to make these compromises, since labor is so weak and both Republicans and Democrats depend on corporate donors to win elections. The exceptional imbalance of US power, with corporations so uniquely in the driver's seat compared to European corporations, helps explain why US climate (and military) policy is so uniquely "extinctive."

7 Inconvenient Truths

Systemic Roots of US COVID-19 Failure

On August 5, 2020, Dr. Sanjay Gupta, CNN's chief medical correspondent, asked Dr. Anthony Fauci, the top US infectious disease scientist, about the US COVID-19 story. Specifically, he asked whether America was failing compared to other advanced nations. Fauci said simply: "Yeah, The United States has the worst corona outbreak in the world."[1] By the end of 2022, three years into the pandemic, the United States still led the world by a significant margin in total COVID-19 fatalities.[2]

While that was under the Trump Administration, by eight months into the Biden Administration, in October 2021, the United States had suffered about 750,000 COVID-19 deaths – exceeding the number of Americans dying in World War I, World War II, Vietnam, and 9/11 combined. The rise of the Delta and Omicron variants plus the high remaining number of unvaccinated Americas – including 20% of adults who say they will refuse any vaccine – has led to recurrent new spikes and shutdowns in part of the United States and around the world. The prolonged American crisis hints that there is something systemic explaining the US failures.

In 2021, data released by the University of Washington Health Metrics Institute suggested the CDC official numbers were significantly lower than the actual numbers, both in cases and deaths. By May of 2021, the University of Washington claimed the US deaths were actually 901,000 rather than 550,000, and the global deaths were 6.7 million rather than 3.24 million. US cases and deaths remained far disproportionate globally to its population, a striking finding given the great wealth of the US relative to other nations. The United States also got worse and worse relative to other advanced countries as shown in Figure 7.1.

The disproportionate US case and death rates show here, actually increased into the Spring of 2022, and the number of cases and deaths in the US declined but remained high in 2023, at this writing, now defined as "normalized" like deaths from familiar influenzas.

DOI: 10.4324/9781003401483-10

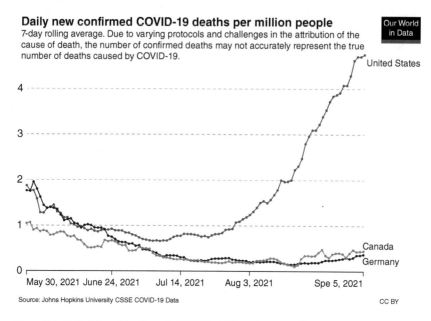

Daily new confirmed COVID-19 deaths per million people
7-day rolling average. Due to varying protocols and challenges in the attribution of the cause of death, the number of confirmed deaths may not accurately represent the true number of deaths caused by COVID-19.

Figure 7.1 Daily New Confirmed COVID-19 Deaths per Million People

It Was Trump – But the US Failure Goes Much Deeper

Well into the Biden administration and after the first mid-term elections in 2022, the 45th president of the United States, Biden's predecessor, is by no means a distant memory. Instead, he remains the face of a resurgent authoritarianism in the United States and is a declared candidate for his party's presidential nomination in 2024. For these reasons, it is important to recall his personal culpability for the COVID-19 pandemic even as we keep our eyes on the systemic problems.

In July 2020, Brian Klaas, a *Washington Post* commentator concluded that President Trump was responsible for the huge US failures to contain and solve COVID-19, a view shared by many progressives and centrists in the country:

> When you compare the United States with other countries, no spin or lies can obscure a basic fact: Trump's response to the pandemic has been a world-leading catastrophe.

Klaas argues that the crisis should be placed squarely on Trump's shoulders, because the United States had advantages that other countries lacked:

> The comparison is even more damning for the White House because the United States had some major advantages going into the pandemic. America is a rich country with low population density. While South

Koreans are packed together with 529 people per square kilometer and Britain has 275, the United States has just 36. Arizona, which has one of the worst state outbreaks, has just 23 people per square kilometer. Those differences make physical distancing easier. Moreover, the dominance of car culture in the United States makes it easier to avoid crowded public transportation. And yet, due to an epic failure of Trumpian mismanagement, those advantages were squandered.

This leaves one damning conclusion: The pandemic was unavoidable, but America's dire circumstances were a policy choice. The rest of the developed world followed the science. The United States followed Trump. In November, voters should look around the world, realize how badly we stack up, and cast their ballots accordingly.[3]

There is no question that Trump horribly bungled the United States approach to the virus. For several months he denied the pandemic was real, calling it "a hoax." In February 2020, he famously said it would "magically vanish" by April 2020. On tapes recorded in interviews with renowned journalist Bob Woodward, he admitted lying about the virus, saying "I always wanted to play it down … I still like playing it down," when Woodward reminded him he repeatedly called the virus no more dangerous than the flu.[4] He never rolled out a national strategy, saying it was the governors' jobs to fix whatever problems they had in their own states.

In January 2020, Trump's top national security advisers told him COVID-19 would become by far the greatest danger to the nation, an existential threat. But Trump chose not to share what he knew. Approximately 400,000 Americans, according to data released in June 2021, died needlessly because Trump did not warn the public of the dangers, claiming the new virus was like the flu, even though he told Woodward in February 2020, that it was five times worse than the flu and "deadly." As one woman whose father died of the virus said, her father's only pre-existing condition was his faith in Trump. Trump lied and Americans died.

Trump's catastrophic failure to develop and fund a national strategy to end the pandemic was, indeed, an American tragedy. The hundreds of thousands of needless deaths should have led to a second impeachment, even before the January 6 insurrection finally led to his being impeached again. But there is something profoundly missing in the progressive consensual view that the US relative to other developed countries is mainly due to Trump's lying and incompetence.

The inconvenient truth is that the American COVID-19 disaster ultimately reflects long-standing and deeply entrenched failures in the nation's own economic and political system, as well as some of its deepest cultural beliefs and values. In Chapter 3, we showed that pandemics are systemic crises in capitalist societies, reflecting capitalism's rejection of activist government, its public goods deficits, and inequalities that have always divided wealthy corporate elites from struggling workers.

In this chapter, we return to this systemic analysis, but with a special focus on the United States. As already discussed, the Reagan revolution ushered in an extreme neoliberal capitalism, that exacerbates extinction threats. President Joe Biden proclaimed he was making systemic and "generational" public investment, a shift from neoliberalism toward a 21stcentury New Deal capitalist brand. And while he has had some major successes, the neoliberalism of the last 40 years will take years to change, and continues to make the US vulnerable to COVID-19 and to the extinction crisis that run-away pandemics can potentially cause.

The American Capitalist Brand: Neoliberalism and Pandemic Economics

In earlier chapters, we have discussed how the "Reagan Revolution" ended the New Deal regime of FDR – a system of social democracy similar to the economies of Western and Northern Europe – and inaugurated the purest neoliberal regime seen in the modern developed world. The eruption of the HIV/AIDS epidemic in 1981 was a harbinger of American neoliberalism as a fertile breeding ground for disease and catastrophic pandemics, one of the inconvenient truths about American exceptionalism.

The idea that pure neoliberalism is a systemic gateway to pandemics such as COVID-19 is not widely discussed. Systemic elements of global neoliberalism, discussed in Chapter 3, open neoliberal societies to pandemics and help fuel a disastrous escalation that can turn them into a form of extinction. We look here at how systemic neoliberal forces playing a strong role in fueling COVID-19 disasters in the United States.

1. De-Fund the Government

President Reagan once famously joked: "the most terrifying words in the English language are I'm from the government and I'm here to help you."

It was funny but Reagan wasn't really joking. He was offering one of the basic creeds of neoliberalism. As discussed in Chapter 5, neoliberalism is built on the principle that government is inherently a threat to liberty and that big government makes that threat a reality. The United States, which had been founded on the principle of limited government, was far more receptive than European or East Asian nations to this inbred suspicion and hatred of "big government." The American mindset was captured by Reagan in another of his well-known quotes:

> I consider all proposals for government action with an open mind before I say "no."

Reagan's humor made it easier for him to destroy the New Deal, and he understood that his jokes helped him stoke hatred of big government. The view of government as tyranny would enable Trumpists to call government mask mandates infringements on liberty and to reject any national government plan against the virus – including even the provision of free vaccines – as a "big government" hoax and form of coercion.

This rejection of government involved some hypocrisy and sleight of hand by Republicans from Reagan to Trump. Like most neoliberals, Reagan and Trump actually were happy to use big government to help the interests of big companies in what we described earlier as "corporate welfare"; an integral part of neoliberalism in the real world. But the big government of the New Deal, crafted to create jobs, social security, and social justice for working people was the true target. And neoliberalism has never stopped seeking to wipe out the New Deal by drastically shrinking government and slashing public goods, public health and social welfare, all a potential recipe for a shriek or whimper pandemic extinction.

The long history of anti-government policy preceded Reagan. The contrast between the United States and European nations in the percent of government spending as a share of GDP has remained dramatic since 1880, as shown in Figure 7.2.

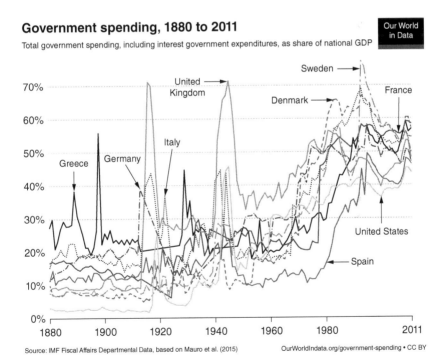

Figure 7.2 Government Spending, 1880 to 2011

Except in the New Deal era, the United States remains below all the other European nations. Spending by government did rise during the Reagan years, reflecting both the growth of military spending and corporate welfare. This helps illustrate the hypocrisy in much of the neoliberal rhetoric against "big government." But despite this growth, US government spending remained lower than that of the European nations.

So what is the connection between small government and catastrophic pandemics? When Reagan said government is not the solution to the problem but the problem itself, that is clearly false when it comes to COVID-19 and other pandemics. You can't fight a pandemic without government, a lesson with fatal consequences as shown by the Trump Administration. Government has to mobilize the population to work together to combat a terrifying common enemy. It alone can raise the funds to pay the huge costs of fighting the virus. It alone can create the administrative infrastructure and national standards to create and distribute enough safe COVID-19 tests, vaccines, PPE, mobile clinics, and other health equipment. It alone can regulate and compel public behavior – in schools, workplaces, and public spaces – to prevent viral spread and ultimately end the pandemic. Only government can limit the iron grip of big pharmaceutical companies that, despite relying on government-funded basic science and being subsidized heavily by government funds keep drugs expensive, profitable, and out of reach of many working people. This includes vaccines and therapeutics developed and funded to a high degree by the government's National Institute of Health.

The Reaganite assault on government got traction in the United Kingdom, but could not become quite so deeply enshrined in continental Europe, such as France, Germany, or Denmark, or in East Asian nations, such as Japan, Singapore, South Korea, or China. Biden's surprising turn toward Keynesianism and public spending is very important, and partly driven by the emergency of the pandemic. But it faces many obstacles and cannot quickly change the American anti-government creed central to US history and its free market brand.

2. The Public Goods Deficit: The United States, Europe, and COVID

The very idea of a "public good" contradicts neoliberalism – and the United States has long had an impoverished public goods system relative to European and East Asian nations. This is a reality that pandemics such as COVID-19 feast on in the United States as there is hardly even the vocabulary to think about a permanently enshrined and well-funded system of public health and a host of other public goods essential to fighting pandemics. President Biden's COVID-19 and "caring economy" investments marked a major US turn, and a source of hope, but it has not yet ended the dangerous US public goods deficit.

The comparison between the United States and the rest of the world on public goods is shocking. Journalist Nick Kristof observes that the US ranked

28th on the 2020 Social Progress Index,[5] a measure based on the quality of public life and access to vital public goods:

> The United States, despite its immense wealth, military power and cultural influence, ranks 28th – having slipped from 19th in 2011. The index now puts the United States behind significantly poorer countries, including Estonia, Czech Republic, Cyprus and Greece ....
>
> The Social Progress Index finds that Americans have health statistics similar to those of people in Chile, Jordan and Albania, while kids in the United States get an education roughly on par with what children get in Uzbekistan and Mongolia. A majority of countries have lower homicide rates, and most other advanced countries have lower traffic fatality rates and better sanitation and internet access.

The richest nation, the United States, ranks only 28 in social progress and public goods. The United States, Brazil, and Hungary are the only of the 163 ranked nations that declined in quality of public life since the Index was first created in 2011, and the US decline is the greatest.

If you compare the spending on public goods, the US falls dramatically below peer European nations over virtually the entire period between 1880 and 2016 (Figure 7.3).

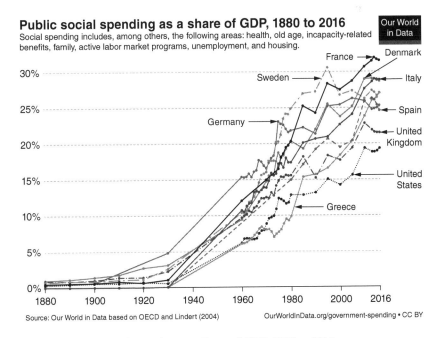

Figure 7.3 Public Social Spending as a Share of GDP, 1880 to 2016

The public goods deficit is a pretty good predictor of COVID-19 systemic vulnerability. The nations providing the most public goods are those in Northern Europe: Norway is number one, and Denmark and Finland are second and third. These Scandinavian countries have begun to suffer from the global neoliberal plague, but have entrenched social welfare programs and still pride themselves on their universal public goods commitments – such as universal health care, free college education, public housing, and child care – for all citizens. New Zealand, the fourth leader, is also a nation known for its generous social welfare programs and provision of abundant social goods – and all the leaders have had relatively low COVID-19 cases and deaths.

In Chapter 5, we briefly discussed why a high public goods deficit creates a high vulnerability to pandemics – ones which historically became whimper extinctions. Consider just one of the most vital public goods: public health. European public goods economies have near – universal public health systems, with access to health care a right guaranteed by the government for all citizens. Moreover, the commitment is not simply to clinical individual medical care but to caring for the health of the community, including public provision of everything from clean water and public sanitation to accessible pediatric and geriatric senior care facilities for all families.

It is hardly surprising that a large well-funded public health system is one of the best weapons against pandemics. During the New Deal era, the US temporarily embraced public goods and public health; in 1946, the US created the Centers for Disease Control (CDC) and the Food and Drug Administration (FDA), which were powerful forces for public health before the Trump administration politicized them. But the CDC and FDA, even before Trump, did not eliminate the large US public health deficit, reflecting the fact that America is committed mainly to a large private system of for-profit medicine for individuals rather than public health for the entire community. For example, US neoliberalism turns nursing homes into for-profit businesses that have been epicenters of COVID-19 outbreaks; to maximize profit, they hire too few workers, pay them poorly and don't protect workers or residents from major health risks. In Europe, senior living and nursing homes are far more likely to be public and have not been epicenters of COVID-19.

Jeneen Interlandi, an influential researcher on public health, has documented the long antagonism to public health in the United States and its devastating impact on the US public health infrastructure. She shows that crises of funding, political antagonism, and organizational dysfunction have undermined the US public health system as a whole, severely weakening even its "crown jewels" such as the CDC, and drastically limiting its capacity to respond effectively to COVID:

> The C.D.C. we have is hardly a monolith: Some of its many pockets are bursting with innovation; others are plagued by inertia. But scientists and administrators who have spent decades working with and for the agency

say that three problems in particular affect the whole institution: a lack of funding, a lack of authority and a culture that has been warped by both. Some of these problems come down to politics, but most are a result of flaws in the agency's very foundation.

From its inception in 1946, the agency's existence hinged on its officers' ability to sell its services to state leaders who were leery of federal interference, and to lawmakers who often struggled to appreciate the point of epidemiology. They did this by taking on the jobs that no other agency wanted, quickly developing a reputation for being the first to arrive at any given emergency, the last to leave and the one with the most cutting-edge technology. But with each success, a pattern emerged. The agency received an infusion of funding in times of crises, and praise and more responsibility when it saved the day. But it was often starved of resources the rest of the time and rived by internal conflicts over how to apportion the money it did receive ....

Today the C.D.C. is both sprawling in its reach and extremely constrained in what it can do.[6]

Public health, and the CDC, were built as adjuncts to a private corporate health system, designed to make that system more profitable but not deliver goods that could supplant for-profit medicine. In certain crises, the CDC could gain substantial funding, but it was never built on a public funding and political foundation that might jeopardize Big Pharma's profits. By fragmenting public health services into local and state domains, where corporations were dominant players, an effective federal or national never was created in the United States. The fragmentation of under-funded public health services at every level created competition and lack of cohesion and coordination that undermined the rise of an enduring and robust public health system.

Interlandi argues that the chronic under-funding of public health is "systemic." In another essay, focusing on the COVID-19 crisis arising early in Texas, Interlandi shows that such systemic starvation undermined the CDC and the fight against COVID-19 early on in the pandemic.[7] The Texan example is interesting because it also points to the capacity to maintain public health and even collective survival in the face of climate change. While she doesn't flesh the connections out here, the COVID-19 disaster in Texas arose at the same time as extreme heat and drought crises in the Lone Star state. The weaknesses of public health investment and political hostility to public goods are simultaneously endangering the ability of the nation to confront the extinction perils arising simultaneously from pandemics and climate change.

The public health system is the most obvious public good shaping a nation's vulnerability to pandemics. But most other public goods have the same effect, whether education, clean water, clean air, and environmental protection, poverty reduction, a high minimum wage, or child and geriatric care. The higher the public goods deficit in any public good, the higher the vulnerability to COVID-19 or other pandemics – and the higher the risk of pandemics becoming extinction perils. President Biden's new major public goods and public health investments – in child care, public transit, green jobs, and infrastructure – offer the first ray of hope in decades for reducing this US public goods deficit.

3. Extreme Inequality: The Upstairs, the Downstairs, and COVID

As discussed in Chapter 3, the capitalist house design is another systemic force or structure, fueling frequent and toxic pandemics such as COVID-19. We've already described capitalist architecture across the centuries as an upstairs/downstairs system. By 2019, the Census Bureau reported that income inequality had become greater in the United States than at any time since it started tracking it five decades ago.[8] It's no coincidence that COVID-19 broke out so disastrously in 2019, just as inequality was spiking to its highest level ever in America.

The United States has by far the worst income inequality among developed countries.[9] This is measured by the "Gini coefficient," with a higher number meaning more inequality as described below in data drawn from the OECD and the World Bank in 2017. The US level of inequality has exceeded that of European nations since the Reagan neoliberal revolution, based again on the Gini coefficient (Figure 7.4):

A high Gini coefficient means the basement and first floor of the capitalist house are teeming with overcrowded poor and stressed people. Because of their poverty, lack of publicly protected sanitation, congested living conditions, lack of access to medical care, good food or even clean water and other systemic conditions plaguing the downstairs, the crowds living there were already before COVID-19 far more likely to suffer multiple illnesses. A Senate report confirms the extreme vulnerability in the downstairs, showing that COVID's impact in low-income areas of New York City is far higher than in rich areas:

> In the coronavirus outbreak, early reports from New York City have shown that low-income, crowded neighborhoods have indeed been the hardest hit. For example, Borough Park in Brooklyn, which has a poverty rate of more than 30%, has one of the highest rates of confirmed COVID-19 cases. Neighborhoods in the bottom quartile (25%) of incomes represent more than one-third of COVID-19 cases (36%) in the city, while the wealthiest quartile accounts for less than one in 10.[10]

Other studies confirm that people living in the basement and first floor are the hardest hit by COVID-19, subject to rates of disease and death which suggest shriek or whimper extinctions among the poor:

> One persistent set of reports in the popular media has focused on the apparently outsized toll that COVID-19. among under-resourced individuals living in urban areas. ...

Income inequality, 1979 to 2013

Shown is the Gini – higher values indicate a higher level of inequality – for equivalized household income.

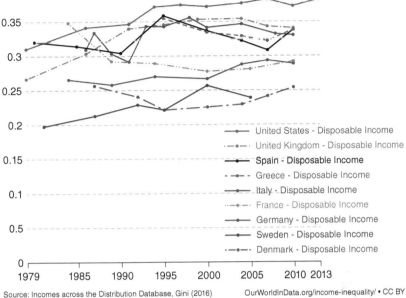

Source: Incomes across the Distribution Database, Gini (2016)   OurWorldInData.org/income-inequality/ • CC BY

Figure 7.4 Income Inequality 1979 to 2013

In addition to problems associated with a greater hazard of death due to COVID-19, individuals living in lower-income communities may also have less access to high-quality health care .... Furthermore, a U.S. Bureau of Labor Statistics report from 2018 indicates that workers with lower levels of education are less likely to work from home, suggesting that they therefore may also be less able to physically distance than those with higher levels of education. In turn, these individuals may be faced with the choice between staying home and not getting paid, or going to work and increasing their risk of becoming infected with the virus. In addition, these people may also have less access to testing and treatment resources, if experience with influenza is any guide.[11]

As noted in Chapter 5, the extreme inequality in the United States created a long-institutionalized tolerance to triage or abandonment of millions of workers, threatening their very survival. It suggests the United States had long embraced a kind of "whimper" extinction of millions of its low-income workers, disproportionately people of color, who have for generations faced a level of homelessness, hunger, job insecurity, and poverty threatening their very survival. A nation hard wired with extreme inequality has basically made a deal with the extinction devil: to incorporate "whimper extinction" as systemic in American life.

In Europe, the numbers in the basement and first floor are lower, because universal public goods and social welfare, as well as strong unions and labor parties, historically protected much of the population from poverty and illness. The European system gives even the poorest European citizens access to health care, job training, and social welfare that are huge buffers against disease, including COVID-19.

In both the United States and Europe, the upstairs wealthy made a windfall of profits while remaining relatively safe from COVID-19. They can pay for the best medical care on the planet, live in the best housing and safest neighborhoods, work in luxurious suites and towers in the best possible jobs, with supreme wages, working conditions and sanitation. They metaphorically live "above" the pandemic; moreover, billionaires buy islands in Fiji and the Caribbean where they can literally purchase immunity from pandemics.

The stock markets in COVID-19 during 2020 and 2021 soared to record highs while the "real economy" was tanking. Inequality expert Chuck Collins told NPR host Terri Gross in a December 23, 2020 interview, that since the beginning of the pandemic nine months earlier:

> 657 billionaires have seen their combined wealth go up a trillion since mid-March ... Elon Musk saw his wealth go up almost 500%, 120 billion. Jeff Bezos has seen his wealth go up about 74 billion, an increase of 65%.[12]

In 2020, Trump and the Republicans sent more than $3 trillion of "stimulus" in the name of small business protection and unemployment relief, but much of that money got into the pockets of big corporations which used the money to buy back their own stock and enrich top management and big investors. The trillions printed by the Fed to keep the system liquid also enriched the top corporate 1%while never trickling down to struggling workers. Biden shifted government policy away from neoliberalism, sending far more money directly into the hands of working families, as in his child credit payments to parents. But the overall wealth gap in the United States under Biden remained huge, as Biden's plans were obstructed by Republicans and big corporations. Seriously curbing corporate power or transforming US capitalism were never part of Biden's agenda; instead, he argued in the summer of 2021, as the markets kept soaring that "capitalism is alive and well in America."

Vaccines: The Hidden Story

Big Pharma – the large super-profitable drug companies such as Pfizer, Johnson and Johnson, and Moderna – have taken the credit for the miracle of COVID-19 "warp speed" vaccines. But while the vaccines were remarkably effective, the real vaccine story is somewhat different. These companies have long turned US health care into a private enterprise designed to make profit at the expense of public health. They create drugs such as statins for an affluent older population that takes the pills everyday for the rest of their lives, making the medication extremely profitable. But Big Pharma dis-invests in drugs that people might have to take only once or twice, reducing profitability. The story of vaccines is a good example of how drugs that might prevent extinction through pandemics have arisen only when government has played a major role in ensuring big profit. Vaccines in the United States are the story of neoliberalism vs. government and public health, and Trumpist Republicans politicizing vaccines and driving massive vaccine resistance in conservative areas. COVID-19 vaccine successes have been possible only because of hidden government and public goods roles slipping into a neoliberal system that devalued them but could not have delivered vaccines for COVID-19 without such "socialism."

Part of the hidden story is that the vaccines were actually a government miracle funded and created by the US government's National Institute of Health labs, a jewel at the center of the otherwise deeply under-funded public health system of the United States. The real story shows that Big Pharma profited immensely but did not serve the nation or world well. While the COVID-19 Pfizer and Moderna vaccines were produced and approved even by the Trump Administration at "warp speed," and protected millions of people as the Biden Administration made vaccination its top priority, Big Pharma was actually ill-prepared for vaccine development, production, distribution and administration, as shown by the major vaccine problems emerging during the "dark winter" of early 2021 and the rollout under Biden. While Americans were dying at more than a "9/11" rate of over 3,000 people a day from COVID-19 in this period, the vaccines were being injected far more slowly than expected into people's arms, leading then-president-elect Joe Biden in late December 2020, to say that his new government's top priority would be to solve a vaccine crisis by vaccinating the whole population against a virus that was creating the most deadly disaster in US history. But despite heroic efforts, deep US economic, political, and cultural forces would prevent his success.

America's history of seeing "big government" as the enemy was a big part of the COVID-19 vaccine problems. A look at vaccine history in the United States shows that the infrastructure for creating vaccines in the United States began and worked best in the New Deal and World War II eras, which changed traditional US attitudes toward government. A war-time New Deal government launched the first robust US public health system capable of creating mass vaccines. It funded and required pooling of technology, research, and distribution of free vaccines for all, as one historical chronicler notes.

Wartime vaccine programs expanded the scope of the military's work in vaccines well beyond its traditional focus on dysentery, typhus and syphilis. These new research initiatives targeted influenza, bacterial meningitis, bacterial pneumonia, measles, mumps, neurotropic diseases, tropical diseases and acute respiratory diseases. These diseases not only posed risks to military readiness, but also to civilian populations ....

Scientists had been laying the groundwork for many of these vaccines, flu included, for years before. It was not until World War II, however, that many basic concepts were plucked from the laboratory and developed into working vaccines.

The newly formed flu commission pulled together knowledge about how to isolate, grow and purify the flu virus and rapidly pushed development forward, devising methods to scale-up manufacturing and to evaluate the vaccine for safety and efficacy.[13]

World War I and then the New Deal opened the door to government that played a central role in World War II in overcoming longstanding corporate resistance and creating a public health system capable of creating and distributing vaccines rapidly.

Scientists often conducted research at their home institutions, which allowed the military to gain access to valuable expertise and facilities in the civilian sector.

The government used "No loss, no gain" contracts that covered the cost of research and, occasionally, indirect costs, but did not provide a profit. Under normal circumstances, universities would have resisted this technocratic reorganization of their research agenda, but the threat of war softened opposition.

Manufacturers also began to work on projects with little to no profit potential. Because vaccines were recognized as an essential component of the war effort, participating in their development was seen as a public duty.

As noted above by Interlandi, this public goods approach in the New Deal was never strong enough to build the robust public health infrastructure of European social democracies. But the New Deal showed reforms were possible in the United States, and a limited public health infrastructure was sustained until the Reagan era, when neoliberalism almost killed it. As in the case of the AIDS epidemic, Big Pharma was slow to respond to AIDS, seeing little profit in a disease striking a mainly stigmatized, relatively small slice of the population. As in any pandemic, the vaccine and other therapeutics for AIDS would be seen as low-profit, since it would only be taken one or perhaps every five or ten years rather than everyday by the masses.

The rapid vaccine developments that began a few months after the COVID-19 epidemic came only because of the once-in-a-century scale of the epidemic and the willingness of the government to lavish billions on research and development in its own labs, while providing the science and technologies for commercial development and production to companies such as Pfizer and Moderna. The companies would take the money on their own terms and never pooled technology, research, nor the vaccines for universal free public access, despite the vast public funding and basic science funded by every American's taxes. The National Institutes of Health, the public health center of science in the United States, while never adequately funded, did sustain a major commitment in recent decades to studying corona viruses as well as inventing the MRNA vaccine technology that became the basis of the Moderna and Pfizer vaccines. While these companies got the credit and the profit, the public funded the research, creation and distribution of the vaccines, in the case of Moderna paying for over 98% of the costs. The US biggest COVID-19 success was due to its public funding by the government, even though the public itself never realized their own money had paid for it while the companies took the credit and profits.

Once the first Pfizer and Moderna vaccines became available, the weakness of the US public health infrastructure created many of the hurdles to follow. Under Trump, there was no national program or agency to oversee the US response to the pandemic. True, Biden made a massive shift, prioritizing the creation of a national vaccine program and a public solution to the COVID-19 crisis; the shift away from Trumpism and neoliberalism significantly reduced COVID-19 hospitalizations and deaths in the United States under Biden. But it would take construction of a new government-funded system – including much broader testing, PPE, community health clinics, mobile health units into rural and underserved community surveillance apparatuses, masks and distance enforcement – to get the public vaccinated.

Millions of un-vaccinated Americans couldn't get the vaccine or resisted it in the name of freedom from government tyranny. They were led by a campaign of Republican governors, such as Florida's Ron DeSantis and Texas' Greg Abbott, who tried to prevent vaccine and mask mandates during the terrible COVID-19 surge in their states during the summer and fall of 2021. The politicizing of vaccines is a tragedy, deliberately stoked by Trumpists who saw it as a road to victory among their most fervent rural and white Christian evangelical base. As we show below in our discussion of culture, the message of the GOP leaders resonated with the anti-science, anti-government, and individualistic cultural themes long central to the United States, representing the cultural side of the neoliberal capitalist creed.

The combination of Trumpist politicizing of the pandemic and the rise of the Delta and Delta plus as well as Omicron variants played a huge role in worsening and sustaining the pandemic even after Biden's leadership on vaccines and public health. But the long-standing structural deficit in public health and vaccine preparedness would haunt the Biden Administration. The systemic public health deficits made the end of the pandemic and a "return to normalcy" anything but certain, with vulnerability to new deadly viruses in 2023 such as the Highly Pathological Avian Influenza.

And these problems in the United States are multiplied by the failure of US corporations to participate in a global response to the pandemic and offer free vaccine doses in desperately poor nations. As the United States was vaccinating more than half its adults in 2021, less than 2% of Africans got vaccines, reflecting the inability to pay for them and administer them. The corporate insistence on maintaining their patent rights on the vaccines helped ensure a COVID-19 catastrophe in countries like India, Brazil, and South Africa that dwarfed the US crisis, creating what appeared to be a potential for a shriek or whimper extinction in the most impoverished and hard-hit countries. This would come back to haunt the wealthy nations, as new more deadly variants developed in India, Brazil and other poor nations, a tragedy eerily reminiscent of the 1918 "Spanish flu," that also spread to India and caused 100 million deaths, a significant percentage of the world's population, bordering on a whimper extinction.

Pandemic Culture: How Core Values Shape Pandemics Differently in the United States and Europe

To understand pandemics and extinction, you have to look at culture as well as economic and political systems. In fact, economics, politics, and culture are intertwined – with neoliberalism driving some of the cultural values, such as individualism and exclusion, that explain US COVID-19 failures. In this final section, we look at how the American Dream and other unique aspects of American culture have played a huge role in enhancing US vulnerability to pandemics, and making it hard to contain them. In contrast, European culture has played an equally big role in permitting European nations to get COVID-19 under better control than in the United States during the first year of the pandemic. Culture is a huge systemic force in the United States, helping make Dr. Fauci so depressed about US COVID-19, as he compares it to the relative success of Europe and the ways in which European culture helps contain pandemics.

We look at three cultural themes below that contribute to the difference between the way the United States succumbed to the virus and Europe contained it, especially in the first year and continuing since then.

1. Individualism vs. Community

The difference between the American Dream and what social critic Jeremy Rifkin calls the European Dream is a conflict between individualism and community.[14] The American Dream – at the center of US culture – is going out for "number one." Each person seeks to follow his or her own star and has the right to look after themselves. In contrast, the European Dream is to connect to a community and enjoy the fulfillment possible in friendship and love of others.

These contradictory values are tied to different ideas of freedom cherished in Europe and the United States. In the United States, freedom is the right to be left alone and enjoy the right to do whatever one wants; it can be called "autonomy." In Europe, freedom is the right to security and support of a nourishing community, which can be called "embeddedness."

These differences are related to the different models of US and European capitalism. In the United States, capitalism promotes "living to work" while in Europe, social democracy promotes "working to live." The American Dream is about accumulation; the European Dream is about quality of life.

These cultural differences play a huge role in the way societies respond to pandemics such as COVID-19. It's obvious in the United States that the focus on oneself rather than others has led much of the public to view masks and social distancing – and even vaccines – as infringements on their personal freedom. Trump has modeled this self-centered approach, not encouraging masks or keeping distances at his rallies or in his speeches; while he quietly got vaccinated himself, he did not encourage his followers to submit to any government guidance including getting the vaccine jab. The reason is clear: it is red meat for his base, who see such public health mandates as unacceptable restrictions on their autonomy or liberty.

Europeans may not like masks or distancing or even vaccines, but they have been raised with values of protecting others. So, while there is some vaccine hesitancy, European publics are more likely to accept masks or distancing or vaccines as the only way to protect their community. And, for them, if their community weakens or collapses, their personal freedom also disappears.

The cultural difference here goes well beyond whether you accept masks or social distancing. Confronting a pandemic such as COVID-19 requires painful sacrifices to protect the community, which individualistic or self-oriented Americans find it very hard to accept. This includes everything from not going to bars and parties to accepting lockdowns of one's workplace, schools, or whole economy. These create unpalatable losses for the individual, but they are essential to stopping pandemics.

Many Americans, following Trump's lead, said schools, workplaces, and restaurants had to open up when COVID-19 hit, even as the virus cases and deaths shot up. What mattered was they were free to lead their normal lives. The idea that it made sense to lock down the economy for the community didn't compute. What mattered was their own personal freedoms; sacrificing drinking at a bar or going to work could not be justified. That attitude became a rallying cry for Trump's base – millions of Americans – and helped fuel to the enduring COVID-19 catastrophe that the United States has suffered.

In Europe and in East Asian communal nations, such as Japan, South Korea, and Vietnam, the culture discourages such anti-social behavior. The people in communal cultures did not like lock-down of the economy any more than Americans, but they were more willing than Americans to make sacrifices to protect the community. Because government was an expression of the community, they also accepted government mandates forcing unpalatable lockdowns. That public acceptance of personal sacrifice for public good led to the kind of national shutdowns that were necessary to contain the pandemic.

The US COVID-19 disaster was, in this sense, an outcome of the fervent individualism of US neoliberalism and the American Dream. American culture not only fueled COVID-19 but also helped explain the failure of the United States to develop a robust public health system and public goods economy, the systemic essentials for preventing pandemics and extinction.

2. Science vs. Religion

It's easy to see that COVID-19 is a viral disease that can only be treated and eliminated through use of medical science and public health strategies. European countries and most other nations have taken this approach. In the United States, though, millions see COVID-19 as a "hoax," a political strategy or the work of Satan. Following Trump and most of the Republican Party leadership, many reject the idea that the problem is something for science and public health to confront; in fact, many see science and rationality or the intellect as the problem rather than the solution.

Karen Alea is a former Evangelical Christian who wrote an illuminating essay in the *Huffington Post* about evangelicals, rationality, and COVID-19. When she was an Evangelical, she always wanted to get closer to God. In her community, people "gathered around to lay hands on me and implore the Holy Spirit to wash over me and show his love to me." Then, she says:

> With more praying and chatting, they realized what could be blocking me from receiving the gift of tongues: I'd graduated from college ....
>
> Later, a leader in the group raised his hand to the sky and commanded the "demon of intellectualism" out of me. I cried. I wanted that too. I was thinking too much ... I was putting God in a box by trying to figure him out with logic.
>
> "Speak out in faith. Just let it come", the leader said. I decided I needed to break through this rational thinking stifling me ....[15]

Karen says she learned from her evangelical peers that science and intellectualism were opposed to God. It should be noted that Karen's story illustrates what Harvard historian Richard Hofstadter argues in his epic 1963 book, *Anti-Intellectualism in America*, that the United States has long been a nation hostile to science and intellectualism. Hofstadter shows that this stems from the evangelical Protestant tradition that the founders brought to America.

Karen writes that her evangelical community's view of COVID-19 was entirely shaped by its anger at and distrust of science and rationality. She says they saw COVID-19 as "a message from God," and that God is using COVID-19 to help us change the world. Certain that God will protect believers, her evangelical friends reject masks and government mask mandates, allowing them to spread the Word without masks. Karen cites polls showing majorities of Evangelicals share this view, and goes on to explain:

> If I hadn't left the charismatic movement that was always requiring God to do tricks and encouraging me to "walk out in faith," I have no doubt I would be attending a church in person. I have no doubt I'd attend purposeful "God is more powerful than COVID-19" gatherings like the young woman who died from the virus ....
>
> As a young idealistic Christian who only wanted to grow in my faith, I was prayed over to sever me from my intellectual and rational thinking.
>
> This global pandemic has revealed there's already a virus inside some American forms of belief – ones that believe God isn't powerful enough to exist outside of gatherings or ones who believe this is in God's plan so he can show his power.[16]

Karen concludes:

> This kind of spiritual terrorism is showing up on a national scale and, as in my own faith journey, only reason can get us out.[17]

Karen's story personalizes the cultural values that explain why the US response to COVID-19 has been so different than that in Europe.

The strength of anti-scientific feelings in the United States, and the power of evangelical movements as the base of the Republican party, will make it perennially difficult for the United States to deal with COVID-19 and future pandemics. When the renowned journal, *Scientific American*, made its first political endorsement for Joe Biden in its 175-year history, it was making a telling statement about the cultural forces against science and truth that are systemic in America and fuel the US pandemic.[18]

3. Inclusion vs. Exclusion: COVID-19 and System Racism

Europe's fight against COVID-19 has been helped by its culture of inclusion, a moral commitment to include and protect all members of the community, whatever their race, religion, or national origin. Inclusiveness underpins European nations' very existence as social welfare states that guarantee everyone free health care, education, and other public goods. It is obviously closely related to the European celebration of community. While discrimination against

North African and Middle Eastern immigrants show the limits of the European inclusivity ideal, the European idea of community is universal since it in principle includes all citizens, whatever their race or ethnicity.

In contrast, exclusion remains a deep part of US culture, and it is a huge hurdle to public health and fighting pandemics, including COVID-19. Inequality experts Dedrick Asanti-Muhammad and Chuck Collins write that:

> While we are several years away from understanding the pandemic's impact on racial asset holdings, the most recent pre-pandemic data is alarming.
>
> Between 1983 and 2016, the median Black family saw their wealth drop by more than half after adjusting for inflation, down to a minuscule 2% of white wealth. Latinos saw only a marginal increase, to just 4% of median white wealth. White households, by contrast, increased their wealth by a third.[19]

We noted at the beginning of Chapter 3 that it is not coincidental that the rise of protests in 2020 against systemic racism emerged as COVID-19 was raging throughout the United States. COVID-19 has decimated US communities of color, with cases and death rates in these groups far higher than among whites. Systemic racism makes people of color vulnerable to COVID-19 in ways discussed by epidemiologists in an article in the *New England Journal of Medicine*:

> Current protests throughout the United States are highlighting the history of marginalization of and discrimination against Black Americans disparities in COVID-19 infections and deaths are laying bare the underlying structural racism that protestors seek to disrupt.[20]

In the first half of the 20th century, infectious diseases – the most deadly being the Spanish influenza pandemic – were a leading source of death in the United States, with African-Americans most likely to die.

Today, history is repeating itself:

> The COVID-19 pandemic clearly illustrates the intersection of structural racism, social risk factors, and health. Data from the Centers for Disease Control and Prevention on COVID-19 infection and mortality rates show high incidences in specific geographic regions. Further investigation within Louisiana revealed that rates of hospitalization and death in Black patients were twice as high as would be expected on the basis of demographic representation.[21]

Neoliberalism's devastation of communities of color since the early 1980s further explains the disproportionate effects of the COVID-19 pandemic on communities of color. This is highlighted by the Senate Report on COVID-19 cited earlier:

> The concentration of confirmed COVID-19 in New York City cases also correlates with race. Six out of the 10 ZIP codes with the highest number of confirmed COVID-19 cases are majority Black or Latino.

In August 2020, The Color of Coronavirus project showed that total deaths and per cap death rates among people of color was drastically increasing compared to white Americans. Dr. Ala Stanford, a pediatric surgeon, founder of the Black Doctors COVID-19 Consortium, summarized the terrible racial disparities:

> To hear that African Americans represent 12 to 13% of the population but 23 to 24% of the deaths is unacceptable in a developed nation.[22]

As in Dickens's era, the epidemics of endless disease – Cholera and TB then, Ebola and COVID-19 now – feast on the intertwining of systemic capitalism and systemic racism creating super-vulnerable populations to disease, that can become crunch, shriek, or whimper extinctions. If you are part of a community of color, you live in an endangered community, subject to extinction, at peril of perishing in the global crisis of biodiversity rooted in neoliberal capitalism.

8   America the Not-So-Beautiful
The US Doomsday Machine

In the nuclear age, war always risks extinction. Many Americans today dismiss the likelihood of a major nuclear war, either because of the end of the Soviet Union and the Cold War or because a major nuclear war has never happened in the approximately 75 years since the weapons were invented. Much of the public discussion is on dangerous new forms of war, such as cyber-war, which is, in fact, a major new peril and extinction threat. There should be a doomsday clock for cyber-war as well as nuclear war. The New Cold War rising between the United States and Russia, most evident in the Ukrainian crisis – and the serious rising tensions with China in a second new Cold War – are creating both cyber and nuclear threats that could spin out of control.

With possible cyber war escalation and the growing hostility under President Biden between the United States and both Russia and China, nuclear war needs to be brought into major focus again. The quickest and most likely way the world will end is through a large nuclear war. The more the nuclear peril is ignored by the public, the more likely that such a catastrophe will occur. We show here that US foreign policy and nuclear planning are designed to almost ensure that, in the absence of public knowledge and resistance, it could become a near certainty, one at this writing looming large in the Ukrainian crisis.

In large part because of US hegemonic foreign policy goals and the design of US nuclear planning, the most likely way that a major nuclear war will happen is through escalation of a conventional war, most likely related to the new Cold Wars with either Russia or China. US nuclear policy is at the heart of the existential risk, and has bred policies by other major powers that increase the extinction peril. These include nuclear policies leading to first strike war doctrines, use of battle field nuclear weapons, proliferation of nuclear weapons, and the weakening or elimination of nuclear arms agreements.[1]

In all these areas, the United States is by far the greatest danger, far ahead of other countries not just in the militarization of its economy and the overwhelming size of its conventional and nuclear military arsenal, but in its never-ending military interventionism and determination to remain the world's hegemon. Escalation could happen intentionally or unintentionally, a risk increased by

DOI: 10.4324/9781003401483-11

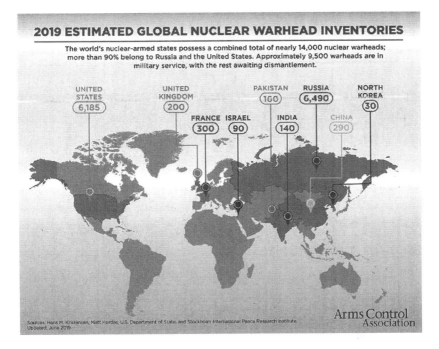

Figure 8.1 2019 Estimated Global Nuclear Warhead Inventories

direct threats that US presidents have historically made and the global deployment of large numbers of tactical and strategic US nuclear weapons in high-conflict zones. Just looking at number of nuclear weapons, the United States and Russia lead the growing number of nations with nuclear arsenals (Figure 8.1).

The United States and Russia have by far the most nukes. But the near equivalence between the United States and Russia is misleading. Consider the total military spending of the world's biggest military spenders:

The pie chart in Figure 8.2 shows global military expenditures by country for 2018, in US$ billions, according to SIPRI.[2]

The United States spends more than ten times on its military than does Russia, while also spending almost as much as all other countries of the world put together. The United States also has far more foreign military bases than Russia, which has few. The United States has more bases, indeed, than any other country in the history of humanity:

> While there are no freestanding foreign bases permanently located in the United States, there are now around 800 US bases in foreign countries. Seventy years after World War II and 62 years after the Korean War, there are still 174 US "base sites" in Germany, 113 in Japan, and 83 in South Korea, according to the Pentagon. Hundreds more dot the planet

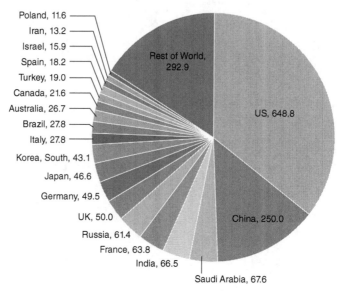

**Military Expenditures by Country
(in US$ billions) 2018**

Poland, 11.6
Iran, 13.2
Israel, 15.9
Spain, 18.2
Turkey, 19.0
Canada, 21.6
Australia, 26.7
Brazil, 27.8
Italy, 27.8
Korea, South, 43.1
Japan, 46.6
Germany, 49.5
UK, 50.0
Russia, 61.4
France, 63.8
India, 66.5
Saudi Arabia, 67.6

Rest of World, 292.9

US, 648.8

China, 250.0

Source: Stockholm International Peace Research Institute

Figure 8.2 Military Expenditures by Country

in around 80 countries, including Aruba and Australia, Bahrain and Bulgaria, Colombia, Kenya, and Qatar, among many other places. Although few Americans realize it, the United States likely has more bases in foreign lands than any other people, nation, or empire in history.[3]

All of this reflects US pursuit of global hegemony since World War II, a policy that military historian Andrew Bacevich, a former military officer, has described as "perpetual war:"

> [Since] 1945 the United States has occupied *the* preeminent place in the global order, a position affirmed with the collapse of the Soviet Union and the end of the Cold War in 1991. Indeed, we have come to believe that American primacy reflects the will of God or of some cosmic authority.

From the early years of the Cold War, we have come to believe that the freedom, material abundance, and primacy we cherish all depend upon the exercise of "global leadership." In practice, that seemingly benign term has been a euphemism for unquestioned military superiority and the self-assigned right to put our military to work as we please wherever we please. Back in the 1990s, Secretary of State Madeleine Albright said it best: "If we have to use force, it is because we are America. We are the indispensable nation. We stand tall. We see further into the future."[4]

Other countries might design their military establishments to protect certain vital interests. As Albright's remark suggests, American designs have been far more ambitious.[5]

America's military and nuclear policies – particularly its role as an interventionist global hegemon fighting endless conventional wars for corporate interests as well its refusal to renounce a first strike or first use doctrine – puts the world on a nuclear hair trigger. There are long-term and often ignored conflicts such as that between India and Pakistan over Kashmir that could lead to a nuclear war and are not primarily caused by the United States (though the US policy on proliferation has facilitated nuclearization of both India and Pakistan).

Horrifying as it would be, a limited nuclear conflict between India and Pakistan over Kashmir will likely not end all human life on the planet. The proliferation of nukes makes nuclear conflict more likely between other states. But any global nuclear war that does threaten extinction of all humanity will almost certainly be a direct or indirect result of US decisions, and involve US nuclear weapons and nuclear policy.

All of this reflects America's deep expansionist and interventionist impulses to consolidate power and profits in the name of protecting liberty or promoting civilized values. After World War II, the United States basically stepped into the same shoes worn by European imperial powers for several centuries. Imperialism is, to a large degree, baked into the capitalist template, as detailed in Chapter 4, but change is possible. Thus, long-militarist European capitalist nations moved after World War II toward rejecting imperialism and hyper-militarism. They have embraced in varying degrees a policy of global collective security, involving an increasing role for the UN and international courts to replace rule by hegemons with global government and international law.[6] Two world wars were close to an extinction event for Europe itself, and it forced post–World War II younger European generations to question war and imperialism, and find other ways to resolve conflicts and exist more peacefully in the world, a trend beginning to be reversed after the Russian invasion of Ukraine and US demands that European nations join them in hiking NATO ambitions and funding. But while we show that European capitalist nations remain far less militarist than the United States, they do not suggest we can end risks of nuclear war or nuclear extinction in a capitalist world. Rather, they show that reforms within the system can give us more breathing room to make the transformative systemic changes necessary to avoid nuclear extinction.

The one advanced capitalist country whose hegemonic aspirations and power clearly benefited from the two World Wars was the United States. By destroying European empires, the two world wars left the global playing field open to the United States, which controlled 50% of the global GDP after World War II ended. In the name of fighting communism, the United States rejected the idea of reaping a peace dividend, seeing the opportunity to take over the "grand areas" that had formerly been controlled by the British and other European Empires.[7] With these Empires in ruin, the US set on the course of hegemonic supremacy. US dominance is weakening today with the rise of China, but in the decades since World War II, it has been the United States, far more than any other country that engages in dangerous interventionist wars that have created chaos and risks of escalation in vital regions, symbolized by the "forever" wars of Afghanistan and Iraq. While the United States and European nations are both investing heavily in their militaries after the 2022 Russian invasion of Ukraine, the United States remains the overwhelming military hegemon.[8]

America's hegemonic build-up strengthened the rising United States and global extinction triangle linking US capitalism to militarism and potential nuclear war. It is symbolically important that the United States won World War II by being the first and only country to actually use nuclear weapons – twice – to force the surrender of Japan in 1945. Hiroshima and Nagasaki not only ushered in the nuclear age, but also marked the rise of the United States as the first nuclear hegemon.

After striking Japan with nuclear bombs, the United States then built a massive nuclear arsenal, developed a nuclear first strike doctrine, and deployed its nuclear forces on land-based missiles, submarines and aircraft. This was tied to a historically unprecedented hegemonic conventional arms and military build-up that allowed the United States to build the most powerful global military power ever seen in history and credibly threaten intervention almost instantly anywhere. And, indeed, the United States proceeded to threaten and carry out hundreds of such interventions during the Cold War and then up to the present time, with its interventionism constantly risking escalation to nuclear conflict. In this chapter, we look more closely at US nuclear policies in the old Cold War and new Cold War with Russia, including an analysis of the catastrophic Ukrainian conflict pitting the United States against Russia, and then, mainly at the end of this chapter, flesh out further the existential dangers of war with China.

Hegemony and Extinction: First Strike America

US hegemony has been the crucial underpinning of global capitalism since the end of World War II. Right after the war, the United States had the most powerful military force ever seen, and the largest economy, producing 50% of world wealth. US leaders saw the 20th century henceforth as the "American Century," as Time magazine founder, Henry Luce, proudly proclaimed. This meant that the United States would develop enough military power to intimidate or force any nation or group of nations to accede to US terms for global security and economic arrangements.

US global hegemony was established crucially right after World War II in US economic dominance, expansion of its conventional and nuclear arsenal and military bases, its push for global control and its "first strike" nuclear military planning. Daniel Ellsberg tells the story so vividly – and with such moral clarity – that every high school and college student and other citizen should read his book. Ellsberg, justly celebrated for releasing the Pentagon Papers that exposed the lies and failures of Vietnam in the early 1970s, trained at RAND, a conservative think tank contracting mainly with the Air Force, where he focused on nuclear war planning. He then went into the Marines as a leading nuclear planner and military officer.

In *the Doomsday Machine*, Ellsberg shows that after World War II, the United States built a militarized set of weapons, deployments, and foreign policy strategies that constitute a literal doomsday machine.[9] It is the ultimate military foundation of today's extinction era. It is also the militarized infrastructure built up since World War II, supported by both Republican and Democratic US presidents and other top leaders, parallel to the fossil fuel infrastructure that makes the United States the leading nation in the race to create irreversible climate disaster.

In his book, Ellsberg shows that since the beginning of the nuclear age, US nuclear planning was guided by plans for nuclear first strike or "first use" on Soviet or Chinese cities that would kill hundreds of millions of people. With the advent of hydrogen weapons in the early 1950s, this would lead to the ultimate moral catastrophe, killing billions of people almost immediately and triggering a "nuclear winter" that would destroy humanity. By the early 1960s, Ellsberg participated in creating a version of such a plan, which he now calls "crazy, criminally insane":

> [As] I would soon discover, the Joint Chiefs' estimates of the effect of carrying out their first strike plans, under a variety of circumstances, foresaw killing more than half a billion humans with our own weapons in a matter of months, with most of them dead in a day or two.
>
> How to describe that, other than insanity? Should the Pentagon officials and their subordinates have been institutionalized? But that was precisely the problem: they already were. Their institutions not only promoted this insanity, they demand it. And still do."[10]

First strike or threat of "first use" – the declared willingness to use nuclear weapons first rather than as retaliation from a nuclear attack – has always been at the core of US nuclear planning. No president has ever renounced this possibility, despite the reality that first strike in US doctrine would target cities and kill hundreds of millions, and possibly trigger a nuclear winner destroying all of humanity. In other words, US nuclear weapons from the beginning were developed and deployed in what Ellsberg repeatedly describes as a "mad" strategy that ensured not simply victory but one that would likely engulf the

United States as well and all other nations in a firestorm of total destruction of humanity. Such policy was "evil" and "insane" as Ellsberg writes over and over again – but it was embraced to ensure unquestioned US power in the world. Ellsberg marvels that he never heard his fellow nuclear planners, or their military and political leaders ask the obvious question:

> Does any nation on earth have a right to possess such a capability? A right to threaten – by its simple possession of that capability – the continued existence of all other nations and their populations, their cities and civilizations as a whole?[11]

The only politician that Ellsberg heard apparently trying to wrestle with this most profound of all moral questions was Bobby Kennedy, during the Cuban missile crisis. Everyone else toed the line. The policy was effectively disguised as the only way to deter a monstrously aggressive Soviet Union. True, US nuclear planners feared the possible invasion of Berlin, and Europe more broadly, by the Soviets. Early US nuclear experts in the late 1940s and 1950s, argued that even conventional attacks on Berlin by the Soviets would have to be met by the threat – and willingness to carry out – a nuclear response, one that would kill hundreds of millions of people. US planners also soon came to believe, moreover, that a doctrinal commitment to US first strike was the only way to ensure that America would not only keep the Soviets and Chinese always in check but would ensure that the entire world and every nation would submit to the ultimate power and national interest of the United States.

Ellsberg, the most knowledgeable and morally anguished official inside the US nuclear planning apparatus, knew that these plans were not only "omnicidal" – likely to lead to total destruction of humanity – but were based on exaggerations of Soviet power and nuclear capabilities. Ellsberg soon recognized that this hyping of the Soviet threat and geo-political dangers was a lie necessary for public consumption. The truth that could not be told was that US nuclear weapons – and the threat of a nuclear first strike that virtually all future US presidents used – were to ensure that the United States had the force necessary to force other nations to accept US power and demands. Rather than simply to deter Soviet attacks, Ellsberg shows that:

> Again and again, generally in secret from the America public, US nuclear weapons have been used for quite different purposes.
>
> As I noted earlier, they have been used in the precise way that a gun used when you point it at someone's head in a direct confrontation. For a certain type of gun owner, getting their way in such situations without having to pull the trigger is the best use of the gun. It is why they have it, why they keep it loaded and ready to hand. All American presidents since Franklin Roosevelt have acted on that motive at times, for owning

nuclear weapons: the incentive to threaten to initiate nuclear attacks if certain demands are not met.[12]

Ellsberg documents a long list of presidential threats to use nuclear weapons not simply repeatedly against the Soviets but repeatedly also against the Chinese, the North Koreans, Iran, the Vietnamese, and many other large and small nations where the United States wanted to force another country to give in to demands, whether about bananas, oil or just "keeping face." He introduces this list – which should be read by every American – with these words:

> The long-secret history of this period, extending throughout the Cold War and beyond, reveals that the assumption of a legitimate and available presidential "option" of first use – American initiation of nuclear attacks as an escalation of conventional armed conflict – is far more than purely symbolic or rhetorical. In reality, every president from Truman to Clinton has felt compelled at some point in his time in office – usually in great secrecy – to threaten and/or discuss with the Joint Chiefs of Staff plans and preparations for possible imminent US initiation of tactical or strategic nuclear warfare, in the midst of an ongoing non-nuclear conflict or crisis.[13]

Ellsberg goes on to document similar first strike threats in the 21st century, from George W. Bush to Donald Trump. *Every* president, both Republican and Democratic, since Harry Truman has carried out US nuclear "first strike" threats against rivals and opponents – from the Soviet borders in Europe to the Middle East to East Asia. This bi-partisan unwillingness by every president to renounce a first strike strategy (including on foreign cities of an enemy), is essentially a "terrorist" doctrine since, as Ellsberg points out, any such nuclear strike would kill millions of innocent civilians for political purposes, the accepted definition of terrorism. The conclusion is stark and an astonishing marker of what Ellsberg calls "the banality of evil," since it was designed by officials who were quite normal people, whether military or civilian, buying into the logic of the imperative of maintaining American power at any cost, publicly defended in the name of preventing submission to an adversary.

US nuclear planning has remained for decades a strategy not simply of deterrence but increasingly for US domination. Ellsberg puts it this way:

> Contrary to public understanding, that strategy has not been a matter of deterrence of nuclear attack on the United States, but rather the illusionary one of improving first-strike capability. Specifically, this has involved the goal of "damage-limiting" to the United States in the event of a U.S. preemptive strike against Soviet/Russian nuclear capability, triggered by a warming of impending attack, possibly in the context of escalation of a conventional or limited nuclear war."[14]

In the global capitalist era rising after World War II, this meant that the United States would effectively be able to ensure that US profits and power would be maximized by ultimate reliance on military force and that the global capitalist system would likewise be sustained by use of US military force, backed up by nuclear threats when necessary. The United States still refuses to renounce the no-first-strike doctrine advocated by the General Assembly of the UN and virtually all other nations in the world. The first strike doctrine is an economic as well as military policy, ensuring that any country opposing American corporate interests faced the possibility of annihilation.

The threat of nuclear war and "omnicide" was not simply miscalculations with the Soviet Union in the Cold War. In the 2022–2023 Ukrainian war, but also in the endless US "regime change" wars – whether for bananas in Guatemala or oil in Ian and Iraq, US interventions could always escalate into a nuclear conflict by accident or planned calculation. In either case, a leading risk of nuclear war was thus always the capitalist (including, as Ellsberg highlights, the military-industrial complex [MIC]) imperative, one central to the foreign policy of both Democrats and Republicans to secure the globe for profit of US global civilian companies.

As the extinction threat grew enormously during the Cold War, the MIC, as discussed in detail in Chapter 4, needs special consideration as an economic force underlying US militarism and the Cold War itself. The MIC has long played a major role in the United States. The major military contractors – Lockheed Martin, Raytheon, Boeing, McDonald-Douglas, and other corporate giants – are among the biggest and most politically influential companies in the United States. President Eisenhower's warning about the overwhelming power of the MIC – as a threat to American democracy itself – has been drowned out by the inflation of foreign threats that the MIC itself, helps produce. While the MIC continues to grow, the critique by antiwar activists of its role during the Vietnam era has largely eroded, along with weakening of the peace movement as a whole.

After the Cold War: America Escalates the Extinction Threat While Europe Tries to Lessen It

In the post–World War II era that Ellsberg chronicles, the US built and deployed thousands of nuclear weapons, constructing a doomsday machine in the name of deterring the Soviet Union. The fact that the Soviets matched the United States in the number of nuclear warheads was a gift to the Americans, offering a pretext not just for building thousands of US nuclear weapons but for deploying them in threatening ways to deter the Soviet "Evil Empire," which, in fact, lacked the conventional global deployments to carry out the endless regime change wars and credible nuclear threats available to the United States. Soviet nukes made the Soviets an unstated partner in

US global ambitions; while the United States and Soviets hated each other, they both needed each other to advance their own global aims. As Noam Chomsky has argued, the United States and USSR were actually co-dependent, hostile partners in the Cold War, helping the United States maintain its global dominance and the Soviets maintain control over Eastern Europe and the Soviet people themselves.

Meanwhile, as the Americans after the Soviet collapse in 1991 continued to build up its conventional and nuclear weapons and policies, the risk of US-fueled nuclear extinction remained palpable. Wars in Iraq and Afghanistan symbolized the new "forever" wars fought for oil and US corporate interests, all now in the name of the war on terrorism. European capitalist nations in this period were moving in the opposite direction. They reduced their military budgets, resisted most of the chronic military adventures and interventions that the United States sought through NATO to make Europeans junior partners, and supported regional and global arms agreements and treaties that would reduce the number of European arms. They stepped back from or banned provocative battlefield deployments such as intermediate nuclear missile deployments (e.g., Pershing missiles) or "defensive" missile systems that the United States supported. Europeans began to envision a model of economic development – though still capitalist – that would not rest on war and military spending. In fact, in direct contrast to the United States, the Europeans have come to see that they can reap economic gains from reducing military spending and avoiding costly military entanglements and wars, a decision, as noted above, that Europeans began to reverse after the Russian invasion of Ukraine. Nonetheless, Europeans still remained far less militarized than the United States.

None of this suggests that European capitalism proves the possibility of peace and the avoidance of nuclear extinction within capitalism. The Europeans operate under the protection of the nuclear umbrella of the United States. They act as lapdogs to neo-conservative hawkish US presidents such as George W. Bush, with European leaders sending forces to aid US militaries fighting catastrophic wars in Afghanistan, Iraq, and many other smaller conflicts in the name of anti-terrorism. The Europeans seek to sustain NATO, giving cover to dangerous US military deployments close to the Russian border. The relentless expansion of NATO east toward Russia after the Cold War made Europe a willing partner of the US-led NATO expansion in Eastern Europe that benefited both Europe and the US MIC.

Nonetheless, the contrast in the foreign and military policy of the Europeans and Americans remained significant, at least until the 2022 Ukrainian catastrophe, and shows that reforms to reduce the risk of nuclear extinction can happen initially within a European-style capitalist framework. The Europeans rejected much of their own history of imperialism and militarism and aspired to more collective security in the EU and the UN. This "dovish" European turn – that lasted from the end World War II until the Ukraine war contrasts sharply with hawkish intensification on the other side of the pond. Since the end of the Cold War, the United States has been ratcheting up neo-conservative war strategies, aggressively pursued by unrestrained global hawks such as Dick Cheney, George W. Bush, Mike Pompeo, and John Bolton, while Democratic "realists," including Bill Clinton, Barack Obama, and, as shown below, Joe Biden, also backed hegemonic and hawkish foreign policies. The contrast in 2019 between the European and American direction was perhaps most visible in Iran, where the Europeans desperately tried to sustain the Iranian nuclear agreement while Trump pulled out of it and pushed a set of provocative deployments promoted by Pompeo and Bolton, including naval carriers and missiles in the Gulf, along with sending 1,500 additional US troops and threatening war if Iran didn't change its government and all of its allies and policies in the region.

Trump and Biden: Ramping Up Nuclear Militarism

While President Trump ran against "silly wars" in Iraq and seemed to campaign on a new nationalist isolationism, he governed with largely the same dangerous policies of the neo-conservative establishment he claimed he would reject. Journalist Mark Landler notes that:

> Shortly before he was sworn in as president, Donald J. Trump vowed that the United States would stop "racing to topple foreign regimes that we know nothing about, that we shouldn't be involved with." He promised to end "this destructive cycle of intervention and chaos."
>
> Two and a half years into his presidency, Mr. Trump is enthusiastically calling for the toppling of one regime, in Venezuela, and energetically undermining another, in Iran.
>
> His administration's escalating economic and political pressure on both countries – alongside a reignited trade war with China – has raised tensions in two hemispheres to the highest levels since Mr. Trump took the oath of office.[15]

The fact that Trump, as Landler concludes, "pushed policies he once denounced" is a measure of the structural forces driving US militarism. More damning evidence is that President Biden, formerly known as somewhat "dovish" on nuclear policies, has not only embraced Trump's nuclear policies but also expanded on them. US economic imperatives weds the United States to its hegemonic policies, no matter who is the President, and creates permanent and growing risks of nuclear extinction. Trump initiated, but Biden has not only continued but actually expanded the following military policies increasing global extinction perils.

1. Massive New Investments in "Nuclear Modernization"

As analyst Aaron Mehta shows, plans drawn up by the Trump Administration in 2019 were to spend billions of dollars on new nuclear weapons and deployments in the coming decade, with Biden, as we document below, planning to spend even more. While the Europeans seek to reduce nuclear weapons, the United States is investing billions in the most dangerous new forms, many, ironically, on European soil and others in outer space. Mehta writes that:

> If the U.S. carries out all of its plans for modernizing and maintaining the nuclear arsenal, it will cost $494 billion over the next decade, an average of just less than $50 billion per year, a new government estimate has found.
>
> The number, part of a biannual estimate put out by the Congressional Budget Office, is 23 percent over the previous estimate of $400 billion released in 2017. That 2017 figure was a 15 percent increase over the 2015 number.[16]

The nuclear build-up includes the following:

- $234 billion on strategic nuclear delivery systems and weapons, including submarines (an estimated $107 billion over this time period), intercontinental ballistic missiles ($61 billion) and long-range bombers ($49 billion, less than the full projected cost of the dual-use bomber fleet); the nuclear warheads for use from those systems; and DOE's funding of nuclear reactors for the submarine fleet.
- $15 billion on tactical nuclear delivery systems and weapons, including tactical aircraft for delivering weapons; management of the warheads for those tactical aircraft; and funding for the new submarine-launched cruise missile.
- $106 billion for DOE's nuclear weapons laboratories and production facilities, where America's stockpile of nuclear warheads are maintained and developed. The department has a longstanding backlog on maintenance and upgrades for its locations.
- $77 billion on nuclear command, control, commutations, and early warning systems, used to coordinate any nuclear-related issues.[17]

Biden's defeat of Trump gave hope to peace advocates in the United States, because Biden in 2020 said the United States had enough nukes and called Trump's build-up a "bad idea." In 2017, he gave a speech to the Carnegie Endowment, warning Trump and neoconservative hawks against their nuclear buildup:

> If future budgets reverse the choices we've made, and pour additional money into a nuclear buildup, it harkens back to the Cold War and will do nothing to increase the day-to-day security of the United States or our allies.[18]

But when he got into the White House, Biden flipped, backing several of Trump's proposals for new nukes and adding new dangerous ones of his own. Biden's nuclear strategy now includes:

> modernizing all three legs of the nuclear triad: the Ground Based Strategic Deterrent, which is the replacement for the fleet of Minuteman III intercontinental ballistic missiles; the Columbia-class ballistic missile submarines; and the new B-21 stealth bomber.... The budget also proposes $609 million for the Long Range Standoff Missile, which is designed to be outfitted on bomber planes. That's $250 million more than what was projected by the Trump administration for fiscal 2022.[19]

US Arms Control groups highlight and express deep alarm about Biden's expansion of Trump's nuclear buildup. The Council for a Livable World said:

> President Biden ran on a campaign to reverse the budget and outrageous policies put forward by the Trump administration, ... However, this budget expands nearly every nuclear program put forward by that administration. This is not acceptable.[20]

2. Use 'em or Lose 'em

Far more dangerous than just numbers of nukes are the kinds envisioned by Trump and now even more by Biden. Both presidents championed increases in the number of "tactical" or "small" battlefield nukes – the type actually deployed on the battlefield. Such tactical weapons make it far easier to justify actual use of nukes in battle, as noted by former Reagan Secretary of State, George Schultz, testifying in the Senate a day before the release of a 2018 Trump Administration call for building "small" nukes:

> One of the alarming things to me is this notion that we can have something called a small nuclear weapon ... and that somehow that's usable... Your mind goes to the idea that, yes, nuclear weapons become usable. And then we're really in trouble, because a big nuclear exchange can wipe out the world.[21]

The Trump plans for tactical weapons were, in fact, tied to a new explicit military policy permitting nuclear use, including first use, under a wider set of circumstances than officially endorsed by earlier administrations. As noted in Chapter 4 and earlier in this chapter, this builds on a long history of the United States threatening actual first use of nuclear weapons to force other countries to do what it wants. In contrast, virtually all other nations have long argued that first strike is never acceptable and that nukes should never be used at all, except to deter or defend against a nuclear attack from another country.

Donald Trump's new explicit nuclear plans – now embraced and expanded by President Biden as we show below – are part of the long exceptionalist US policy. Beyond the development of a new generation of tactical battlefield nukes, Trump's 2018 Nuclear Posture Review (NPR), a Pentagon doctrine issued every few years to state official nuclear policy, authorizes first strike nuclear use under a wider range of circumstances against non-nuclear countries or even terrorists. The key point is the explicit endorsement of United States plans to use nuclear weapons not just for nuclear deterrence but as a strategy to advance the nation's "vital interests," a way of saying America will do what is necessary to maintain hegemony or power, even if it means destroying whole nations and risks global conflagration. The NPR states that the United States is prepared to use nuclear weapons in conflict with non-nuclear countries or groups seen as threatening US interests, defending against, for example, "non-nuclear "strategic attacks":

Significant non-nuclear strategic attacks include, but are not limited to, attacks on the United States, allied, or partner civilian population or infrastructure, and attacks on United States or allied nuclear forces, their command and control, or warning and attack assessment capabilities.[22]

As journalist Mehdi Hassan cogently commented during the Trump era,

Got that? Trump wants to be able to retaliate against a non-nuclear and perhaps even non-military attack on U.S. infrastructure – say, a cyberattack on the power grid? – with a nuclear strike that could kill hundreds of thousands, if not millions. To call such a move disproportionate would be a severe understatement.[23]

This is a vivid way of talking about how US nuclear policy – which has long been first strike and escalatory – has increased extinction risks today. Rather than dropping Trump's plans for new "useable" nukes, Biden is supporting and expanding them – even in the face of fierce criticism from arms control advocates and progressives in the Democratic Party. Biden's military budget plan for 2022 massively increased funding for the military budget and dangerous "low-yield" weapons, citing not only Ukraine but heightening Trump's rationale that we need options that are more credible for first use against Russia as a deterrent:

Most controversially, the Pentagon's request maintains the W76-2 low-yield warhead that is now outfitted on submarines and sets aside $5.2 million for a new sea-launched cruise missile capable of carrying a nuclear warhead. Another $10 million is being requested for the warhead in the budget for the National Nuclear Security Administration, an arm of the Energy Department.

The low-yield warhead, which has less explosive power than other atomic bombs, was recommended by the Trump administration's 2018 Nuclear Posture Review, which concluded that Russia's growing reliance on such weapons in war planning required the United States to develop more "flexible" options to deter their use.

"Expanding flexible U.S. nuclear options now, to include low-yield options, is important for the preservation of credible deterrence against regional aggression," the review stated.[24]

These weapons are designed for battlefield use against Russia or other nations or groups seen as posing a military threat, especially on the Russian border or in the Middle East. Biden and future presidents could be on the path to nuclearizing the war on terrorism, about as frightening a path toward extinction as anything one can imagine.

Biden's hawkishness reflects the hegemonic US policies that have long kept the US militarily dominant on the global stage. In fact, Biden rejected Trump's isolationist rhetoric, when Trump wanted immediate withdrawal from Afghanistan and Iraq. While Biden did withdraw from Afghanistan, his foreign policy is run by the same national security elite that waged endless wars in the name of fighting terrorism and assumes US dominance as a condition of US security and economic health. As noted earlier, many Democrats, in fact, tended to critique Trump by claiming he was too isolationist and unwilling to maintain traditional global leadership in military and national security affairs, particularly denouncing his being too "soft" on Russia. Biden's embrace of intensely militarized US foreign policy led to his massive increase in his proposed 2024 military budget to $886 billion, which with expected Congressional add-ons for specific conflicts leads to the first trillion dollar defense budget.

"Building back better," Biden's campaign slogan when he won in 2020, was partly an assertion of re-asserting toughness with the Russians and reclaiming the mantle of US hegemony, re-installing the global power the United States had enjoyed since the end of World War II. The 2022 Russian invasion of Ukraine reflected Putin's own pursuit of imperial policies and a huge rise in the risk of nuclear conflagration in the new Cold War, as we show in the next section, also leading to Biden returning to the traditional anti-Russian militarism after the invasion of Ukraine.

War with Russia: Ukraine, the New Cold War, and Nuclear Extinction

Four days after Russia invaded Ukraine on February 24, 2022, the mayors of Hiroshima and Nagasaki in Japan sent an urgent letter to Vladimir Putin begging him not to drop a nuclear bomb. As mayors of the only two cities ever bombed by nuclear weapons their letter carried special significance. That bombing by the United States at the end of World War II destroyed these two great cities and awakened the world to the new age of extinction. The two mayors feared the Ukrainian crisis could now create mushroom clouds over Europe or the whole world, reflecting all out nuclear war between two super-powers in a world war that could destroy all humanity.

Indeed, the Russian invasion of Ukraine changed the world. It inaugurated a more dangerous stage of the New Cold War. The first Cold War came close to destroying the world, most famously in the 1962 Cuban missile crisis. The New Cold War, beginning in 1990 after the collapse of the Soviet Union, never ended the hostile rivalry between the United States and Russia. From 1990 until 2022, in the first stage of the New Cold War, the United States and Russia remained in constant tension in Eastern Europe, the Middle East, Afghanistan, and throughout the world, as both nations sought to defend and expand their own power. But it was not until the 2022 Russian invasion of Ukraine that the more dangerous stage of the New Cold War erupted, raising the prospect of nuclear extinction so powerfully that the Hiroshima and Nagasaki mayors wrote those ominous letters, reminding us that the world remained on the precipice of nuclear extinction.

Indeed, while much of the world's population still did not pay extremely close attention to the nuclear risks, the Ukrainian conflict carried multiple risks of escalation to nuclear war from the very beginning. In the first few days, Putin expected to quickly conquer Kiev and other major Ukrainian cities. But Russian forces encountered unexpected fierce resistance from the Ukrainians while Putin's planned blitzkrieg was undermined by his own military's unexpected logistical, supply, equipment and morale problems. As the United States and West cheered and massively resupplied the Ukrainians, Putin explicitly reminded them that he had the world's largest nuclear arsenal and raised the Russian nuclear alert status, strongly hinting that he might resort to a nuclear strike to prevent Russian defeat or disgrace.

In the first two weeks, as the war changed from a blitz into what looked like a merciless, indiscriminate bombing of Ukrainian cities, a vivid humanitarian catastrophe emerged in Ukraine, captured and conveyed around the world by Ukrainians videoing the bombing of their maternity hospitals, suburban neighborhoods and even nuclear power plants. Putin's willingness to subject millions of civilians to what appeared to be genocidal violence, including hints at possible use of chemical and biological weapons against Ukrainian cities, was itself a provocation for escalation that could go nuclear. The violence was so horrific that Putin knew it could increase Western public opinion pressure and tempt the United States and European leaders to stop the massacre with escalation of great – potentially even nuclear – force.

Indeed, the United States and NATO nations were so horrified by the wholesale destruction of Ukrainian cities and killing of civilians, as well as inspired by the courage of Ukrainian President Zelensky and his people, that the United States almost immediately began a massive and provocative Western escalatory response. The United States led a major resupply effort to get stinger ant-aircraft missiles, anti-tank Javelin weapons and eventually attack – drones to the Ukrainian military, typically delivered through intermediaries that US leaders thought would not immediately provoke a Russian attack on the United States itself or NATO. President Biden was careful to reject Zelensky's repeated calls for a "no fly zone," making clear that he would not approve US planes shooting down Russian plans, anti-aircraft and other Russian military, a risk of all-out war with Russia that he would not take.

But, just as Putin was being reckless about nuclear risks, Biden and European leaders and strategists on each new day of the war contemplated further and more dangerous escalations to help defeat the Russians. While they rejected a full no-fly zone, they began to consider targeted and restricted zones of United States or NATO engagement to protect Ukrainian nuclear plants or humanitarian corridors and help Ukraine with their air-defenses. Likewise, while they wouldn't fly American planes or pilots into Ukrainian air space, the Biden Administration began discussing ways to get US jet planes or attack-drones into German or Polish or Dutch hands, who would quietly or secretly transfer them to Ukrainians at their borders. While this was defined as keeping the United States out of war, it looked more and more like the United States was getting involved in the war that not only Putin but legal and military scholars might agree represented a perilous escalation of intervention in the conflict. And these initiatives were accompanied by funding huge military re-supply depots for Ukraine in the Russian border nations, such as Poland, where virtually every form of weapon could be supplied quickly to the Ukrainians, at the same time that Putin was declaring the supply of such weapons an engagement by the United States and a "legitimate target."

Indeed, the Americans were escalating their own involvement in ways that Western media saw as "reasonable" but could easily be seen as reckless because of potential for direct engagement with Russian forces. In the name of protecting NATO allies, the United States began transferring thousands of US troops into Poland, Hungary, and the Baltic states of Lithuania, Latvia, and Estonia, where miscalculations could easily lead to firing and killing across the Russian or Baltic borders. Likewise, US strategists quietly designed and escalated cyber-war initiatives that could target Russian critical infrastructure, including military command centers, as well as financial and energy companies; such cyber-war initiatives remained shrouded in secrecy but had already become a major part of 21st-century warfare. Moreover, these direct, if unconventional, engagements in the war were accompanied by arguably the most serious economic sanctions ever deployed against another nation against whom the United States was not in war, sanctions that would be catastrophic to Russia and that Putin had already called a "declaration of war."

One other extinction risk aided and abetted by the United States in Ukraine involves energy and climate. As the war continued, US sanctions against Russia increasingly focused on oil and gas, essential to the Russian economy and also important to Europe, which consumed 40% of its energy from Russian gas. While the solution might have involved massive and urgent dis-investment in fossil fuels, both in the United States and Europe, this was hardly a priority. Instead, US oil and gas companies, that made enormous profits off the sanctions of Russian oil, successfully promoted US bi-partisan demands for more domestic production of US oil and gas to ensure energy independence. Canadian dirty oil coming through the Keystone Pipeline and others stopped by climate activists, were being raised by bi-partisan American politicians as the real solution to dependency on Russian energy. A far better solution would have been massive immediate investment in renewables, both in the United States and Europe, a way of diminishing both climate and war risks simultaneously. But while advocated by climate activist leaders such as Bill McKibben, and promised as a later step by the Biden Administration, it was never viewed by United States or Western leaders as the most important and immediate solution, despite its double-whammy blow to extinction dangers arising from both climate and war. Indeed, in March, 2022, Biden announced he would release a huge amount of oil from the US Petroleum Strategic Reserve as part of the economic war against Russia. Biden boasted that: "The scale of this release is unprecedented: the world has never had a release of oil reserves at this 1 million per day rate for this length of time."[25] While he was hoping to gain politically by lowering the price of gas at the pump, he was cutting way back on the massive clean energy programs that he had initially proposed in his Build Back Better agenda.

Returning to nuclear extinction, while Putin's risks of nuclear escalation were not denied by Putin himself and widely condemned, the nuclear risks of United States and NATO escalation were framed in more careful language and were rarely highlighted by even the more liberal Western media, such as MSNBC and CNN, as posing dangerous risks of escalation to nuclear war. This reflected partly Western rage at the Russian invasion and barbaric humanitarian attacks, consistent with the Old and New Cold War framings of Russia as a monster. Such a tyrannical monster would take such nuclear risks, while the United States and Western image of themselves as democratic freedom-protectors, and of American exceptionalism, embraced by Western media and bipartisan political leaders, increased the asymmetric view of how such a war could escalate into the unthinkable. Only state tyrannies such as Russia, not capitalist democracies like the United States, could go that route. Should it happen, it would only be by Putin's "unhinged" state of mind, rather than an unpredictable escalation by both sides that has always been a major way that nuclear war could erupt from a conventional conflict. This became the accepted view of the majority of both Democrats and Republicans.

The ugly truth is that both sides in this war saw the conflict in existential terms. Indeed, both sides defined the war as world-shattering, likely to shape the future of 21st-century security arrangements and their respective nation's power within them. Both had been great Super-powers, and both were confronting a 21st century in which they perceived themselves as in relative decline, partly because of the rise of China and other Asian nations as a competing world – hegemonic force. They were both willing to go to the brink, because they had come to view their own survival, power, and prestige as dependent on the outcome of the war.

This was more obvious in the case of Russia. Russian power and prestige in the world had declined precipitously in the 21st century, as its form of crony capitalism and increasingly dictatorial rule under Putin had destroyed much of the economic, political and cultural power of Russia and the earlier Soviet Union. It was well known that Putin had long dreamed of a restoration of not just the Soviet Empire, but the great ancient Russian civilization that had dominated such a huge part of the world in the 17th, 18th, and 19th centuries, as well as during the Old Cold War. As New York Times columnist, David Brooks wrote, Putin was pursing his version of Russia's "identity politics," to resurrect the great civilizational identity that Russia sustained through many centuries, from Peter the Great to its huge role in defeating Hitler in World War II.

Putin had already demonstrated that restoring Russia to its rightful place as a great world power was his vision of his own legacy. Before invading Ukraine in 2022, he had shown how willing he was to use brutal force to achieve his ends. He had not only subjected Chechnya to unrelenting destruction for several years after its revolt in 1998, but had also invaded Georgia in 2008 and annexed the Crimea and supported Russian separatists in the Donbass region, in Eastern Ukraine, in 2014. In all these conflicts, he had made clear that re-uniting ethnically Russian and Russian-speaking peoples in all the former Soviet Republics was the inevitable destiny and rightful place of Russia in the world. But as NATO had moved eastward since 1990, the exact opposite had taken place. Nations in Eastern Europe and the former Soviet Empire were all turning away from Russia, with Ukraine, the largest border nation now clearly turning toward Europe rather than Russia as its home.

Ukraine was thus the decisive battle-ground for Putin; if he lost, his legacy collapsed and Russia would become a third-world petro-station for Europe. All of this was existential for Russia. It had to prevent Ukraine from being lured to the West, and Putin, a former KGB strongman, was determined he would never accept such an existential defeat. It was thus not surprising that he might resort to his ultimate card – his huge nuclear arsenal – to ensure his vision and the survival of his own regime in Russia.

By April 2022, Putin had already begun to make explicit nuclear threats. As the west continued to supply more lethal weapons to Ukraine, Putin repeatedly threatened "unpredictable consequences," code words for the use of Russian nukes. As the war dragged on, and President Biden repeatedly accused Putin of "war crimes" and "genocide," Western security analysts and media began to focus on the Russian nuclear threat, with many analysts predicting that unexpected Russian conventional losses, combined with increasing western military support of Ukraine, made Russian nuclear use more likely than at any time since the Cuban missile crisis. As in that crisis, many Americans began for the first time in 50 years to worry about what they would do if nukes started falling, contemplating fleeing into northern Canadian woods or building nuclear shelters in their basements.

Nuclear strategists echoed this public sentiment. Political scientist Michael Klare argued, in April 2022, that Americans and NATO strategists had concluded that Putin's threats had fundamentally changed the nuclear risks and global security. Putin's willingness to threaten openly and repeatedly a nuclear strike in the middle of a major war was seen as a decisive turning point, opening the door to a new set of conflicts between great powers in which nuclear threats would become normalized and used to achieve military objectives in conventional wars. The nuclear genie was now fully out of the bottle, enshrining in future wars generalized fears of nuclear annihilation in all great power wars that went beyond the limited case of the Cuban missile crisis. Klare argues that extinction by nuclear war would begin to eclipse climate change as the greatest threat to all life.[26]

The Russia case certainly makes clear that capitalism is not the only economic system that can lead the world to extinction. Of course, many argue that Russia had become a "crony-capitalist" system under Putin, who had turned the nation's economy over to the billionaire oligarchs with many tied to the West, wealthy from involvement in Western real estate, energy and other partnerships and investments. Some also see Russia as "state capitalism," since it played in the Western global economy more or less by the trade rules of that global capitalist system. Nonetheless, the Ukrainian nuclear extinction peril makes absolutely clear what has been a premise of this book. Capitalist nations are deeply involved in fueling extinction, but they are not the only ones. If there were any doubt, Russia's invasion of Ukraine makes clear that the end of the world could come about because of the leaders and structural conditions of nations not designed according to Western capitalist systems.

But the role of the United States and Europe in the nuclear peril surrounding Ukraine also reinforces our view that the great capitalist societies play the nuclear game and are willing, even eager, to take risks of the "unthinkable" in the pursuit of their own systemic power and aims. While Putin pursued the restoration of the great Russian Empire and the Soviet Union, US leaders by 2022 had been struggling with the fate of US hegemonic world power since 9/11 and the failures of the wars in Iraq and Afghanistan. Just as important, the 21st century was emerging as an era in which broader US economic power was under deep challenge from China, which was emerging as the true new economic Super-power rival to the United States.

American leaders such as Biden, as well as Trump, saw the relative decline of American economic power – and the new challenge from China – as the over-arching challenge facing the United States. As noted in Chapter 4, Harvard political scientist, Graham Allison wrote in his influential book, the world was entering another "Age of Thucydides." Just as Sparta and Athens had to compete for dominance as the latter began to challenge the former's power, so the United States would be faced in the 21st century with containing China and maintaining its own economic and political hegemony. A defeat in Ukraine would very likely spell a great victory for China in this epic struggle, with the United States being subordinated in the world's eyes to both Russia and China, should it lose in Ukraine.

In the concluding section below, we deal with China, that has also begun a major nuclear arms development project along with its economic global ambitions. But it is essential to see that US leaders were as invested as Putin was in the resurrection of their own national and civilizational destinies and future leadership of the world. Like Putin, no US leader would willingly accept defeat in Ukraine, even if the cost of victory involved risks of nuclear escalation. The defeat would not only condemn the political prospects of Biden and the Democrats but also would deprive the Republicans of their traditional self-proclaimed identity as guarantors of global freedom by en-suring that the United States never be defeated in a major confrontation such as Ukraine.

Despite his careful and nuanced words, Biden understood the stakes of fail-ure in Ukraine. For 30 years, Biden had been an intimate player in the politics of the national security state and the Senate committees dealing with US for-eign policy. He has always functioned comfortably in the circle of American "realists" who seek Western allies rather than unilateral control but remain totally committed to US traditional hegemonic policy and its existential stakes in remaining the "leader of the free world." His enormous military budgets in 2023 and 2024 make clear that Biden was committed to massively funding not only Western victory in Ukraine but a broader US global military dominance, with his proposed 2024 budget of $886 billion more than four times that of China and ten times larger than Russia's.

In a different context, the United States and the West might have avoided the nuclear risks of Ukrainian engagement and escalation. It could have limited itself to humanitarian aid. It could have rejected many of the steps that each day led closer to US military involvement in the war itself. As Jonathan Steele, chief former foreign policy correspondent of the Guardian has argued, the United States could have considered a kind of "surrender," in a negotiation with the Ukrainians and Putin which would have avoided millions of Ukrainian deaths and saved many of its cities now demolished into rubble, while achieving from Putin and the world community guarantees of neutrality, international protection, and recognition of Ukraine as a nation with sovereign rights other than entry into NATO.[27]

The very idea of "surrender," even if it achieved the essential Ukrainian ends and preserved their basic sovereignty and millions of Ukrainian lives would never be accepted by a West steeped in triumphalism and hegemony. The admiration for Ukrainian courage and desire for freedom was real and understandable. But it does not have to take the form of a growing United States and Western militarism in the New Cold War that is seen as indispensable to maintaining US global power and humiliating its most formidable nuclear rival. Such humiliation, itself, might be conceived as another escalatory risk, since Putin's abject defeat would likely increase his likelihood to think the unthinkable and take down the rest of the world with the collapse of Russia and of his own regime or survival. Only in a militaristic West long willing to risk nuclear perils to ensure its power would admiration for the courage and values of the Ukrainians be inevitably tied to a victory in war that could destroy not only Ukraine itself but much of the rest of the world.

As the war dragged on and millions of Ukrainians died or became refugees, the United States and Europeans both turned to increasingly militaristic agendas. In his 2022 budget, Biden abandoned much of his early progressive "Build Back Better" climate and "caring economy" policy, and shifted new funds mainly to massive increased military spending in both his 2023 and 2024 defense budgets. Biden has continuously proposed large increase in funds to all three cornerstones – land, air, and sea – of the US nuclear arsenal. Meanwhile, European nations made a major shift in their own budgets, breaking constraints on military and nuclear spending of their own that had been put in place after the horrors of World War II to prevent World War III. The commitment to protecting Ukraine and saving the peace took the turn of greater militarization of all the major players in the conflict, ironically increasing the likelihood of World War III and accelerating the race to extinction.

War with China?

President Biden's aggressive response to Russia is paralleled by what many view as a more dangerous and hostile policy to China. Nobody has been more deeply unsettled than the man who counts: President Xi. In July 2021, the *New York Times* spotlighted President Xi's bellicose reactions to what the Chinese perceive as escalation of US hostility to China's rise:

> It is not clear whether the Chinese leader, Xi Jinping, has formally signaled a change in foreign policy strategy, but judging from public

statements and actions in recent weeks, patience with the Biden administration has worn thin.

China has retaliated against American and European sanctions over
China's political repression in Hong Kong and Xinjiang with sanctions
of its own. It has reined in the public offerings of Chinese companies on
American stock exchanges. And it has stepped up military activity in the
South China Sea and in the water and air around Taiwan in response to a
more visceral American policy of support for the island democracy under
Mr. Biden.[28]

President Xi's responses suggest the United States is laying the groundwork for
war with China:

> The quickening tempo of military operations increases the chances of
> armed confrontation – even if accidental. The incendiary language ema-
> nating from some officials and state media in China would make climb-
> ing down even more difficult, given a nationalistic mood at home.
>
> Mr. Xi used a speech on July 1 celebrating the 100th anniversary of
> the founding of the Communist Party of China to warn that anyone who
> challenged the country's sovereignty would "crack their heads and spill
> blood on the Great Wall of steel built from the flesh and blood of 1.4 billion
> Chinese people."[29]

Leading US security officials have been laser focused on "the China threat,"
introducing several frameworks predicting US–China conflict as central to security and survival. As discussed above, political scientist, Graham Allison, has
argued that a modern "Thucydides Trap" – a point of extreme danger involving hegemonic transition – now lies at the heart of major global war prospects.
As Chinese economic and political power grows extreme rapidly, the United
States sees a mortal threat to its own hegemonic primacy since World War II-
one Allison sees as realistic:

> Today, China has displaced the United States as the world's largest econ-
> omy measured in terms of the amount of goods and services a citizen can
> buy in his own country (purchasing power parity).
>
> What Xi Jinping calls the "China Dream" expresses the deepest aspi-
> rations of hundreds of millions of Chinese, who wish to be not only rich
> but also powerful. At the core of China's civilizational creed is the belief –
> or conceit – that China is the center of the universe. In the oft-repeated
> narrative, a century of Chinese weakness led to exploitation and national
> humiliation by Western colonialists and Japan. In Beijing's view, China
> is now being restored to its rightful place, where its power commands
> recognition of and respect for China's core interests.

As noted earlier, Allison's reading of history is that hegemonic transition eras make China and the United States dangerously close to war. To avoid war, he argues that:

> Managing this relationship without war will demand sustained attention, week by week, at the highest level in both countries. It will entail a depth of mutual understanding not seen since the Henry Kissinger–Zhou Enlai conversations in the 1970s. Most significantly, it will mean more radical changes in attitudes and actions, by leaders and publics alike, than anyone has yet imagined.

Many other influential analysts dispute parts of Allison's analysis, with Allison's Harvard colleague, Joseph Nye, actually arguing the greater danger is internal disruption or drastic weakening of China as it confronts numerous internal and external economic, ethnic, environmental, and political conflicts that could be a more likely cause of Asian and global destabilization. Allison is not emphasizing enough that the United States may be misreading China out of fear. China's military funding and policies are regionally assertive but do not suggest China is seeking global military dominance. It is not building global military bases, a military budget even remotely close to the American one, a worldwide naval and submarine capacity, and other worldwide military infrastructure enabling US global hegemony. It appears, rather to be asserting that it will no longer tolerate the kind of subjugation to the West that it experienced in the last two centuries. China's partial alignment with Russia during the Ukrainian crisis was, in this view, a strategy to help weaken the West in that conflict, while opening a new path to Chinese hegemony.

President Trump's bellicose trade sanctions and labeling of COVID-19 as the "China virus," are signs that the prospects of war may arise mainly from United States desire to keep China an important but subordinate player in the US-led global order. Biden's calm temperament and progressive domestic policies belie the perpetuation of a hegemonic US foreign policy that sees a viable and free world as possible only under American leadership, backed by US force. European powers were notably cool to Biden's claim that "America is back;" they share the view of many US progressives who want to rein in Biden's "return to normalcy" and prevent the return of Cold War policies underlying the "forever" US wars from Vietnam to El Salvador to Iraq.

Analyst Daron Acemoglu argues that US relations with China are rapidly militarizing in ways that parallel the old Cold War.

> Despite steady deterioration in Sino-American economic and strategic relations, few thought the rivalry would turn into a Cold War-style geopolitical confrontation. For a time, the US was overly dependent on

China, and the two economies were too closely intertwined. Now, we may be heading toward a fundamentally different equilibrium.

Three interrelated dynamics defined the Cold War. The first, and perhaps most important, was ideological rivalry. The US-led West and the Soviet Union had different visions of how the world should be organized, and each tried to propagate its vision, sometimes by nefarious means. There was also a military dimension, illustrated most vividly by a nuclear-arms race. And both blocs were eager to secure the lead in scientific, technological, and economic progress, because they recognized that this was critical to prevailing ideologically and militarily.[30]

The rise of two blocs, with the US fighting to ensure it continues to be the dominant leader of the dominant bloc, is hardly surprising. President Biden was a leading player in US top national security circles that helped create and manage the Cold War with the Soviets. As discussed earlier, the Soviet enemy helped to justify US wars as a defense against the global evil threat of Communism. The United States and the Soviets were useful to each other as each side invoked the threat of the other to militarily advance their own economic interests and fund enormous military arsenals. President Eisenhower warned that the US Military Industrial Complex might be the biggest beneficiary of the Cold War, with the Soviet threat a source of unlimited new military investments for an ever-expanding military.

The major new Belt and Road Chinese infrastructure investments in East Asia, Africa, the Middle East, and Europe are suggestive of major initiatives by China to create its own autonomous "world order," clearly rejecting any continuation of its history of exploitation and humiliation by Western and Japanese colonial control. From China's point of view, Biden is even more hostile than Trump, reflecting the familiar militarism promoted by the US national security elites in the Cold War. The claims of the United States to be the champions of democracy vs. the national autocrats aligned with China, are, in China's view, deeply misleading and hypocritical. Western colonial powers, and then the US Cold War hegemon, preached a democracy they violated in their relations with their Third World clients, a kind of Western "democracy" that the Chinese will no longer tolerate, especially now that the US status as a democracy is itself in deep peril.

The war dangers of this new Cold War will likely mirror in new contexts those of the old Cold War:

It is an equally grave mistake to think that the Cold War fostered international stability. On the contrary, the nuclear arms race and brinkmanship on both sides prepared the ground for war. The Cuban Missile Crisis was hardly the only time that the US and the Soviets came close to open conflict (and "mutually assured destruction"). There were also close calls in 1973, during the Yom Kippur War; in 1983, when Soviet early-alert systems sent a false alarm about a US intercontinental ballistic missile launch; and on other occasions.[31]

The old Cold War brought us the Cuban Missile crisis and the 1973 Middle Eastern crisis, both events being the closest the world ever came to global nuclear war. The new Cold War has innumerable potential parallels, whether it be explosive US–China conflict over Hong Kong, Taiwan, the south China sea, North Korea, Iran, the WTO, the development agendas of the UN, punitive trade sanctions and tariffs, cyber technology and cyber-war protocols, and AI.

Indeed, on July 26, 2021, reports emerged that China was more than doubling its current number of land-based nuclear silos in a second new nuclear missile base, with no information about whether the actual number of missiles were being increased. China has long had a policy of "minimal deterrence," maintaining a small nuclear force estimated at 300 nuclear weapons compared to more than five times that number of operational missiles held by the United States and Russia. Robin Wright argued in 2022 that the Chinese have decided to increase their nuclear force to as many as 1,000 nuclear weapons. Chinese motives are unclear but may be a defensive response to threatening developments in American, Russian, and other nuclear arsenals:

> There are several theories. The simplest is that China now views itself as a full-spectrum economic, technological and military superpower – and wants an arsenal to match that status. Another possibility is that China is concerned about American missile defenses, which are increasingly effective, and India's nuclear buildup, which has been rapid. Then there is the announcement of new hypersonic and autonomous weapons by Russia, and the possibility that Beijing wants a more effective deterrent.
>
> A third is that China is worried that its few ground-based missiles are vulnerable to attack – and by building more than 200 silos, spread out in two locations, they can play a shell game, moving 20 or more missiles around and making the United States guess where they are. That technique is as old as the nuclear arms race.[32]

While there is uncertainty about Chinese motives, the move came in a period of growing tension and anger with the United States, signaling that China was serious about never again allowing itself to be a subjugated nation in a US hegemonic world order. A decision to expand its nuclear force is a reminder of the existential risks of the increasingly militarized US–China relation one that might explode in a growing intense conflict over Taiwan.

China clearly will no longer tolerate US dominance and is striking back hard. In late July, 2021, when Biden sent Deputy Secretary of State to China for meetings with Xie Feng, the vice foreign minister responsible for US relations, she got an earful, as summarized in the *New York Times*:

> Mr. Xie accused the United States of committing genocide against Native Americans and botching the response to the coronavirus pandemic, which has left 620,000 Americans dead.
> The Biden administration's policies are nothing but a "thinly veiled attempt to contain and suppress China .... It seems that a whole-of-government and whole-of-society campaign is being waged to bring China down," Mr. Xie told Ms. Sherman.[33]

The overt tension between China and the United States has grown steadily. In 2022 and 2023, angry exchanges between the United States and China escalated over everything from US shooting down of Chinese spy extreme militarization of all sides around Taiwan to Chinese rejection of any lectures about democracy and human rights from United States that was imposing proxy rulers abroad and losing its democracy at home. In the Chinese point of view, the new Cold War against China is being led by the United States – and constitutes a new crusade for Western dominance. It all hints that another Cuban missile crisis, this one pitting the United States against China, could emerge in the 21st century, with the new Cold War potentially ending the human prospect the way that the old Cold War almost succeeded in doing. The question for Americans is to what degree their government, as in the old Cold War, is complicit in risking global survival to save its position as Number One – and what can be done about it.

Part III
The Slender Path Forward

9 Lessons from Abolition

The reader is to be forgiven if, at the end of a book describing the systemic sources of our grief and possible extinction, they feel a little depressed or even hopeless. Indeed, in describing the triangle of extinction, one may well ask if we have written an obituary for the future. For those who have long believed with Dr. Martin Luther King, Jr., that the "arc of history bends towards justice," surely this book has made the case that time may no longer be on our side. The faith of 19th-century enslaved folks that "time is longer than rope" may be misplaced in the 21st century. In all honesty, however, we cannot amend our arguments to conjure up any magical solution guaranteeing that the 200 millennia during which the human species emerged and flourished will be prolonged in any desirable way. Instead, what we draw from history is *a slender path forward*, one filled with challenges and difficult decisions but one which we believe to be viable.

"Signposting" the route forward is, of course, a matter of strategy. And such matters presume a "subject," i.e., an agency, a social force, able to effect such a strategy based on its present and/or anticipated resources, be they material, intellectual, or spiritual. We take as our subject the broadest of all possible coalitions, a Front for Survival, one which we believe to emerging in tacit and occasionally explicit practices of social movements, non-governmental organizations, and political actors, be they actual political parties or even state-based entities. The anticipated Front is based on all people who are working class, i.e., the overwhelming majority of humanity, whatever their race, nationality, or gender. To understand the cross-cutting shared reality of class exploitation, a social fact that does not deny other lived realities, is to discover the potential for working people as a whole to unite across caste, color, gender, borders, and even income. Would-be working-class leaders in the coming period will be defined by their creativity in converting the potential for unity into an active, if you will, kinetic energy for survival.

In the struggle for survival, the Front organizes and helps build a new economy structured to produce public goods that serve the needs of the community rather than our current system that is organized to make profit by producing endless commodities. The Front's collective capacity to rally much of

DOI: 10.4324/9781003401483-13

humankind on a positive platform for survival and against extinction is where we find hope. Their ability to activate this capacity is not only logically possible but also long anticipated by the 19th-century abolitionist movement. As the following text suggests, we believe that the abolitionists faced the same kinds of critical organizational, political, and structural challenges that we face today, but that they were able to bend history their way, at least at critical junctures. One defining characteristic of the 19th-century abolitionism of William Lloyd Garrison and David Walker was the emphasis on *immediate* abolition and the rejection of gradualist solutions. Even as their movement would wax and wane in the 30 years before the Civil War resulted in the emancipation of the enslaved, the emphasis on immediate abolition constituted an unwavering pole in the debate, one which ultimately succeeded. As we confront the prospects of human extinction, the abolitionist's "fierce urgency of now," has particular resonance as our movements for the *immediate* abolition of fossil fuels, nuclear weapons, and extreme inequality – in all its expressions including mass incarceration. In other words, latter day abolitionists or anti-extinction activists should revel in the radicalism of their demands, even if they may be, like Garrison and Walker, relatively isolated, dispersed and disorganized in their day.

In prefiguring the Front, the abolitionists are joined by succeeding radical social movements as well as many intellectuals and political philosophers, but especially in recent times by writers of speculative fiction, people less bound by the dictates of academic disciplines or political parties. In the spirit of these writers, we offer the following "interview" to suggest the route ahead.

★★★

The 2062 Transcript on the Approaching Bicentennial[1]

In this two-part interview, Katarina Martinez talks with the legendary Maxi Muzor, one of the earliest leaders of the Front for Survival that seemed to precipitate out of thin air in mid-twenties. More than four decades ago, Maxi's cohort rightly saw themselves in a "decisive decade" during which the critical choices made then would determine whether or not humanity still had a realistic chance to prevail over the extinction threats that it had conjured for itself and the rest of the planet. Maxi was one of the pioneering bridge builders who remade the political landscape by connecting disparate masses of working people through myriad campaigns some of which seemed incremental, others obscure, and still others, people realized after the fact, were the decisive ones. Among the topics that the interview covers are the Front's strategy, "the Slender Path," that centered on revitalized public and social sectors, how single issue and identity-based struggles wove themselves into larger more universal? social change movements, how they worked with what seemed to be contradictory strategies, and how it was that they prevailed, leaving us more hopeful today.

As we approach the bicentennial of Lincoln's Emancipation Proclamation, January 1, 2063, the lessons and inspiration that the Front for Survival and its partisans drew from the now very remote 19th-century abolitionist movement and its heirs in the 20th and early 21st centuries appropriately open the dialogue:

Katarina Martinez (KM):	*A long time ago, in less hopeful times, you made the case for "a slender path forward," one that had to be followed if humanity were to survive the multiple existential threats that seemed to doom it to extinction. In thinking about this overwhelming topic, I know that you were greatly inspired and learned from the 19th-century abolitionists. Can you say a little bit more about that?*
MM:	Let me paint a picture for you – a picture that I hope will make clear how abolitionism illustrates the universalizing struggle we had to build to dismantle the extinction threat. In the middle of the Civil War which delivered the knockout punch to the US slavocracy and ended legal slavery in the United States, although not to white supremacy, a huge crowd gathered in Boston ...
KM:	*Boston! I love that city and the way it is recovering from the last tidal surge!*
MM:	Yes, it is a great city. I want to take us back to a cold winter morning, January 1, 1863. A crowd converged for a reading of a long-anticipated message coming over the telegraph wires – one containing the Emancipation Proclamation issued at midnight by President Lincoln. Gathered in the crowd were well-remembered personages of the abolition movement – Harriet Beecher Stowe, author of the bestselling *Uncle Tom's Cabin*, poet John Greenleaf Whittier, Ralph Waldo Emerson, perhaps the preeminent public intellectual of the time, Minister Leonard Grimes, a "conductor" in the Underground Railroad, William Lloyd Garrison, editor of *The Liberator*, Julia Ward Howe, the poet who would found "Mother's Day," and the legendary Frederick Douglass, who declared then that the proclamation was "the first step on the part of the nation in its departure from the thraldom of the ages." In New York, the crowd that gathered at the Cooper Union sang a tribute to John Brown, the armed abolitionist whose Harper's Ferry raid, paved the way for the decisive Civil War. In fact, Douglass

would underscore this point a few years later at the same Cooper Union venue: "Good old John Brown," he declared, "was a madman at Harper's Ferry. Two years pass away; and the nation is as made as he. Every general and every soldier that now goes in good faith to Old Virginia, goes there for the very purpose that led hopest John Brown to Harper's Ferry."

Now my point in naming these various individuals is that they played very diverse roles and had very different visions and strategies for how Emancipation would be won – I need to say a bit more about this because the diversity of visions shows how the struggle against extinction would begin to be won in the 2020s.

Garrison was a pacifist who deplored politics and parties; Whittier supported political parties and looked to the Federal government to achieve emancipation; Grimes, the minister ferried escaped enslaved individuals to freedom – in direct violation of the Fugitive Slave Law, Stowe was ambivalent about the role of free African Americans in the United States and, in fact, supported their "colonization" to Africa; Douglass, perhaps better than anyone else, understood that abolition and emancipation could only be won through a diversity of strategies and tactics – a point to which I will return; and, of course, Brown responded to the violence of slavery with the armed means at his disposal, whether in Kansas, Missouri, or, ultimately, Virginia.

In spite of the diversity that I have described, they were able not only to unite in victory, but also in so far as each created conditions that others sharing their broad ambitions could exploit for their own strategies. Let's look at two opposites who nonetheless "collaborated" in a variety of ways. Harriet Beecher Stowe was a member of the American Colonization Society that hoped to end slavery by "returning" formerly enslaved individuals to Africa – Liberia primarily – where they hoped these Americans in Africa would also serve as a front for Christianity and development. This strategy sat well with Stowe's moderation. Some radicals even flirted with the strategy at different points – including the abolitionist Paul H. Clark reputed to be America's first black socialist. However, Stowe's bestselling novel

did as much as John Brown did for paving the way
to the decisive confrontation of North and South.
Southerners saw her bestseller – depicting the brutality of servitude – as an affront resulting in the book
being banned in many states and pro-slavery writers
composing their own counter-novels. In the North,
it produced spinoff works, dramatizations and public
performances. Only the Bible outsold Uncle Tom's
Cabin in the 19th century. In short, notwithstanding
her moderation, Stowe's book produced the cultural
polarization, a veritable "culture war," that forced a
decisive battle against slavery. It also demonstrates that
abolitionists, far from being a fringe element, were
central to the public conversations of the day, and the
mainstream Stowe ended up stoking the same liberation forces as the revolutionary John Brown.

In fact, the diversity of the movement was built
into its expansive character. Abolitionists across many
institutions – congregations, workplaces, higher education sites, lyceums, legislatures – developed a "lec-
turing agency system" which saw ex-slaves, students,
intellectual and activists touring the country and developing a greater understanding of their movement
and its diversity. Manisha Sinha, one of more astute
21st-century students of the movement pointed out
that this agency system constituted one of the reper-
toires that succeeding movements, including the Populists, would emulate.

Frederick Douglass whom we still celebrate today,
probably had the most sophisticated understanding of
the diverse and multiple forces and practices required
to take down slavery. Appreciating this viewpoint,
Katarina, helped me, in the twenties, to make sense of
our diversity and not turn my nose up at things I did
not immediately recognize as helpful. And this was
hard. For example, many people turned their noses up
at European teenagers who were raucously denouncing their governments and corporations for failing to
live up to climate agreements. Many of us thought
that they were really and appropriately exercising their
privileges as people who had benefited from centuries
of power. At the same time, still others were rejecting
the very militant struggles of anti-extraction struggles

of indigenous people in say Ecuador or the Niger Delta at the time. I'll say a bit more about this diversity later; I just want to illustrate that thinking about 19th-century abolitionism helped me make sense of our situation 150 years later.

KM: *If I may interrupt to learn more about the context before you tell us more about Douglass: why was the defeat of slavery more than a 150 years earlier such a big deal for you in the 2020s?*

MM: Yes, that is a vital question. For a long time, indeed much of the 20th century, scholars and propagandists alike presented slavery, even as it was experienced in the 19th century, as an anachronism, something on its way out. People even pointed to the once venerated American Founding Fathers who assumed, at the end of the 18th century, that slavery was dying out naturally. Of course, that was before cotton became the central raw material driving industrialization and, in the South. Absent other sources of labor, slavery provided an answer to who would grow and reap cotton.

By the early 2000s, most scholars came to realize that slavery was central to the development of capitalism in the United States – quite the opposite from being a brake on its development. It helped develop the stock market as people could buy shares in the financing of slavery – rendering the institution both much broader based that just the Southern slaveholder and also an extension of Northern capital. The many related accounting methods, the insurance industry, shipping and ship building, not to mention the Northern industries depending on Southern cotton – in essence then, nearly the entire world of American capitalism at that point, all received decisive boosts from slavery even if they were not wholly dependent on it. When Southern slaveholders proudly declared that slavery had created the "greatest material wealth" known to humankind, they were simply telling the truth, albeit at the expense of the enslaved and their home continent.

By no means was slavery merely an American institution, one nurtured in the backwaters of the 17th, 18th, and 19th century world economy. Without going into too much detail, and to return to Frederick Douglass, the British and French economies, with the former being at the cutting edge of the 19th-century capitalist economy, were extremely dependent on Southern cotton – so much so that abolitionists the world over feared that either or both Britain and France would intervene in the US Civil War on behalf of the South or, at best, that they would prevent the North's blockade on the South's exports.

KM: *Okay, I now get the picture that even where slavery was outlawed, as in the North or in France and the UK, the capitalist world depended on it. So where does Douglass fit in? And how does all of this relate to the 2020s fight to save the planet?*

MM: Yes, as we have seen that global capitalism fueled the 2020s extinction crises, Douglass understood the institution of slavery as not only deeply integrated into the US capitalist economy as a whole but also as a global institution. Fortunately, the abolitionists as a whole rose to the challenge. I remember reading one book in the teens, *The Cause of All Nations*, which discussed the global character of the movement – something that was inspiring to read given the global character of the triangle of extinction that was driving our challenges of militarism and environmental destruction together with the political confusion that the periods' extreme inequality caused. What we learned from the abolitionists was that our movement had to be profoundly global in character. And here's where Douglass's practice was exemplary – he spent a great deal of time in the UK building support for the abolition movement back in the United States. His appearances there reached millions through the newspaper reporting on his speeches. His work was paralleled by other American abolitionists touring Europe, including that of Sarah Remond Parker, for example.

Notably, too, Douglass was ready to tie his cause with that of other freedom struggles with Europe and the UK. Thus, Douglass built strong ties with the Irish freedom movement. Of course, there were others too. In the early 21st century, we were slow realize how closely the abolitionist movement was tied to other progressive movements and how these proved decisive.

Global networks had emerged out of the failed European revolutions of 1848. In fact, German 1848ers in the United States were among the strongest supporters of the emancipation of the enslaved. One of Lincoln's advisors and representatives in Europe, an acquaintance of Karl Marx, Carl Schurz, insisted that Lincoln and the Republicans frame the Civil War not only as a war against Southern succession and for American unity, but as a war for emancipation, sounding the very themes of the 1848 revolutions. This framing helped make the Civil War "the cause of all nations."

For example, the person most associated with Italian unification, Giuseppe Garibaldi, rallied European workers from his jail cell through letters that celebrated the Civil War as a war for emancipation. These rallies, in turn, helped prevent the French and British governments from recognizing the South and intervening on its behalf.

So, you may say that in the 2020s, one big lesson that I took from the Civil War was that our struggle against extinction has to be global, that we have to build alliances based on common, universal principles. In this case, principle had clear pragmatic payoffs – it created the networks of support and mutual aid throughout the world with direct impacts on what governments did. To underline what will be a theme: our movements were often faced by what seemed to be dichotomous choices, however, in practice, our movements had sufficient breadth and diversity to take both paths at the same time – what was critical was that we were able to leverage each other's choices and gains.

This ability to handle a complex interaction of sometimes contradictory strategies was well recognized by people hoping for social change. In the 2020s, Noam Chomsky, the leading public intellectual in the United States in the preceding sixty years, noted that as a movement we needed these diverse strategies even if individuals would have to commit to particular ones that most move them. I will return to this point when I get to explore the Front for Survival. But Chomsky might as well have been talking about examples from the Civil War: the abolitionist movement was deeply conflicted over how to engage in politics. Some engaged in the "lesser evil" politics constituting themselves as the Radical Republicans in pushing for emancipation and eventually supporting Lincoln who could not be counted among their number prior to the election.

Earlier, some abolitionists formed their own independent party, the Liberty Party, to run in presidential elections with mixed results. Nonetheless, they helped contribute to the decline of the Whig Party and the rise of Republican Party more inclined to abolition. At critical points during the Civil War, when Lincoln was rumored to be wavering, to be contemplating compromise with the South, there were attempts to revive the Liberty Party.

Still others, including William Lloyd Garrison, eschewed party politics altogether, questioning the moral and constitutional foundations of the United States itself. Of course, Frederick Douglass, grounded in his organic connection to African American struggles, navigated and worked across these different currents. Again, the big takeaway here is that politics and its currents change, but the big structuring issues – including the government institutions and the underlying economy relationships – are constants, and social change makers cannot will away either politics or the big social questions, one has to consciously engage with them.

I notice the quizzical look in your eyes! By "constants," I mean that whatever our diversity of approaches, we were all reacting, albeit in diverse ways, to underlying structures and forces that existed independently of how we felt about them. As such, reaching across certain divides was not merely a choice but a necessity. Only by working across our many divides could we fully grasp the nature of the underlying system.

KM: *I get the feeling that this is a segue to more about Douglass – and how his universalizing and global view of abolition also informed the 2020s perspective on preventing extinction?*

MM: Yes! Douglass was condemned for spending a great deal of time in England. In part this was pragmatic – in the United States he was a "fugitive slave." But it also indicated his comprehension of the universal – multi-front – character of slavery. He recognized that abolition was also a cultural struggle: Douglass attacked the reigning pseudoscience of his day: scientific racism. In entering this terrain, he was debating established scientists, including Harvard University's Louis Agassiz, a figure venerated well into the 21st century despite the decisive debunking of his theories and Samuel George Morton who led the Philadelphia Scientific Society.

Standing his ground, Douglass used history to debunk their arguments that humanity has multiple origins that yielded separate races with different temperaments and talents and, consequently, variable claims to "greatness." Egypt, which Douglass visited 1887, provided the evidence of greatness that Agassiz and Morton denied possessors of a black skin. Douglass was therefore very conscious that scientists "write to please, as well as to instruct," and that therefore power relations in a society impinged on science. For us, in the 2020s, science was largely on our side in most issues, however the imperatives of profit often fueled pseudoscience, works written "to please."

In recognizing that science could be compromised, Douglass chose to extend his engagement with science into other nuanced contests – he embraced the technology of his day to wage cultural battles, much like anti-extinction climate and COVID-19 and anti-war struggles in the 2020s also involved culture wars and use of new cultural technologies. In fact, Douglass, was the most photographed person of the 19th century, consciously using new imaging technology to challenge depictions of African Americans, most notably with his own portraits. Similarly, he challenged the depiction of Africans at the 1893 World's Fair in Chicago. Where others recommended boycotting the fair, Douglass used it as platform to argue not only against racism but for the full embrace of democracy and therewith the full participation of African Americans in public life.

If I could circle back using the life of Douglass as an example, 19th-century abolitionism – it bears mentioning that in his very existence Douglass gives lie to the idea that the abolitionists were a small bunch of relatively privileged radicals and zealots. He demonstrates that African Americans were central players in the movement, and they were not passive but gave strategic leadership to the movement. He also embraced abolitionism as part of a broader emancipation movement that worked for women's rights, Irish freedom, and was global in scale. These broad commitments were never an obstacle to local actions, be they desegregating rail roads or fighting to prevent the return of "fugitive slaves" to South. He was also always ready to consider a diversity of strategies and tactics – indeed John Brown invited Douglass's participation in the Harper's Ferry raid. Of course, Douglass failing to find military-strategic benefits declined. Later, however, Douglass would come to understand the raid's political-strategic value in polarizing the North and South on the matter of slavery, much as Harriet Beecher Stowe's all-together different initiative (the publication of her book) did.

In this, we have to recognize the critical role of the abolitionists in creating the cultural and political context for the Civil War. Once it was underway, Douglass, following in-person entreaties from Lincoln, actively took part in recruiting African Americans into the Union army, enlisting his own sons into the famed Massachusetts 54th Regiment. The active participation of African Americans in their own emancipation issued from the organizing work of abolitionist organizers like Douglass. Of course, ever since W. E. B. Du Bois, we've known that a critical part of defeating the South was what he dubbed to be a "general strike" by enslaved African Americans. Du Bois was borrowing from and co-opting the language of the rising socialist movements of his day, as would the 2020 movements against extinction threats like climate change.

There is another sense in which Douglass and his experiences provide a more complex picture of abolition movement. Once discerned, this picture furnishes an abolitionism that was so very relevant to the circumstances of the 2020s. I have already mentioned the Fugitive Slave Law and the movements throughout the North to defend their rights. Picturing their work everyday life, the quotidian life of the abolitionists if you will, provided insights into what we had to do in the 2020s.

Douglass and his comrades, in their newspapers, in
large and small in-person gatherings, in courtrooms,
in boisterous demonstrations, used every opportunity
to engage the broader public on the topic of slavery.
Each "fugitive" brought the national institution of
slavery into direct, local view as federal authorities and
courts litigated whether or not the "fugitive" could be
returned to slavery. While some championed the boy-
cott of goods connected with slavery, these escapees
from slavery brought not only an immediacy to the national institution but the work to raise funds for and to
resettle escapees created a culture of work and radicalism that engaged the whole public. Many abolitionist
women in the 19th century found that their work for
emancipation was an avenue to their becoming public
beings, ones who could speak out on matters of public
concern. Their work often embraced whole congregations and communities. They routinely documented
the stories of the enslaved, got these into print, and
into widespread circulation. Douglass, as an in-person
presence of a runaway slave, added to all of this. Not
for nothing do people recognize him first and foremost as an orator. This provides obvious lessons for
us in the twenties: in working with personalities and
events, the decisive element was not the personality or
the event, but how we could use both to communicate
our concerns to the public at large.

One place where Douglass spoke frequently, one
which he wrote about in his first memoir, was a meeting venue in Boston. It was founded by an abolitionist
who was also a member of the temperance society. Often denied access to other venues, including the famed
Faneuil Hall, the abolitionists created their own space.
In this case, the Marlboro Hotel and Chapel wel-
comed future woman's movement leaders, people opposed to the imperial war against Mexico (1846-48),
leaders of the Transcendentalist movement, early trade
unionists, and, of course, the members of the anti-
slavery organizations. Often there was a great deal of
overlap between these movements.

Interestingly, too, if you'll permit a small but perhaps instructive digression, the owner of the Hotel and Chapel, was also the founder of Boston's fire

department. In a city based on very flammable wooden buildings, he helped end the chaos of multiple private fire contingents deploying to put out a fire but which, in their competition with each other, often aggravated matters! Even in their everyday lives, abolitionists recognized the need for public goods – in this example, fire safety!

Boston was also among the first cities, along with Chicago and New York, where a powerful youth movement, the Wide Awakes, emerged to support Lincoln in campaigning for president. He won their support after speaking out in New Hartford against slavery *and* for the right to strike, in one speech, demonstrating the common cause between emancipation and working-class politics. In effect, the Wide Awakes were "woke" before we used that term in the twenty teens! By the way, Douglass would sound Lincoln's wisdom connecting chattel slavery to wage slavery long after the victory over formal slavery, declaring in 1883, the year which gave us May Day, that the "slavery of wages must go down with the other." In this story about Wide Awakes, the twenties' activists found inspiration in their example for youth but also for making the connections between young people and employment matters, i.e., "the slavery of wages."

I should add, especially after focusing on the local movement, that in the course of their struggles, the abolitionists developed their own community-level institutions that would be vital for developing consciousness and, at a face-to-face level, negotiate the diversity of the movement. A brilliant student of the Abolitionist movement in my time, Jesse Olsavsky, called our attentional to "Vigilance" committees that emerged across the North and that were often staffed by volunteers or stipended individuals from the African-American community or even runaways from the South. These committees documented slavery in the most personal of ways, helping catalogue the experiences of individuals, while sharing the resulting knowledge broadly, and involving both "free" African American and white abolitionists. Moving from the individual experience of slavery to involve a diversity of forces took the day-to-day work of these committees. The result was a more connected and universalizing world view. Olsavsky tells the story of one factory worker, John Murray Spear, who was imprisoned for helping an enslaved person in Massachusetts. As a result of his work in the committees, Spear came to socialize with, as Olsavsky described them, "the most brilliant minds of his generation." This resistance work liberated what Jermain Loguen, a "fugitive abolitionist," described as "invisible mental powers," and as a result "turned society on its hinges to let in a new dispensation on learning, religion, and life." Yes, movement work, then, in the 2020s, as now, brings together people – with each other and with their ideas.

For us, in the 2020s, wrapping our heads around these examples, in which tactics and strategies against slavery played out at every level of society, from the household to the relations between countries, and which cut across issues proved to be extremely valuable. Our equivalent to the escaped slave as a focal point for organizing required little imagination: there were regular climate catastrophes and extreme weather events, myriad wars which threatened to spiral into apocalyptic outcomes, and ever more health threats. We quickly discovered that, in themselves, these events did not produce new consciousness, instead, it would require grounded organizers with the imagination and will power of the abolitionists to tell these stories in every possible context and to always increase participation in the solutions that we were advocating.

KM: *It is all well and good to show that abolitionists were able to rally large numbers of ordinary people to their cause and to ensure that the Civil War broke in the direction that they wanted it to. However, let's face it, the amendments that followed the war, that ended slavery, that recognized African American citizenship, and that extended the franchise to African American males, seemed to have benefited the corporations and also seem to have ended slavery but not white supremacy. How could you find inspiration in what seems to be an ambiguous legacy at best?*

MM: Absolutely! A great question. In fact, in the 2020s, a hundred and sixty years after its conclusion, we were still dealing with the incompleteness of the victory over slavery. However, let me enumerate some of the takeaways from the victory over the slavocracy. Noted earlier in this conversation, slavery was integral to the capitalism of the 19th century and our abolitionist counterparts of that period defeated it. Where the "Slave Power" once prevailed, it was forever defeated. Every attempt to reconstitute and to elevate it to national power was defeated. A hundred years later, in the wake of the Civil Rights movement, Republican elites pursued a "Southern Strategy" and with not inconsiderable success awakened a new coalition, one cemented by an anti-Black racism, but at no point did they succeed in erasing the gains of abolition movement.

In fact, the very amendments that you cited, and that you correctly observe to have been successfully exploited by corporate power, formed the legal grounds for challenging any rollbacks, much as we use them and the amendments of the 2030s to fight attempts to reopen old oil and gas fields today. There we have it: a victory over a once-all powerful system, cemented in constitutional reforms, serves not as a guarantee but as a resource for ongoing struggle. So even as we approach the anniversary of the Emancipation Proclamation, we have to understand that there are no "forever guarantees," only gains to be actively defended and extended.

Importantly too, we have to accept that the gains are often paradoxical in nature. The Emancipation Proclamation shares its bicentennial with the Homestead Act. It extended the practical frontiers of the United States to the West and with it the annihilation of indigenous communities and the further privatization of the commons. It was premised on and reinforced stereotypes against Native Americans. It failed to acknowledge – no passive failing – the role of indigenous communities in stewarding the land and embodied the idea of privatization long before the neoliberal era. In effect, it is another example of the American enclosure of the commons.

But there is another suppressed series of victories won by the abolitionists that to a certain extent matter much more to us today than even their victory over slavery. Du Bois appreciated these. This was the abortive attempt after slavery to rebuild the nation and develop the South – Reconstruction. In a political and intellectual sense, it was the discovery even before Bismarck's reforms in Europe, that the market could not provide for the building of robust African American communities or even the rebuilding, in general, of the war-scarred South. If the revolution that was the Civil War allowed for the growth of Northern industry and yielded within two decades to a second industrialization of the North, capitalism nonetheless could not provide for the common good. With Reconstruction, came active efforts to build public education, public health systems, and other common, public goods. They also fostered the building of cooperatives and encouraged freedmen to join trade unions. Abolitionists were instrumental in all these efforts, mobilizing their numbers to go South and assist in all these efforts. Less well connected to the abolitionists in the public imagination but nonetheless very instructive, is the fact that their movement helped call attention to the wounded Civil War veterans and their care, a matter that came to involve the federal government in the care and health initially of veterans and then later broader issues, including public welfare. As our conversation progresses, I will be happy to talk more about this public goods and anti-capitalist dimension of the abolitionists' victory.

KM: *Yes, that point really gets to what my producers want us to talk about! But do continue.*

MM: Thanks, one final point in this vein. The abolitionists did not simply declare victory and disappear. Theirs was an unfolding agenda. Certainly, some abolitionists moved in the direction of capital and imperialism after the Civil War. In the main, however, they continued their work for social change. Wendell Phillips expanded his work on labor reform. Douglass continued to champion antiracist struggles while also supporting the suffragettes – attempting to heal wounds caused by the postwar strategic differences. Notably, when William Lloyd Garrison shuttered *The Liberator* after four decades and 1,800 issues, with the passage of the 13th Amendment, *The Nation* magazine was founded to continue the struggle for social reform. Garrison's son, Wendell Phillips Garrison, served as its literary editor. In the 2020, a young socialist, the son of West Indian immigrants, became its president. In a couple years, the magazine will be approaching its own bicentennial. All of this to say, the abolitionists were outstanding examples for us, not only because they won certain victories, but also because they understood the need for ongoing struggle and vigilance.

KM: *Okay, this really helps. In the 2020s, then, 19th-century abolitionism stood as an example of a very diverse and diffuse social movement, often very divided on matters of strategy, let alone in mobilizing resources, yet one capable of rallying humanity as whole – both within the United States and globally, both in day-to-day struggles and longer-term campaigns – around the banner of emancipation, forefronting the struggles of the oppressed but relating these across many different kinds of intersections. And what makes their effort so consequential was that they challenged and defeated the reigning model of capitalism of their day by taking advantage of political openings and conflicts as they arose. In turn, in ending slavery, they laid the foundations for future struggles, not only on racial justice but across the board too – to the struggles of the working class, women, oppressed nationalities, people with disabilities, and so on. Not coincidentally, the abolitionists were at once peace movement leaders, suffragettes, labor organizers, builders of cooperatives and so on. Most inspiring!*

I expect that we should go on to address the Front and how it worked for the Common Good and planetary survival. But I would like to learn more about Maxi Muzor's own journey.

MM: Sure, Katarina, let's get the personal journey stuff out of the way (laughing). In the teens and twenties, I was working on many projects but my heart and mind melded in the struggles for health and universal health care coverage. Keep in mind, Katarina, that public health is one of the central pillars of the public goods economy at the heart of our anti-extinction struggle. Now, I know that look on your face! Nobody in your generation believes that we actually had a huge fight on our hands to win those battles. Yes, "how can something so commonsensical as universal healthcare been in need of so much effort?" you must be wondering. But back then there were powerful forces that reaped huge rewards, "profits" was what they called it, by rationing care based on income. I went into the battle thinking this was an easily winnable campaign. All the public opinion polls showed the broad public to be on our side. There were large numbers of "front-line" care workers – nurses, doctors, social workers, and hospital and clinic staff – who lined up behind the push for universal health care. When that failed, we pushed for what we thought was a much more winnable campaign, this time focused purely on the insurance side of things. It was called "single payer." But even that failed at the federal level. Everyone still believed that the battle could be won.

So, we shifted targets. Instead of going for the federal victory, we went after the big "blue" states, those controlled by the Democratic Party, where overwhelming majorities supported single payer. If you're blue, we thought at the time, why not be *true* blue? Even that was proving to be a slog. Then came the first of the big pandemics. Not only was it foreseeable, it was foreseen! Top scientists and other public health experts had pushed for early warning systems and public health measures in just such an event. And, by the time the first big one came, we discovered just how bad things were. But all that is better known today, we all know now how devastating neoliberalism and capitalism in general could be with respect to the institutions that served all of us. Save it to say that those who survived the major pandemics, slowly and unevenly at first, came to understand the global nature of our problems at just about the same time other crises were becoming much more evident and only promised to get worse.

If those of us working in health-related campaigns came to understand that we were fighting a huge social system, capitalism, my friends working on other issues – housing, energy, poverty, prisons and "mass incarceration" as that time's forced labor system was called, environmental protection and recovery, disaster relief, gendered violence – also came to see all these matters as related to the same social system which we were slowly realizing was at the heart of our extinction crisis. But our knowledge of each other's campaigns and struggle was quite limited. We spent all our waking hours putting out fires in our own campaigns, so we didn't have time to think about what other movements were doing. Absent this knowledge, it was impossible to leverage each other's strengths and know when to combine strength and identify strategic openings.

Katarina, this may sound like an impossible situation. Despite, maybe because our precarity – I guess the correct word would be "precariousness" – our lack of really steady employment, we came to grasp the bigger picture or at least big parts of the picture. Here's why: in that period, I moved around a lot. Before we won a universal basic income, social movements and trade unions supported me with various kinds of income-producing jobs. Their solidarity allowed me to work with community organizations, local and global campaigns and many different kinds of organizations and networks. If you recall Jermaine Loguen's words, this solidarity helped turn "society on its hinges" to let in new ideas.

At first, everything appeared to be a bewildering mess, an intertwined spaghetti-like bowl of issues, causes, and campaigns. But then we became very conscious of the fact that people like me – there were thousands if not hundreds of thousands of us – doing what we felt to be very hard and necessary work.

Even with our precariousness, we were weaving together a huge number of ideas and dialogues to build the global conversation that became "The Slender Path" and the resulting Front for Survival as a global convergence. Often, it meant taking the common sensibilities about our problems and talking it through, sometimes talking with more than just words …

KM: *Sorry to interrupt Maxi, but what do you mean by "more than just words"?*

MM: Yes, that must have sounded quite cryptic. The dialogues between would-be partners were hardly ever simple conversations or collegial exchanges. They could get quite heated, involve protests, and even sharper forms of engagement even when we shared many values and overlapping identities. If organizations and communities looked like they had a good fit or shared interests on paper, in the real world, we had to take that as starting point but we then had to work things out between them and this was nearly always more complicated than the simple idea of unity.

To be very clear, though, out of the daily struggles of literally billions of people, there was a dazzling array of organizations and projects. Further, the vast majority of humanity by the 2020s were people dependent on the market for a living – even those who still had access to land needed to get maximum returns for whatever they could sell on the market in order to win their subsistence. This near universal dependence on the market did not render us all alike in all or even most respects. But there were hints at commonalities. And we also came to recognize that we were really at the whims of the people who controlled vast amounts of capital and who therefore were making most of the big investment decisions.

Once worker organizations in the most privileged countries and places came to recognize that their protections could not be sustained unless they were spread to everyone else, in effect, raising the floor, things began to change. Instead of seeing uprisings of the most exploited workers and communities as threats to their gains, a few of the unions organizing those workers began to pour resources into many movements, that's how I got to survive as an activist by doing what we called "movement work." I should interrupt myself to say that most working people got the notion that we had to stand together across industries and geographies – that is to begin universalizing. It just took a while longer for organizations and unions to translate that into campaigns and budget lines – and, conversely, to recognize that all this labor organizing was ultimately essential to saving life on the planet!

This was something of a sea change. Added to this, unions that once were wary of investing in union drives among "harder to organize" workers slowly changed their calculations. See, workers whose workplaces constantly turned over many workers or who toiled in what were called "right-to-work" states were unlikely to meet mainstream unionists. Instead, they had to organize their workplaces by their bootstraps or if they were lucky with insurgent but resource-strapped unions like the century-old Industrial Workers of the World. Soon however, in fact, by the late teens and into the twenties, places like the ubiquitous Starbucks coffeehouses, Amazon warehouses, schools and medical facilities in what were called "right-to-work" states which prevented union drives were more likely to meet with better organized union insurgencies. Workers began, suddenly, to organize like wildfire!

You know Katarina, once we prioritized the Universal Basic Income (UBI), we knew we had discovered a catalyst – a reform which would allow us to win more! Where we won UBI, many thousands of activists were suddenly freed up to do much more movement work. It was chaotic at first, but our social movements had already developed tools and techniques to facilitate conversations, build consensus, and plan campaigns. Those tools were learned and shared by people like me although all one had to do was search the internet for any number organizing institutes and academies. What was missing initially were the in-person engagements that would allow us to thoughtfully apply and develop these tools. That was a quickly overcome as we became more and more aware that our organizing work required thoughtful deliberation and the processing of what we learned on the streets.

Initially, most of our work focused on getting communities to talk with one another and to figure out common projects and also demands. We had a lot to overcome – city residents were often forced into competition with each other, newer, wealthier residents against older, previously settled ones, and the same things played out in the suburbs. We had to build consensus – essentially with each other and against some of the most powerful people and institutions of our time.

KM: *Earlier you mentioned, "common sensibilities" – which were what exactly?*

MM: Yes, there was a growing shared sense about several matters. People on the left and right generally understood that that many of our problems had their origins in the way we were all forced then to limit conversations about the economy to what worked for the very wealthy. We also understood that our problems had a global character. It took a while, but we also came to understand that even if we were all impacted by the crises of environment, some of us were harder hit, and often sooner than the rest. However, consciousness that some people benefited enormously and in fact were the same ones making the decisions that locked us into the planet-killing fossils fuels, also became a shared sensibility in the mid-20s. Even with the threat of nuclear annihilation, then a daily reality, some communities paid and understood the costs of militarism much sooner than others and with it came the realization that parts of the very wealthy were profiting from military investment. Yes, common sensibilities were emerging out of the many struggles. But the most important one of them all – that all of humanity, many other of our planet's inhabitants, and whole ecosystems are threatened with extinction – was a little slower to emerge, even though I am telling you all this because it was this work that slowly morphed into our struggle against extinction of all life.

Helping that awareness emerge – and naming the names of those who benefitted from and were causing this threat – that was the calling of my generation of activists. In practical terms, mornings could find me – as one of a new generation of activists in different movements unifying around survival of the planet – in mobile home and trailer park communities several freeway exits down from big cities and afternoons had me talking with middle-class planned communities of the exurbs, while evenings had me talking with largely people of color land trusts in and around big cities. So we organized in homes, communities centers and warehouse parking lots. And we helped those different communities learn about each other. Some people referred to this as "recomposing the working class," others felt that we were "building the beloved community." That was the very foundation level of the Slender Path.

KM: *I can understand the calling to do this work. But what I don't readily get is that idea of a "Slender Path." It suggests peril if one should stray from it. In any case, given the kinds of divisions you're suggesting, how do/did you keep people to the path?*

MM: Sure. Let's start with the "Slender Path." To be honest, Katarina, there were many terms floating about back in the twenties. All trying to convey the idea that humanity had to consciously choose its next steps, never for a moment surrendering thoughtful deliberation, debate, and planning to the market. Yes, the market. It was a concept that had mythical status back then even if the majority of the world at that time was rightly skeptical of its power to deliver the changes that had to be made.

"The Slender Path Forward," if I recall correctly, was the title of a book chapter by a pair of activist intellectuals deeply troubled but energized by the multiple extinction threats that they noted were driven by a triangle of extinction. And they were grounded in their relationships with different communities dealing with these matters on a daily basis. What they argued was that our main way of making investment decisions back then produced bad decisions, simply put, private profit came before people and planet. To use the cliches of the time, the wants of the few and the powerful came before the needs of the many. And people were upset then. Given our 2062 realities, it is easy to imagine the twenties: the hurricanes and droughts, firestorms and floods, things that we face today, then routinely took thousands of lives; communities were abandoned to rebuild on their own or compete for the charity of one or other billionaire who may feel some connection or discern some reputational benefit for helping out. Times were brutal and in trying to deal with problems as individuals, things just got worse. Heatwaves forced people to buy AC systems. Everyone who could ran out and bought what they found. The moment the mercury accelerated through the 80s into the 90s and with ever-increasing frequency into the triple digits … Then the whole energy grid would overload …

KM: *What are the "80s," "90s," "triple digits"? Something to do with temperature?*

MM: Forgive me. Yes, back then, the country that imagined itself to be exceptional, the so-called the "United States of America," used what was even then an antiquated system of measurement, one different from the rest of the world and also from their entire scientific establishment. So yes, we're talking about temperature, roughly. In the 40s, 50s and even occasionally the 60s Celsius in some places. As an aside, you can imagine why the Good Ole USA could have such a profound cultural split within itself and with the rest of humanity – even something as basic as how hot or cold things were resulted in two different vocabularies, most regular people in US then spoke in one language, and many demagogues also embraced their language and vernacular, but then the scientists and the educated, and pretty much everyone else in the world spoke a different language.

But let me get back the Slender Path …

10 Front for Survival

Movements, the State, and Public Goods

KM: *I'd like to turn to the point you raised about public goods and your remarks about capitalism. Given capitalism's celebration of individualism, how did a sense of the common good and public goods emerge? Today, capitalism is sometimes talked about by a few people in romantic terms, but it has really become a kind of dirty word. From what I gather, however, it was seen as an all-powerful system dominating every aspect of life. Even socialists who tried to reform it ended up being sucked into talking about capitalism in such terms. Is that correct? Perhaps starting with these two concepts – capitalism and public goods – will help us understand the birth of the Slender Path and the Front for Survival?*

MM: Maybe I should begin by recalling that my generation was very influenced by the sense that capitalism, then our reigning economic model, fueled our extinction, driving climate breakdown, biodiversity loss, and ever more destructive and diverse forms of warfare – all this, in addition to jaw-dropping inequalities in life chances and extreme poverty. But I was also part of a generation of organizers and activists who reflected a widespread sentiment, one held by significant majorities across many nations, that there were steps that could be taken by governments and movements to increase the chances of our survival and expand the sense of the common good. We began talking about public goods – the bundle of security and rights guaranteed to everyone – that were essential to the common good. For these steps to succeed, we needed actions and policies that were not driven by the profit motive or sectional benefits of the wealthy minority that traditionally drove policy and dominated the state.

KM: *Okay, I get that. But can you say more about the policies and reform packages?*

MM: I will – but, I am afraid, there's another "but!" Look, the reason people come to talk with me is that I was an on-the-ground, in-the-heat-of-things organizer who turned to the grassroots and who saw their participation, buy-in and interests as central to our survival. So, you're not going to get a policy wonk's or political theorist's answer. Instead of a list of programs, I will emphasize the more intangible

DOI: 10.4324/9781003401483-14

processes and qualities – judgment, negotiation and coalition building. These activities help craft movements and policies and these are largely invisible activities; we tend to only talk about the results – the sausage, but not how it gets made (laughs). To the extent that I appeal to theory and concepts, it is about how these could be helpful or unhelpful in building movements and coalitions. The scale and diversity of our extinction threats meant then as they do now that we had to build vast and diverse coalitions. And for that reason, I will ask which concepts or ideas are helpful or not. For example, if we have the time, I will talk about how people debated stratification and divisions within the working class – my goal will be to emphasize the intra-class dialogue that allows us to "universalize" our claims rather than to produce a sociological accurate but static picture of social classes.

If it will help, I'd like you to look at several charts that we experimented with in the twenties to map out our challenges. With each of these, we'd start out with a blank chart or board and then ask people questions about what they wanted or needed, who they thought should help bring it about, and who could be counted on for support. And the answers would be all over the place but, gradually, clusters would emerge with discussion and debate. So you'll see that the charts were starting points and themselves very incomplete.

The Common Good

Public Goods	*The "Commons"*
Examples	*Examples*
Health	Energy
Education	Food
Security	Water
Biodiversity	Clean Air
...	...

Strategic Focus Points

The "State"	Understand the many levels of governance and public institutions that take public goods and the commons as their mission
Commanding Heights	Sectors of economic power that drive other sectors.
	Sectors that are critical for human survival
Global Cooperation	Treaty processes that involve national states but also grassroots movements and actors across borders

Visions, Movements, and Programs (Examples)

"Narrative of Connectedness"	Identity-based	Green New Deal
Democratic Socialism	movements	Leap Manifesto
The "Beloved Community"	Class-based movements	Universal Declaration of the
One "No," Many "Yeses"		Rights of Mother Earth

Coalescing into a Front for Survival

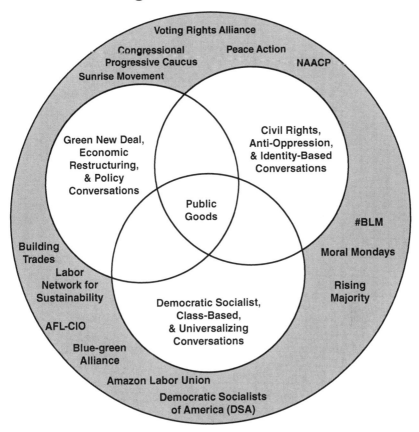

Figure 10.1 Coalescing into a Front for Survival

KM: *Great, I will look at them! But perhaps you could tell me more since I go-*
        ing to be sharing this as audio – and I want people to know about how you
        worked to achieve the common good necessary for survival.

MM: As you will have noticed, in talking about social change, we are also
        talking about changes from one system to another. For a long time,
        we thought about capitalism as an all-encompassing system that com-
        pletely exhausted the whole of society, bringing every space under its
        influence and discipline – we know that it compels growth and tries
        to introduce the logic of the market and profit maximization into
        every relationship. And yet, we also noticed that people have turned
        to the state to demand public goods that the market failed to provide.
        Here, I am using the "state" to designate the times people invoke

the sense of the collectivity and the "social fact"; sometimes people would use the word "society" to designate this whole (collectivity) even though "society" and "state" are often counterposed to each other and I apologize for the resulting confusion!

I choose to use the word "state" because most people recognize the institutions and different levels of governance that we call "the state." Ironically, of course, capitalists found ample uses for state – to stabilize markets, provide research and development funds, educate workers (or "human capital" as they would prefer), protect capitalists from other capitalists, pacify rebellious populations, and so on. As a result, the state, be it at the local, regional or federal levels, always had contradictory pressures placed on it. Its logic of operation was never simply read off the needs of corporations, instead different social struggles forced other logics onto it and even the capitalists had to constantly battle to subordinate the state to their logic and needs. To give you one example, everywhere capitalists tried to ensure that the state was ultimately dependent on their corporation's health, their tax payments, etc., in order for the state to carry out its activities. In other words, they set up the system so that government depended on corporate investments to collect revenue through payroll taxes, corporate taxes, and so on. However, this was never a foregone conclusion – in many cases, the state under the right combination of forces could expand its role in the economy to fulfill the same investment function that capitalists so jealously protected as their own. Remember, that if capital stopped its investment and re-investment in the economy, it would effectively stop everyone else, the state included, in their tracks. However, the more that the state actively invested in the economy – from providing critical infrastructure to meeting emergency needs, the more people realized that the state – assuming it was a democratic one – could itself fulfill the investment function and in ways that are more rational, more subject to a needs-based logic over a for-profit logic. In other words, society does not need the capitalists to organize investment.

Understanding capitalism as a powerful system, one always ready to subvert the public good for private profit, was critical. But so too was the idea that other logics and economic systems are possible and available to be struggled for…

KM: *Okay, I see where you going: to get to where we are today, with a fighting chance of saving the planet from the many extinction threats, you effectively had to understand capitalism in two ways – first how it animates the drive for profits and secondly people responding to its pressures drive back in the opposite direction. I expect that that was how you got beyond capitalism. Just*

as the abolitionists pushed back against slavery and embraced the state during
Reconstruction, so too, in the 2020s, did the anti-extinction forces...

MM: Yes, it seems so straightforward now. Back then, many of us were
trapped in capitalism, finding that every road out apparently curved
back on itself and returned us to capitalism. No less a revolutionary thinker than the great Noam Chomsky even despaired by the
2020s, temporarily setting aside his anarchism, he accepted a large
role for business in shifting course from the extinction capitalism of
the day. With good reason, we used to hang on his every word, and
I remember him stating that "[B]usiness has always rejected the sui-
cidal doctrines that are piously preached. Rather, the business world
demands that a powerful state, under its control, intervene constantly
to protect private power from the ravages of an unconstrained market
and to sustain the system of public subsidy, private profit that has been
a cornerstone of the economy."

He went on to note that "It's of no slight importance when 'More
than 300 corporate leaders are asking the Biden administration to
nearly double the emission reduction targets set by the Obama administration,' including big boys like Google, McDonalds, Walmart."
Perhaps, for tactical reasons, Chomsky did not call attention to the
possibility that this activist role for the state could also be a departure
from the rule of capital. But he stated quite firmly, "Like it or not,
there is no alternative now to large-scale governmental projects. The
reference to the New Deal is not out of place."

It was easy to agree with Chomsky on this point however there
was also something of a challenge. The adoption of prudent policies by the state, including when it "goes big," seems to be cred-
ited exclusively to the needs of capital and its discretion. What was
missing is the fact that – in addition to initiatives from capital –
pressures from below, from working people, created the demand
and even occasionally the design of such programs. Moreover,
"dialectically" speaking, to use an old vernacular, the more capital turned to the state, the more its weaknesses and dependence on society as a whole was revealed. State interventions,
especially in democratic societies, provided a glimpse of a world
beyond capital where the collective good guided decisions as opposed to individual, sectional or profit-seeking ends. This hinted
at and even inspired a hope that we could move to a different
form of society.

The problem of departing from capital had bedeviled every social movement, reformist and revolutionary, from the moment radical thinkers first began thinking of the economy as being defined by
a system. One step out of the dilemmas of revolution versus reform

and toward the Slender Path was prompted by the need for a "Front for Survival" – a coalition that encompassed all anti-extinction forces, even those like big business whose short- and long-term strategies presumed the very capitalism that was destroying us. The strategic starting point wherein the anticipated partners of the Front could find common ground lay in the state and in the provision of public goods. Within the Front, there could therefore be struggles over the state, both its look and feel and in its substance.

The Front could even work with the corporate "big boys" on government, by embracing green projects and infrastructure investment that forced even corporations to support public goods. An important first step!

One thing was clear, especially after the 21st century's first major pandemic, the neoliberal state, in which capital largely defeated the working class and its social movements, was just not up to the task of addressing either the immediate needs of people or the tasks of adapting to or recovering from the radical changes in climate and related emergencies. Ironically, in the two most advanced neoliberal states, the United Kingdom and the United States, faced with the pressures of capitalist collapse during the pandemic, neoliberal orthodoxy was quickly jettisoned in favor of expansionary budgets and huge deficit spending in 2020. None of this heralded a counter-logic to capitalism but they immediately engendered expectations that it was the state's responsibility to save all of us! My job, or more accurately, it was the responsibility of my fellow activists to shape how the state carried out that responsibility and in ways that were accountable to, if not designed by, our constituency of working people – sure we supported reforms but never giving up on the right to revolution, something that made reforms even more likely.

With the pandemic response came other elements for the Front for Survival and the Slender Path that it would move forward. To look back at how this worked, although the neoliberals and corporate "big boys" turned to government spending in 2020 and the early COVID-19 years to keep the bottom from falling out of their capitalist market, they would soon pivot. They took the inflationary pressures that came with expanded government spending in the context of pandemic-induced supply-chain disruptions, as an opportunity to cut back and to reimpose austerity logics on working people. However, that is where the popular fight back occurred: everywhere, grassroots coalitions pushed urging more government intervention to overcome the supply chain bottle necks and provide urgently needed services ...

KM: *For example?*

MM: Sure. When people needed personal protective equipment – including masks – government intervened to provide these. Even in matters of energy that until that point were seen as the space of big business and large utilities, community coalitions demanding clean and renewable "public power" emerged – eventually forcing the state to get involved in the production of energy and not just in regulating private providers.

Of course, this was a messy, messy process – some steps forward, some steps backward – the push and pull of the class struggle. Victory was by no means guaranteed. In some contexts, governments fell quickly, other contexts like the United States, a large federal system, with many nodes of power, hierarchically organized but also with divided government, there were many different spaces for contest – places where defeats in one level of government could be countered by victories at other levels or in other jurisdictions. For this reason, politically speaking, even in the worst of times there were often blurry or opaque but realistic grounds for hope. This was particularly true in the US Northeast and West. For example, in California and New York, then the world's 5th and 10th largest economies respectively, progressive forces could rally majorities for effective policies that spoke to urgent needs and moved the state in the direction of the Slender Path even when certain branches of the Federal government came under the control of the extremely irrational forces of the Right (or remained under the hegemony of centrist or liberal reformers who could be equally irrational, especially about technology and capitalism). I will say a bit more about both the Fight and about the bundle of ideas and strategies that constitute the Slender Path.

KM: *I get the sense of push and pull and the to-and-fro movement of politics and yet, given that we have survived to this point, there must have been a sense of direction? Somehow, something in the events of the 2020s must have pushed you toward the present in which we can legitimately maintain hope.*

MM: Let me say more about the political climate of the 2020s and how it conferred a sense of urgency upon us. In addition to numerous hot wars between global powers and their respective proxies, another defining dimension of the period was the increasing ferocity and frequency of extreme weather events. In themselves, these events did not generate new political analysis or awareness. It is worth noting how extreme these were to our early 21st-century eyes. I will give you one example: the Pyrocumulonimbus.

Following once unthinkable fires in the tundra of Siberia, the rainforests of the Amazon and Indonesia, and altogether more predictable ones, albeit on heretofore unimagined scales, in Eastern Australia, British Columbia, North Africa, the Eastern Mediterranean, and of course, US West – including the Great Plains, Mountain States, and the entire Pacific Coast – the Pyrocumulonimbus entered common parlance. It was an extreme manifestation of the cumulus cloud, i.e., the white, puffy, and marshmallow-like cloud we readily imagine on hearing the word, "cloud." "Extreme," for several reasons: it is characterized by glowing red-brown hues created by the fires that generate these clouds; additionally, however, the upward thermal currents cause it to reach stratosphere where it flattens out giving it a recognizable anvil shape and the sometimes mushroom-like form recognizable since 1945.

If the Pyrocumulonimbus' appearance, combining huge scale, thunder, lightning, flames, and smoke, is unnerving, so is its lifecycle. It is a weather event that generates its own weather! Ground-level, explosive fires, often following drought and years of accumulating tinder, fuel violent updrafts or thermals, propelling tons of super-heated air, debris, sparks, and embers upwards, producing a fiery, atmosphere-borne cauldron whose static electricity generates billions of volts unleashed as cold and hot lightning, phenomena that themselves spark more fires. As the flames exhaust their fuel and the uppermost layers cool, the flow is reversed, down drafts replace the upward-moving columns of air. And if the lightning were not enough to spark more fires, the downdrafts themselves become enormous natural bellows – blowing more oxygen into the flames and dispersing embers, sparking yet more fires.

Early in his administration President Biden would pay tribute to the firefighters "who run toward the flames," the professionals earning less than $13/hour, and who, as can be expected, are suffering from "low morale."

Immediately, Biden's comments should convey why the state in neoliberalism was simply inadequate to needs of the moment. But therein lay the challenge for those of us thinking about how to respond to the new 2020s normal in which extreme weather events demanded both immediate large-scale mobilizations and long-term policy responses: only governments have the wherewithal to command the necessary resources, override concerns about property, and coordinate across jurisdictions and borders. Equally important, only national leaders have the bully pulpit to comfort the afflicted, reassure the nation, and explain the brutal combination of social relations, laws of nature, and policy choices that introduced us to the Pyrocumulonimbus.

KM: *So how did this get you to strategy and alliances?*

MM: It forced so many of us activists to set aside the kind of either-or thinking that left us polarized against ourselves. For example, we recognized: (1) that we need pressure, influence, and organization relative to all centers of power; (2) that in dividing over which center of power to target and prioritize, we were in fact, in our diversity, pressuring all of them if inadequately in some cases; (3) but that we were unlikely to push people off their chosen strategies; and (4) that we needed a way take advantage of this diversity and internalize each other's victories.

By way of example: people who won more federal spending on necessary programs as a result of their electoral and lobbying work needed to ensure that the programs were effectively implemented and in ways that built more support for these programs. As such, local and regional power was necessary to ensure that programs met the needs of people on the ground and that people on the ground recognized that these programs came out of organizing and their own power. The skill sets for national electoral and lobbying work, not to mention the resources for the same, are extremely different from the face-to-face work involved in local community organizing. The critical work for those of us who believed that we could appreciate the "whole picture" – which encompasses not only our theories of power and where we saw society headed but also the needs of particular communities – was therefore to network and coalesce these many layers of organizing, power and society in deliberate ways. In this networking function across the layers of power, we discovered a critical guidepost of the Slender Path – that our social change work has to be multi-scalar in character. One could not privilege the local over the global or any other layer as at every level we used different strategies to pursue our shared public goods agenda.

If that was a guidepost of the Slender Path, then the corresponding activity of the Front for Survival activist was to engage in actively building bridges across the different levels of society and power. And the activists could be placed in various places, in community organizations concerned about housing, trade unions organizing their members or winning contracts, non-profit organizations focused on particular issues like heat pumps or public education, professional organizations developing and framing research needs, political parties mobilizing voters or building alliances, or government employees filling their mandates. The key dimension here was that they were all taking the threat of extinction seriously and mobilizing their particular networks of influence to push for political change, government action, and public goods.

KM: *So, the Slender Path and the Front for Survival correspond to program and agency, the Path answers the "What is to be done?" question and the Front answers the "Who?" question?*

MM: Not quite! Rather than a program, the Slender Path was a set of guideposts or principles that emerged in the course of our debates. We recognized that we had to be nimble and adapt to quickly changing circumstances. A 10-point program would likely have been outdated and irrelevant before it could be edited...

KM: *If I may, Maxi, you have often said, "we," and by that I understand you're referring to your comrades at the time, your milieu as it were. At other times, I wonder if you're referring to members of the Front for Survival.*

MM: You're right, Katarina, that "we" for me is a very fluid idea. But let me try to narrow it down before returning to a few thinkers who "we" were both reacting to and who helped us. Here was the problem in getting to a clean definition of "we": the problems to be addressed were global in scale and yet they were experienced by people in everyday life through any number of overlapping containers – be they political units like nation-states or city governments – and also through different associations and networks. Within nations it was sometimes easy to define "United Fronts" in terms of clear blocs of formal political parties with designated numbers of delegates. But our "we" was constantly shifting, sometimes acting across political boundaries and at other times sharply defined by these boundaries. There was another obstacle to clear definition as well: parts of the "we" worked with one another without clear formal relationships.

        But let me stop with the excuses! If you force me to come up with a definition of the "we" – the membership of the front – I will want to distinguish between a "core we" and an "actual we"! For the core, I would describe them as consisting of individual organizers and activists in various layers of government and society who clearly saw the extinction threats posed by capitalism but who also recognized the specific issues, strengths, opportunities, limits and problems associated with their particular organization or role. They became part of the "core" by utilizing their unique locations to reach out to and work with other like-minded but differently situated activists and organizers. This active networking function helped define the core of the Front.

        For example, when I was working on health care and very focused on winning a version of Medicare for All at the state level, I reached out from my advocacy, non-profit coalition, organizing job to like-minded people working in local, county, state and the federal government, in trade unions, and also to people working in the broader labor movement. Each of us had access to different kinds of resources and networks and our sharing of these built the trust and relationships needed to win. It is also important that we not personalize this too much. We were part of the core due to our relationships not only with each other but also with our respective "constituencies" and bases.

The resulting connections, projects and alliances, helped define in a temporal and geographic sense the "actual" Front as any one point in time or space. You know, we used to create a number of graphics to illustrate the "members" of the Front, but these were invariably outdated by the time we were ready to circulate them. This is because organizations moved in and out of the Front and often also because there were groups and individuals who were functionally members of the Front but did not choose to explicitly identify as such. Among the reasons for people not formally calling themselves part of the Front, especially in the early days, had to do with the fact that they had organizations that were addressing the core concerns of the Front and they just took it for granted that they were members of the Front. Recall if you will that the Abolitionists similarly did not have membership cards with the word "Abolitionist" blazoned across it.

That said, there were emerging and rising core individuals and organizations like the Democratic Socialists of America and Progressive International but they were not widely known in the early 2020s and people better recognized leaders within these organizations and their signature programs.

I will say more about these as we explore this topic. However, even with these organizations, there were many individuals and other organizations that identified with them and their goals without ever joining them. There were also very specialized organizations or informal groupings that were associated by outsiders with the Front. To give you one example, "The Squad" of the late teens and early twenties was an informal group of US Congress people who embodied the spirit of the Front.

KM: *Let me press you further on this. I like the fact that you've started to name names. So, who was in the Front for Survival?*

MM: Maybe I should push back a little. There is an easy answer. It is to simply name many of the historical figures over the last four decades who contributed to the building of the Front. However, that would be a mistake for several reasons. First, singling out particular people will deny recognition to many other people and organizations whose contributions also proved to be indispensable. Second, even with the progress we've made to date, there remains only a Slender Path forward for the foreseeable future, and as such, it would be better to describe the Front for Survival in terms of functional roles that its members adopted. Thirdly, and somewhat painfully, one has to recognize that some people and organizations Front were vital members in one period or moment only to become less so or even the opposite in another period. So, Katarina, I am going to compromise by naming some names but get directly to a more functional kind of description. That is, I hope that my description provides a tool to identify continuing and future members of the Front for Survival.

Earlier, I described my local and regional work as cutting across all sorts of divides and building coalitions. Of course, I was not alone: had I been so, we would not be alive to have this conversation! So, members for the Front were networkers and bridgebuilders working on issues that mattered to their community. Here's one example. By the end of the teens, the idea that government – representing the institutional face of the public as a whole – should be a key player in ensuring our health – an absolutely central public good – was pretty much shared by large majorities.

Programmatically, it took the form of the Affordable Care Act (ACA). The far right and corporate types however weaponized it, derisively emphasizing its popular moniker "Obamacare." As a result, many Americans in so-called "Red States" lost out on many of the program's benefits. However, even in the centers of the worst reaction, subtle and pragmatic coalitions emerged. Running against Republican governors who refused to expand Medicaid in accordance with the ACA, progressives ran referenda in states like Idaho, Oklahoma, Missouri, Nebraska, Utah and South Dakota – and they won. The importance of these victories cannot be overstated. They came after the right-wing loaded Supreme Court ruled that governors could refuse Medicaid expansion. The coalitions won over Republicans and independents to build majorities. The organizations involved include health care workers' organizations and unions but also professional ones like the states' American Heart Association affiliates.

The organizations involved in these kinds of efforts housed activists and organizers who became members of the Front for Survival, schooled in the fight for public health goods intensified by the COVID-19 pandemic. Similarly, in many cases due to neoliberalism devolving state or public functions onto voluntary organizations, every town and county would have publicly-oriented, volunteer bodies addressing environmental and social welfare matters. With the not-for-profit missions of these organizations, many Front for Survival members emerged out of this sector. The local green, recycling or environmental club in schools and counties were among the places where this consciousness emerged. Now it could have resulted in a technocratic kind of managerialism. In many cases it did – prompting very apposite critiques of the professional managerial class character of such individuals and organizations. In other cases, however, in association and dialogue with trades unions and community-based organizations a more radical consciousness emerged and flowered into the Front for Survival.

Now similar accounts can be given for the literally thousands of higher education-based research institutes and centers. In some cases, these centers were more accountable to their corporate sponsors; in other cases, particularly those funded by governments, unions and progressive donors, a very different dynamic took place enabling creative coalitions to emerge – proto-Fronts for Survival, if you will – linking university-based knowledge creators with still other knowledge and public good creators in workplaces, unions, communities and government. Nobody in the twenties could have a legitimate excuse for not knowing about the Front for Survival despite it not having an address. There were simply hundreds of entities in every locale ready to provide an intellectual and organizational home for people who were concerned about where humanity was headed and how to change course.

And you saw a plethora of entities spread across the nation. In some political campaigns for local government, candidates would invoke the Green New Deal, if not that, Red New Deals or Black New Deals or even Blue-Green alliances. They would champion the kinds of coalitions for social and environmental public goods that I refer to as the Front for Survival. Mayoral candidates or school board officials who created coalitions with parents, teachers and bus drivers concerned about the effects of diesel fumes on themselves, their neighborhoods and their students were members of the Front in a very practical sense.

All this diversity to the members of the Front suggests that the critical task was knitting together the coalition, building consensus, agreeing to disagree, sequencing debates, growing trust. I remember one old-fashioned leftist telling me, "Look I agree with the goals and am ready to give the coalition my all. But I will only do so after the bickering and factionalism is overcome!" I replied to him, "Actually, the real work involves the investment, patience and fortitude, the problem solving needed to overcome the bickering and factionalism. Once that is done, the rest is relatively easy!" Later, he came to agree with me.

One of the early challenges in identifying members of the Front was that there were many forces that while recognizing the dangers of capitalism nonetheless imagined a domesticated, reformed, or even a re-conceptualized capitalism. Of course, reformed versions of capitalism were as old as capitalism itself. For example, by the twenties, Harvard University economist Rebecca Henderson, argued for a "Reimagined Capitalism," one in which more socially responsible values are maximized. Among the mainstream Democrats in the twenties, an economic nationalism emerged. It too, at times, attacked capitalism or at least its neoliberal incarnation. As a consequence, talk of "Green Growth" and "sustainable capitalism" gained currency. One disturbing trend, involving the World Economic Forum, was the call for a "Great Reset." It premised its claims on a fourth industrial revolution. However, these models invariably floundered on the rocks of their elitist and anti-democratic characters. They were usually ready to talk about involving all "stakeholders" including various representatives of labor, consumers, communities, etc. But they tended to assume that corporations – or governments controlled by the corporations – would be the agenda setters and have a voice that is at least as loud as any other without regard for the fact that they represented only a tiny fraction of humanity whereas the oft-silenced voices of labor and community, especially where these reached around the world, spoke for the vast majority of the humankind.

So as various green capitalist schemes, including many very technocratically inspired forms of renewable energy, unraveled, members of the Front for Survival came to sort out who could and could not be counted on to challenge the extinction tendencies of capitalism and pose genuine, effective and democratic alternatives.

KM: *Okay, I get the point, but surely there is an identifiable core or even a set of principles?*

MM: You're right! And I am sure that my deliberate blurring of lines is getting tiresome. This, eh, tactic, if you will, of finding shades of grey where things could be painted in black and white stems from my interest in conveying how social movements as opposed to organizations grow and develop. In real time political work, especially for those out of power, understanding the grey areas and leveraging them to build broad alliances is critical. It was true then, in the twenties, and it remains so even though we may have turned to corner with capitalism no longer the driving force. I always remember a statement that my Dad, also a radical, made to me when I was very young: the measure of a revolutionary is not their capacity to exclude the enemy – the system does that just fine – it is their capacity to include! Guided by this insight or strategic consideration, I came to understand that the core of the Front for Survival was that group of individual activists who were members of organizations or parts of various social milieus who recognized that their jobs involved not only fostering the interests of their organizations and constituencies but to build enduring relationships with other individuals and organizations – therewith constituting the broad Front for Survival. Therefore, what was key was to reach out to and develop relationships with those individuals fighting for public goods in their own very different ways. It was hard to predict who they were. That person might be a recent college graduate working for a community youth group or a new social worker attached to a retirement community or someone working their first job who wants to unionize their workplace. To the extent that they recognized that their challenges required connections with people outside of their immediate networks, they were primed to become part of the core of the Front. In talking about networking and individuals, I should emphasize that I am referring to activities and people within the vast and diverse working class as opposed to members of the ruling class – although we had plenty of defections from them.

KM: *Hang on for a moment! Surely, all they people had to be operating with a set of principles and core ideas?*

MM: Yes, certainly! And many people in the period were creating their lists of core ideas. One thinker, Bhaskar Sunkara, barely 30 years old at the time, offered a list of 15 principles for action in that period – ones that he saw as necessary to win social democracy and on which ground the working class could advance toward democratic socialism. His list saw elections as decisive, centered on the working class and the building of a political party, and advocated for the universalist framing of demands. While those generally appealed to me and my politics, I also recognized that many people would feel excluded.[1]

Another big-picture thinker in the period, Timothy Snyder, a student of the 19th and 20th century crucible of nationalisms and fascisms in Central Europe, looked at the rise of 21st-century fascism in the United States and came up with his list of 20 points. These had a strikingly individualist ethical dimension with warnings and injunctions for individual action – "Beware the one-party state" was one, others were to "Believe in truth," Investigate," "Be reflective if you must be armed," and "Make eye contact and small talk." Today, shorn of their context, these points must seem insipid and almost trite! However, with the rise of armed militias and when national leaders appealed to "alternative facts," these had a certain appeal for how one comported oneself. What I found most lacking in his list were the positive principles that we could use to deliberate among ourselves and across our divides.

KM: *So you're saying that there is nothing wrong with a universalist framing, but the important thing is that the universal has to be constructed out of many particularisms? Out of the intersections, if you will?*

MM: Indeed. We have already noted the multi-scalar starting points and corresponding networking function. But what is particularly important here is that we also had a theory for networking our movements and strategies. Like Sunkara, we recognized that the vast working class was subject to contradictory pressures under capitalism. On global, national, and regional scales, people were constantly being forced into and out of labor markets as capital's needs shifted. To use the language of the time, the working class was constantly being recomposed and decomposed. This gave it a profoundly intersectional character. At one time, it may have been convenient to capital to tap into rural young women as workers – as it did at the birth of the Industrial Revolution in the United States and again as it exploited decolonized Southeast Asia – and at another time it may depend on highly educated, high-skilled workers drawn from all countries and all genders. It may also depend on both at the same time albeit in different neighborhoods or hemispheres. With technological change and constantly evolving production chains, the strategic location of one sector of the working class may increase relative to that of another. In this context, many despaired of Marx's 19th century-hope for a self-emancipating working class that would develop awareness of itself and challenge capital.

And this is where the Slender Path, with quite a practical and non-ideological intent, really delivered on some of Marx's early promises. At the time that Marx in the mid-19th century wrote, nowhere was the working class a majority. Where it existed, Marx realized that it was subject to diverse influences and visions for the future. And so, for the barely 30-year-old Marx, it was very important that working-class activists never stand apart from the class or take the standpoint of just one or other part of the class. Activists had to take the perspective of the class as a whole!

Now Marx never really spelled out how we would get to that perspective, but he left some great lessons which more ideological people than me could walk through. However, for me, in the 2020s, what was most vital and alive in Marx's legacy was the sense that the world had finally arrived at a moment in which it could be appreciated as a totality and not only in the sense that we could think globally (and utter the many yeses) but also in the temporal sense – we could look back into our pasts and ahead into our possible futures. In a cruel sense, capitalism and is civilizational malcontents had seeped into every pore of the planet, subjugated or otherwise threatened every population and species and in so doing, birth a diverse and multifaceted working class while creating the tools for comprehending the possibility of a global civilization. Yes, at the very same moment that it threatened to extinguish us all, what we called "The Greatest Emergency of All Time," we came to recognize that our multi-scalar or multi-level existence is a global one. As such, political parties targeting national states were wholly inadequate, although necessary, to the global tasks of our survival.

By the 20s, one important expression of the need for global political awareness, coordination, and action, was the formation of Progressive International. In the late teens, both Bernie Sanders of the United States and Jeremy Corbyn of the United Kingdom became early sponsors of the effort, but it encompassed vital experiments and projects for public goods all over the world. From Mississippi, it brought in Cooperation Jackson's Kali Akuno and Arizona-based thinker Noam Chomsky, and the Cameroonian philosopher Achille Mbembe, but it also included active political leaders like Barcelona's mayor then, Ada Colau, and the former guerilla leader who positively upended Colombia's militarized state by winning the presidency, Gustav Petro. If the Slender Path and Front for Survival had precursors, they were to be found in the diversity of forces brought together in Progressive International.

KM: *So what was the Progressive International?*

MM: As you will notice from my listing of personalities, Katarina, it was a very diverse coalition of individuals and projects – some of them political parties, others were individuals with huge constituencies like Colau and Petro whom I just mentioned. But they were brought together through an initiative of Yanis Varoufakis, a former Greek finance minister, and Bernie Sanders, who helped reawaken American socialism after a century-long slumber. They recognized the global character of the threats facing humanity as a whole, and developed a list of 12 broad principles, enumerated as single words, like, "Democratic," "Plural," "Egalitarian," "Sustainable," "Ecologic," and "Post-capitalist." Such was the heightening awareness of the movements at the time, the growing polarization, and the extent of the crisis that words with such broad meaning could be readily understood and stand as broad markers for a political position. The International's inaugural summit expanded on these into a set of 25 principles that emphasized increasing organization of social forces and the need to develop movement infrastructure. Significantly, it provided means for individuals to join it directly as well as a process for organizations to affiliate. Check out its full set of principles in the chart.

Declaration of Progressive International, September 2020	
Principle (PI)	*Summary/Excerpts from Explanatory Text (MM)*
I. Internationalism or Extinction	Internationalism is not a luxury but a strategic necessity.
II. A Definition of Progress	Progress that is democratic, decolonized, just, egalitarian, liberated, feminist, ecological, peaceful, post-capitalist, prosperous, plural, and bound by radical love.
III. Peoples of the World, Organize	"international organization: to combine forces across borders ... to reclaim the planet as our own."
IV. We Build Infrastructure	"the forces of progress remain fragmented, while wealth and power consolidate .... We build the scaffolding of a planetary front."
V. Unity, Not Conformity	"The present crisis demands the strategic alliance of all progressive forces. But coordination does not require submission. We aim to build a broad coalition, while making space for creative contention inside of it."
VI. Partnership by Mutual Power	"partnership without mutual power is just another name for domination. In our work, we aim to rebalance rather than reproduce disparities of power ...."
VII. Capitalism Is the Virus	"We believe that exploitation, dispossession, and environmental destruction are written into the genetic code of capitalism."
VIII. Internationalism Means Anti-imperialism	"Our internationalism stands against imperialism in all its forms: from war and sanctions to privatization and 'structural adjustment.'"
IX. Language Is Power	"Linguistic barriers strengthen class domination, white supremacy, and indigenous dispossession. We aim to transcend linguistic barriers to find our own common language of resistance."
X. Freedom at the Frontline	"Our internationalism is intersectional ... we center the frontline struggles for liberation at the base of global economy: for food, for land, for dignity, and for emancipation."
XI. An Internationalism of Liberation	"Our opposition to oppressive hierarchies is the foundation of our internationalism."
XII. Decolonization Is Not a Metaphor	"Our demand is full reparations for past crimes and the immediate restoration of land, resources, and sovereignty to all the dispossessed ...."
XIII. Feminist Politics, Feminist Practice	"Our aim is to break with the patriarchy while disrupting the binary structure of gender on which it relies. We direct our politics toward care, cooperation, and communal accountability"
XIV. *Buenos Vivires*	"We do not measure progress with growth ... and we define our success by the quality of our collective coexistence."

(Continued)

Declaration of Progressive International, September 2020 (Continued)

Principle (PI)	Summary/Excerpts from Explanatory Text (MM)
XV. No Justice, No Peace	"… peace can only last in the security of social justice. We work to dismantle the war machine, and replace it with a diplomacy of peoples based on cooperation and coexistence."
XVI. Revolution, Not Regime Change	"We support popular movements to transform society and reclaim the state. But we stand against attempts to overthrow regimes in order to protect the interests of capital …."
XVII. Winning Elections Is Not Enough	"Elections are opportunities to transform politics and turn popular demands into government policy. But we know that winning elections is not enough to fulfill our mission."
XVIII. Power from Pluralism	"Our coalition is bound by a shared vision of collective liberation. We do not import this vision, or impose one program over the rest. Instead, we weave together our needs, knowledge, and policy priorities to build a common program that derives power from pluralism." [complete explanatory text]
XIX. Relationships Are the Foundation	"Our internationalism is intimate. New technologies promised community and connection, but sowed discord and disillusionment instead. We believe that we cannot succeed unless we know and trust one another on equal terms." [complete explanatory text]
XX. Dialogue is Not Enough	"Our aim is collective action …. Our activities prepare us for planetary mobilization, matching the scale of our crises to the scale of the actions that we mount …."
XXI. Not For Profit, Not By Profit	"We do not accept money from for-profit institutions and the representatives of fossil fuel companies, pharmaceutical companies, big tech companies, big banks, private equity firms, hedge funds, agribusinesses, and the arms industry."
XXII. We Are Not an NGO	"[R]eal change comes from movements of people, not the benevolence of philanthropy. We are accountable only to those movements and the communities from which they grow."
XXIII. Fight on All Fronts	"Our coalition reflects the diversity of struggle …. We welcome unions, parties, movements, publications, research centres, neighbourhood associations, and individual activists in their lonely struggle. Together, this coalition is greater than the sum of its parts, and powerful enough to remake the world."
XXIV. From Each, and to Each	"Our model of membership is simple: from each, according to ability; and to each, according to need …. And we strive to support members in all the ways that their struggle demands."

(Continued)

Declaration of Progressive International, September 2020 (Continued)	
Principle (PI)	*Summary/Excerpts from Explanatory Text (MM)*
XXV. Solidarity Is Not a Slogan	"We believe that solidarity is an action. The expression of sympathy for our allies is common. Our task is to recognize their struggle as our own, to organize our communities to take part in that struggle, and to join forces across borders in a common defense of people and planet." [complete explanatory text]

Source: https://progressive.international/declaration/en

KM: *Did you join them?*

MM: Yes, I did! In joining them, I received regular emails and videos about their and their affiliates' work in different parts of the world. This helped me develop a sense of my own work and contributions. It was not only inspirational, but in a strategic sense, I could talk with other members of the core of the future Front for Survival about the work that was being done. This helped us develop objectives and benchmarks. As you notice in the next chart, we worked with a variety of concepts that we'd map out during internal workshops and strategy sessions with communities. Concepts and ideas were "popcorned" and consolidated into clusters. We add names, goals, places, etc. to ideas and therefore we were very "undogmatic" and open as to what the content of the Front and the Slender Path required. But what you'll notice is the short distance between the ideas in this chart and many of the points listed by Progressive International.

Ideas and Concepts from the Front for Survival and the Slender Path	
Goals and Objectives Do these goals give us the capacity to challenge the rule of capital and face down the extinction threats posed by war, climate breakdown and disease?	*Public Goods* The Commons Commanding Heights "Variegated" State
Visions Do these visions inspire people to action and cooperation?	*"Beloved Community"* Democratic Socialism "Narratives of Connectedness"
Activities What kinds of organizing embodies these goals, objectives and vision?	*Multiscalar Organizing* Active Networking Participatory Organizing Negotiating the Universal

What I would like to emphasize at this point, though, is that all these topics are deeply interwoven with one another. That is, it was typical to talk about organizations, networks, political jurisdictions, programs, social theory, and vision as discrete topics. They are! But they are also interconnected. Much of the ferment of the twenties should be seen as part of a broader transition underway at the time. So, what I hope is that my description of Progressive International, one of many global projects that I found inspiring, demonstrates that conscious work was being done to build the political agency necessary for forestalling the extinction threats and for imagining a better alternative. This was part of the work of recomposing and coalescing the diverse and fragmented working class.

Unlike Marx, many of his successors took the working class to be a thing with fixed and defined characteristics given by their workplaces. What we recognized is that the working class is a political project in the constant throes of composition and recomposition. What later working-class activists like Antonio Gramsci recognized is that this process is struggle involving diverse elements including class conscious intellectuals who emerge from both within and outside of the working class to solve the problems of the class as a whole.

KM: *Ah yes, the famous "organic intellectuals" that I read about in college!*

MM: For sure! Activists like me found my marching orders in figuring out how to bring the diverse parts of the working class into dialogue with each other.[2] The threat of extinction was therefore both a source of frustration with its impossible urgency and a source of motivation.

One particularly productive framework for me emerged on the fringes, from within the Green Party, then a "third party" within the United States – the Green New Deal which invoked the 1930s heritage of the New Deal in the context of the environmental and militarist challenges of our day. It went "viral" – an unfortunate term of the time for something that keeps spreading – and communities and activists around the world began using it as a framework for thinking about the world and their own communities in holistic ways – how to generate both good jobs while attending to urgent environmental and energy needs. In fact, a prominent labor movement historian and activist Jeremy Brecher dubbed many local efforts to be a "Green New Deal-from-Below." By the way, while thinking about class and knowledge, this labor activist also turned to heuristic devices developed in the academy and elsewhere to put them in service of the working class. In so doing, Brecher, who celebrated working-class creativity in both his historiography and practice, cut across the dichotomization of specialist and popular knowledges.

In the vein, projects run by young people, some open to the unfair charge of being unaccountable NGOs and embodiments of the Professional Managerial Class, like the Sunrise Movement or New York State's Public Power Coalition, were really pioneering efforts agitating on both non-class, humanity-as-a-whole, lines and class lines building dialogues not only with organized labor but also the other disparate unorganized parts of the labor movement. They were working to save the entire planet – even if they didn't always talk or think about the extinction of all life.

KM: *If I can take stock for a moment: the Slender Path and the Front for Survival has its origins in the problem solving and networking activities of activists trying to overcome the fragmentation of the working class? And the working class in your view seem to encompass the vast majority of humanity including what were popularly called the middle classes or even professionals?*

MM: Yes, in short, that *is* it!

KM: *But what about the political content? What about the rise of fascism, still a somewhat present threat in the 2060s though obviously nothing on the scale of the 20s and 30s?*

MM: Sure, to this point, I have remained vague about politics and actual policies, even where I named the Green New Deal. My reason for this is that politics varied across contexts, and we had to remain flexible and avoid unnecessary either-or choices. In one important respect, both the Slender Path and the Front for Survival are matters of affect, attitude, and outlook. It is a certain flexibility in a world of hard choices and inflexible but complex laws of physics and nature. In some ways, it was and is about an ethics of how we treat each other within the movement – have we developed ideas about each other and each other's priorities that allow us to engage in a dialogue to build a bigger picture, a more complex working-class point of view? I'll seek your forbearance one last time, with another example before …

KM: *Before directly answering the question, "what was the Slender Path?"*

MM: Yes, for sure! In retrospect it was quite simple really. Working people everywhere at the time needed more. Yes, simply more. In fact, more than a hundred years earlier, an American labor leader on being asked what the American workers wanted, responded simply, "More!" Well, there was a bit *more* to it. But everyone recognized the need for more stability, more employment and housing security, a stronger social safety net, better health and healthcare, and so on. Instead of these necessities, more planet-killing trinkets and commodities were being produced, often combining deadly chemicals, fossil fueled energy sources, and generating all sorts of energy intensive activities to bring those products to the market. These were precisely the things that the "degrowthers," as they were called then, wanted to eliminate. Between the demand for "more" and the degrowthers, a consensus was emerging, one envisioned by the authors of "The Slender Path." Growth had to be radically rethought. Rejecting both the assumption that working people simply needed more of what the market was either already producing or failing to adequately produce, and also the caricature that the Degrowthers wanted already-deprived people to live more austere lives – to make do with less – the consensus was we need to be deliberate about our forms of growth. And that we needed democratic and decentralized ways of deciding what we needed and figuring out how to produce our livelihoods in ways that are conducive to Earth, to our general well-being and everyone involved or other impacted by the production. The idea that we should democratically plan our production – in the form of expanding public goods – may seem mind numbingly obvious today. Even back then, at a time of great optimism about using technology to help us with all manner of problem, there were sizable numbers of people who took that for granted. But there were sizable intellectual fortifications that denied this. Some people claimed that planning was exactly what the discredited state socialism of the 1900s embodied. That idea soon gave way to the recognition that the old-fashioned mega-corporations of the 2020s were in fact engaged in planning on a routine basis. Indeed, they were using the very technologies that everyone else was using to gather decentralized information and data points (for example, tools that coordinated people's calendaring preferences to identify convenient dates for everything from holding toddler's birthday parties and scheduling great sports events involving dozens of players, coaches, support personnel, to hundreds of journalists, and millions of fans. If I remember correctly, Degrowthers came to be so impressed with the planning tools and their efficacy at huge scale that they increasingly cited one of their greatest critics, someone named Leigh Philips, who was critical of corporate power while extolling its planning capacity.

KM: *Tell me a little more about the Degrowthers.*

MM: It's quite straightforward really, almost everyone at the time was bemoaning the super large vehicles that corporations spent billions shaping tastes and attitudes to in turn generate demand for their planet killers. This outrage extended well beyond the beard-stroking lefties in the academy as working women in particular revolted at the impracticality of many of these types of goods and it merged with people whose entire communities were being destabilized by the associated mining and heavy industries that shaped the early parts of the production chains of the planet killers. "Living lightly on the planet" became a set of values that whole generations of young people, communities of faith, and middle-class professionals of all stripes, many incomes and employment statuses came to accept as common sense. These values fueled the practical, consciousness raising and agitational work of both self-conscious Degrowthers and thousands more activists for whom the term degrowth was quite alien. Urban hipsters, whose food, clothing, and shelter, mostly likely depend at the time on huge industrial processes easily boarded the "living lightly on the planet" bandwagon. In fact, those urbanites, millions of residents in the big cities of the world, became more and more agitated over the disruptions to their lifestyles and often livelihoods as 21st-century disasters became the norm. They too began to joke, tweet, complain, and eventually organize to secure certain common and public goods that city life required but by the mid-20s that came to be in short supply. They wanted green spaces for recreation and to soak up storm surges; they wanted their only child to have great accessible schools near where they lived and worked. Increasingly, even the better earning, more stable urban residents wanted better work conditions, job security, and health for all the gig workers they met in their everyday life's. For the baristas, librarians, nurses, first responders, janitors and others, winning the public goods of better housing, health, and incomes all meant that everyone else would benefit. Percolating up from millions of random conversations, there was a new awareness that the most efficient and just way to achieve this necessary leveling up had little to do with "More," and everything to do with a new social contract one that had to be discussed and negotiated by democratically chosen representatives of these different layers of the working class. One hundred eighty or so years earlier, socialists had envisioned that factories would bring thousands of workers together, facilitating their common consciousness and fomenting a radical will to overcome private property. In the cities of the 21st century, struggles over space and for survival allowed these workers of different incomes, industries and sectors, and lifestyles to challenge their segregation and increasingly through myriad struggles, defeats, and victories came to understand that they needed certain things, public goods, that their employers routinely undermined, rationed, or destroyed in the hope that they could profit from either their provision or the insecurity of its scarcity. Even then, it was a contested terrain as some employers understood that the failure to provide high quality healthcare was depriving their workforces of people and introduced a radical instability in the workplace, particularly as pandemic waves and strains succeeded one another.[3]

It may be added that workplaces were, of course, very diverse places varying not only by industry but also by relationships to ownership. While democratic, worker-owned workplaces were largely discouraged by the capitalist marketplace, the more governments – local, state, federal – and even international treaties came under pressure to support worker ownership, the more viable these entities became. These emerged as non-capitalist models, prefiguring a greater democratization of society much at the broader anti-extinction movement did. Democratic workplaces, while still facing the production imperatives that governed most other workplaces, tended to recognize that their workers were whole human beings, not just hands for work or brains to write algorithms. As such, the resources of these workplaces could be devoted to anti-extinction ends much as capitalist workplaces were oriented to private profit. When one of the largest cooperatives announced that it was not only going fossil fuel free, but it also would turn its huge buying power to help its neighboring communities, often places where its worker-cooperators lived, do the same – go fossil fuel free – that was a shot in the arm for the anti-extinction movement! Another point about cooperatives and the anti-extinction movement, one that we have not explored but assumed throughout, is that these movements were at one with the democracy movement. In arguing for democratizing investment and the "variegated state" needed to respond to the extinction threats, we were at the same time embodying the "democracy movement."

KM: *I can see how that worked! Also, your illustration of growth versus degrowth helps me understand why you needed to cultivate new habits of the mind that rejected dichotomous thinking!*

MM: Thanks! There were clearly understandable starting points for the Slender Path and principle of multi-scalar organizing from local to global. One to which we have already alluded – with the Reconstruction and other breakthrough moments like the New Deal of the 1930s – is the contested public sphere delivering public goods. Now capitalism had always co-existed with public goods, the provision of which operated on not-for-profit lines and often resulted in universal access of various forms. Think of roads and bridges, and also of hospitals and schools. But even with those examples, you can imagine that there would be a fair amount of contestation even if we called them public or universal goods. You can think of things like Obamacare, a medical access program we discussed earlier, that prefigured the actual universal healthcare that we won in the 30s. It was an example of a public good that the Federal government delivered. But so too are public schools which are often won at the local or near-local, regional scale. Often certain people benefited through contracts with the state for the provision of public goods or some communities were better served than other communities in the provision of these goods. When you recognize that most public health goods have to be global in character then you can immediately see that it was and even today remains very unequal and differentiated in its delivery. Nonetheless, armed by both working class struggles and long-evolving ideas like human rights doctrine, the provision of public goods grew and as did the demands for these in proportion to the increasingly evident disasters. Shared knowledge platforms, Facebook and Twitter were popular at the time, became places for struggle and knowledge formation in the face of these challenges. Increasingly, neoliberal doctrine that demanded a tiny state whose main function it was to provide social order, increasingly gave way to struggles for "decommodification." If the word doesn't roll of the tongue easily, the concept behind it was well understood – "decommodification" meant that whether your child had enough safe water to drink did not depend on how much cash was in your pocket. The corresponding policy was also straightforward: the state had to take responsibility for the production of critical goods. The debate was not over the state's role but what level of state.

KM: *A moment, Maxi, what do you mean by "level of state"?*

MM: For your generation, this may seem like a strange term. When I was growing up, we were very aware of many different levels of governance and we thought of the federal government in the US as the highest level of state. But everything was really in a state of flux although we did not quite realize it at the time. Closest to us, were local and regional governments, increasingly, though, the functional region – like the metro-system that got me around from my home in a suburb to the downtown, or communities served by particular food distribution hubs, did not conform to a single government in which we had voice and so there were many struggles at the local level to construct an accountable level of local government.

There were also straightforward public goods like schools, childcare, neighborhood clinics, local parks, and even ice-rinks – you may not remember those! – that were taken care of at the local level and people did not even see that as either "public goods" or "government" and yet they were both. By the late twenties, there were also many voluntary projects that had some measure of public accountability, outside of formal government, but also outside of the markets: they ranged from community gardens and workshops to art festivals and concerts. "A Woodstock A Week" an old activist labeled the government-funded but locally planned and administered concerts and lectures that spread throughout the country. In fact, someone familiar with the 19th-century abolitionist movement reminded me how important those public gatherings were for spreading awareness of the "slave's cause." So yes, a renewed sense of government emerged.

Increasingly, through many social struggles and Green New Deal-from-Below kinds of activism, rather than a monolithic state, the kind we imagined of the old 20th-century state socialisms to have embodied, the state was seen as a variegated kind of entity with many different levels and avenues of accountability. Not only was a huge amount of power devolved to the near and local, but there were also public bodies outside of the state, lacking its coercive dimensions, that filled public functions and were accountable and transparent to local communities. Even where their leaders may have resembled the PMC of old, they were tightly controlled by staff unions and other stakeholders. So, corresponding to the multi-scalar organizing and networking, we have a diversified and variegated state. It constitutes if you will a key element of the Slender Path.

KM: *Wait, "variegated state"?!*

MM: Yes, rather than the monolithic state we used to imagine, we were institution-making and institution-changing activists who re-made what was considered the state – constructing levels – plus nooks and crannies! – that conformed to our capacity and needs as working people challenging the rule of capital and enabling our survival.

Given this role for the state, one of active involvement in the satisfaction of human and environmental needs, those activists making up the Front for Survival needed a strategy – where to deploy the state? Often times, we had educated each other about strategy and the fulfillment of our needs. Indeed, given our great needs – not only ones generated by the extinction threats but also long unfulfilled needs involving centuries of deprivation and want – we really need strategy! In fact, our needs routinely outstripped the resources on hand. At the simplest level, we had to discipline our thinking: if we needed 10 of a certain resource, but only had 2 on hand, we had to ask if 2 could do the work of 10 or if 2 could be used to get 10.

KM: *And the point being?*

MM: We had to take complicated and large social goals and break them down into a series of winnable achievements that would get us to our goals. These kinds of calculations are conducted democratically, i.e., in participatory ways involving real deliberation at various levels as opposed to simple majority voting, was the stuff of the Slender Path. Participation, following multiscalar organizing (corresponding to a "variegated state") and networking, was therefore another principle or guidepost for the Slender Path.

Here's one example: in our county, working people were divided on race lines, and there was a strong cultural-political polarization. We had to win over people who were just not talking to each other. More practically, early on, we only had enough people power – a combination of volunteers, small organizations, sympathetic government officials – to conduct campaigns in one electoral district! How then to win majority support across 15 districts, some of which were simply no-go, "MAGA" districts? Put differently, how to get eight districts when you only have enough Front allies for one? Well, we did something unusual, we supported an ally, one not wholly onside in the first district, where we could have one on our own, and then we conducted a powerful drive for more clinic funding in several of the districts where we had very little support at the electoral level but where this public health demand had strong resonance. As a result, we (1) won zero seats in our own name, but (2) built support for a common policy in a majority of the districts. It is also true that that kind of longer-term strategizing set us up for winning a majority in our own name within a few electoral cycles. But notice, the policy did not have to wait for our electoral victory. The fact that these kinds of strategic experiments abounded in the twenties blazed the Slender Path forward in its earliest days.

But we had to go further: the Pyrocumulonimbus example taught us the meaning of urgency. As such, another concept had to be rehabilitated from the 20th century. The idea here was simple there are some strategic starting points that are more important than others as we secure our livelihoods and survival. By the early 1990s, following decades of concerted attack and eventually also the fall of statist socialism, the idea of these starting points, called "commanding heights" was also discredited. However, in the transition from fossil fuels, energy had become an obvious commanding height to be developed by the state. More powerful human rights movements came to assert other commanding heights too: the provision of water and health-related services. To be sure, there were strong technocratic dimensions to all of this and fortunately the Slender Path's third principle – participation – formed a healthy antidote and resource to be invoked by grassroots social movements. For example, early in the 20s the Biden Administration bought into the commanding heights concept in practice if not name – it sought to subsidize microchip manufacturing and foster lithium mining. These policies seemed compatible with some dimensions of the Slender Path and the Front for Survival – we certainly need lithium then for energy storage and we needed the most efficient computing power afforded by advance chip manufacturing. By explicitly labeling energy a commanding height, the Front for Survival liberated the topic and deliberations from the realm of technocrats and big private investors and brought it into the democratic light of day. This reframed the conversation from what brings profit to what meets needs!

KM: *To take stock again: the Slender Path is about multi-scalar organizing in a variegated state – from the local to the global and everything in between – to expand public goods informed by human rights doctrines and with a strategic choice of public goods?*

MM: Yes, exactly that but as you will notice, each involves human actors, the activists of the Front for Survival, uniting all of humankind in self-conscious ways, exercising their judgment, including their senses of what's right or wrong, what's just or unjust, what achievable or merely utopian. And so, while I point you to the decisive 2020s, I am not citing specific policies or politicians instead I am trying to convey our activism as self-conscious, morally-inspired makers of history, people operating with an imperative to save the planet not merely our own hides, but also understanding our makeup as people who did not own or control capital – except when we combined in our workplaces and communities, and through the state!

KM: *You'll have to forgive me! This all sounds a bit too simple. As I noted earlier, in the twenties and into the thirties, there were powerful fascist movements very reminiscent of their century-old predecessors! Your narrative seems to skip very easily over them.*

MM: Okay, I can see why you'd say that. Let me start by saying that at a very personal level, I took the re-emerging fascist threat quite seriously. I had no choice: one group of fascists, calling themselves the Patriotic Front, marched on my offices and physically threatened me in the teens. Fighting fascism was therefore a constant reminder that we were not only fighting against the physical and military threats associated with climate change and nuclear war, but we were also radically fighting another force unleashed by capitalism itself: the strange alchemy wherein some of capitalism's victims allied themselves with its victors in various nationalistic projects. It is easy to call this an extension of American nativism and white supremacy – after all in the run up to the Civil War, plenty of non-slave owning white poor and working-class people allied with the plantation owners. But this was a global experience: in India, it took the form of Hindu fundamentalism, in Brazil, parts of the military allied with agricultural elites, right-wing media tycoons and industrialists, and poor farmers, in an old-fashioned fascist coalition, and so on. Even in South Africa, former radicals aligned with community-based strongmen in a xenophobic, anti-immigrant coalition, ironically against other Africans from countries that once gave those ex-radicals refuge!

A central challenge that we had to overcome in addressing the rise of fascism and to confront that fact that a good portion of the white working class had turned in that direction was the cultural war in which science and race were variously weaponized against broader working-class unity. If we took comfort in the fact that Du Bois recognized in the Civil War – some 100,000 poor whites deserted the Confederates and followed the nearly half-million ex-slaves north and away from slavery, we knew a lot had to be done to counter fascism and its ideas.

This was accomplished by a mix of measures. Some on the left were tempted to "run straight at the propellors" and attack right-wingers whose demonstrations were designed to intimidate. With experience and much debate, we learned to develop cross-cutting campaigns that acknowledged some of the more universal dimensions of right-wing grievances by reaching directly into their communities. I will describe a few of the early attempts and also the language and framing choices that we had to make.

We also had to recognize that part of their anger was directed at neoliberal elites with whom parts of the working class and people-of-color movements often sided. As we developed inclusive language that also gave voice to our shared anger at neoliberal elites, the polarizing dynamics of fascist agitation was attenuated. In addition, the more we consciously drew on political figures who spoke in cultural and political terms to parts of the white working class, without ever undermining our commitments to women, immigrants, and people of color, the more we were able to weaken the fascist coalitions. Surprises emerged in the process: evangelical groups which added to the electoral might of the MAGA crowd and gave structure to some of the fascist-adjacent projects were somewhat neutralized as our campaigns, especially those at the local level, spoke to some to the needs and anxieties that they were expressing. Women, people of color, and immigrants who were part of the evangelical groups proved to be important footholds, intersections, if you will, that allowed us to engage with people who otherwise would have nothing to do with us.

But to be sure, there was plenty of data to indicate that all the policies that we stood for corresponded to deeply-held values, ones that often cut across even the left-right divide. Our best thinkers knew this and affirmed the agenda of recomposing the working class through on-the-ground struggles and intra-class diplomacy if you will. Yes, I know I sound like glitchy recording – activists who would network the various layers and factions of the working class were and are central! One of the best at the time was Heather McGhee. In a brilliant work, *The Sum of Us: What Racism Costs Us and How We Can Prosper Together*, McGhee showed us working people divided by white supremacy and racism, fell into what she called a zero-sum model racial competition. As a result, public goods and amenities were paved over rather than shared. At the same time, McGhee showed us many examples of how this could be overcome, precisely by the kind of intra-class diplomacy and knowledge sharing activities we have already described. She found exciting examples of people reaping what she calls a "solidarity dividend," the results of working people choosing to collaborate across divisions of race, religion and immigration status. She provides an example from Lewiston, ME, which she calls a "beachhead of solidarity" wherein old Maine residents of Francophone backgrounds find commonality with new immigrants from Central Africa or unemployed white workers find employment in dressmaking for Somali women, recent immigrants to the state. She made "five discoveries": by the 20s old-style zero-sum, racist policies reached their zenith in destroying public goods, and (1) we had no choice then but to seek a "solidarity dividend" which meant (2) refilling the "pool of public goods," but in doing so, we should (3) never assume a one-size-fits-all approach (recall our variegated state) even as we reach for universal goods, further (4) we must revalorize the idea that "we truly do need each other," and finally, (5) its time to "move forward with a new story, together" – I hope that you heard my exclamation mark after "together!"

If prior to talking about McGhee, I identified key elements of the Slender Path including multiscalar organizing, a variegated state, participation, and commanding heights – I must add two more in view of her theses, ones already alluded, negotiating universal goods and weaving together a narrative of togetherness without dissolving our particularities.

Now McGhee was but one of many people sounding these themes in diverse places and rallying people – a thread or strand of the incipient Front for Survival constructing and propelling the Slender Path forward. There were others who stood among the many like the members of Progressive International, the Congressional Progressive Caucus in the United States, the lightning rod that was known back then as "The Squad" and so on. Two who immediately come to mind are the Swedish-born Yale philosopher Martin Hägglund and Berkeley legal scholar Ian Haney Lopez. Hägglund, informed by decades of social democracy and the ensuing neoliberal turn took a journey through Hegel and Marx to understand the totality of human experiment over time before landing in the universal class politics of Dr. Martin Luther King, Jr., and the latter's sense of a "beloved community," Some completely consistent with McGhee's "new story, together!"

Ian Haney Lopez also moved from a political orientation that valued the concerns of oppressed identities to one which sought unity in the universal and shared class interests while still naming the various identities to be united. That is, Lopez, like McGhee, recognized that we get to the universal by working through the particulars and our identities.

Writing in the Marxist tradition of that time, the political scientist Victor Wallis also acknowledged the specific struggles and traditions of oppressed genders and races but nonetheless found strategic value in class as a basis for building alliances and fronts to transcend the capitalist-fueled extinction threats. Another example, one less well-known in the United States but also of global significance, was that offered by the Indian architect and social movement commentator, Jai Sen. His "Movements of Movements" initiative, bearing great resemblance to anarchistic projects, assembled a fantastic diversity of social movements to bring each into dialogue with both some and all other movements. It started from the premise that a space needed to be constructed, an open-space, if you will, that consciously builds these dialogues. The common thread here, is that in face of the threats, early 21st-century activist thinkers were thinking big – not assuming but building – a consciousness of humanity as a whole – without smuggling the interests of the capitalists into a definition of that consciousness.

KM: *So, you've shown us that there were ingredients for a Front for Survival to plot a Slender Path forward, and that activist thinkers understood the universal challenges facing humanity and aspired to universal solutions but that they were aware that they had to work through difference and find/negotiate the universal …*

MM: Yes, this parallel intellectual movement was by no means confined to activist intellectuals. However, starting with one of them, historian Peter Linebaugh, who takes a long view, one predating capitalist, one grounded in resistance to privatization of common goods, he also valued both the universal "commons," warning that "The commons is invisible until it is lost." But he also promised against the enclosures that "There's a hole in every wall and thus a commons behind every enclosure." And corresponding to this sense of a hole, an opportunity, a place to gain purchase for resistance, a space for a Front for Survival, was a whole movement in the arts, in science and speculative fiction for example that opened up spaces for hope. Instead of dying for capitalism, they imagined new alternatives for us without ever underestimating the challenges we faced then and face now albeit with more grounded hope. One fiction writer, celebrated by Barack Obama, Kim Stanley Robinson captured the mood of the early 21st century when he wrote that "[M]ore and more our daily reality and our recent history resembles science fiction, it becomes more true that the genre formerly known as near future science fiction is now simply realism itself, and as such the best description of the felt reality of our daily lives ...." In the spirit of that realism another pioneering writer, Octavia Butler observed, "The world is full of painful stories. Sometimes it seems as though there aren't any other kind and yet I found myself thinking how beautiful that glint of water was through the trees." That's my last bite at the apple defining the Slender Path, it's the "glint of water" through the trees! I should add, in the spirit of public goods, that Octavia Butler found shelter, inspiration, and space to become a writer in the nooks and crannies of her local public library – for her, the state was not necessarily remote, impersonal, and oppressive, in fact, it could be quite the contrary, an entire intimate space albeit a public one and home in her own community.

KM: *Let me riff on our long conversation! I have learned a great deal from what you have said. Certainly, I am inspired by how the abolitionists challenged and defeated the capitalism of their times even if it yielded to a different form of capitalism following the defeat of Reconstruction. I also understand now that many organizations and individuals came to be part of the Front for Survival. Unlike earlier United Fronts focused on national states, the Front for Survival had to be at once local, regional and global. Individuals and organizations carrying out networking functions across parties, institutions and borders were at the core of the Front. The ideas and strategies that united the Front, also known as the "Slender Path," included multiscalar organizing for public goods in a variegated multi-level and highly diverse state. In thinking about public goods, the old socialist and Labour ideas of economic commanding heights and the commons were strategically important and intimately related to a sense of the universal. But, the universal could not be an abstract distillation of many particular needs and demands, it had to be negotiated within the Front and between the Front and other parts of society.*

This process of negotiation was the active and conscious work of organizers who could be found throughout society.

All of this leaves me with a final question, one that could require a huge amount of time but one that I trust you'll be able answer quickly.

MM: Yes?

KM: *I noticed that you spoke about pandemics and about climate and about public goods. You also spoke about international cooperation. But surely war making and international rivalry – both threatening to escalate into immediate extinction – were important topics for the Front for Survival.*

MM: I probably repressed that topic given that international rivalries, largely driven by huge capitalist investment in war-making capacities, were a critical and frustrating dimension of our work. The short answer is that those of us who emphasized climate issues worked hard to demonstrate the international cooperation was central to the Slender Path. We were assisted in this by the fact that climate-, disease-, and war-related mass migrations underscored the need for deeper cooperation, rendered the international local, and allowed for more people-to-people peace building – again requiring the constant attention of active peace makers within the working class. I should add that as the costs of the various climate, health and war dislocations increased everywhere – in both imperial countries and those of the Global South – neoliberal foibles about limited state intervention in the economy went out the window! With the rich countries that grew while spewing carbon reneging on their Loss & Damage commitments to the Global South, it became clear that the countries of the South had to energize their states to provide public goods – and given the scarcity of resources, popular mobilizations had to be evolved to directly provide necessities and build solidarity. Of course, it was a messy process but models emerged here and there and the Front managed to share and globalize the success stories.

KM: *Thank you, Maxi!*

Notes

Introduction

1 George Monbiot, "The Earth Is in a Death Spiral. It Will Take Radical Action to Save Us," *The Guardian*, November 14, 2018, https://www.theguardian.com/commentisfree/2018/nov/14/earth-death-spiral-radical-action-climate-breakdown.

2 Ellie Silverman, "Indigenous Activists Come to D.C. with a Message for Biden: Declare a National Climate Emergency," *Washington Post*, October 11, 2021, https://www.washingtonpost.com/dc-md-va/2021/10/11/indigenous-protest-dc-climate-change/.

3 Edward Helmore, "Tornadoes in Mayfield, Kentucky Caused Profound Losses: 'Some Are Never Going Back to Their Homes'," *The Guardian*, December 26, 2021, sec. US news, https://www.theguardian.com/us-news/2021/dec/26/tornadoes-mayfield-kentucky-caused-profound-losses.

4 Peter Prengaman, "Ghanaian Girl Cuts through Jargon, Tells COP27 Delegates to 'Have a Heart,'" Stuff, November 18, 2022, https://www.stuff.co.nz/environment/climate-news/300743427/ghanaian-girl-cuts-through-jargon-tells-cop27-delegates-to-have-a-heart.

5 "Earth Strike International," Earth Strike, accessed January 23, 2022, https://earth-strike.com/.

6 For a summary of the Act's climate benefits, see Candace Vahlsing, "New OMB Analysis: The Inflation Reduction Act Will Significantly Cut the Social Costs of Climate Change | OMB," August 23, 2022, https://www.whitehouse.gov/omb/briefing-room/2022/08/23/new-omb-analysis-the-inflation-reduction-act-will-significantly-cut-the-social-costs-of-climate-change/. While the Sunrise Movement helped create the ongoing momentum toward climate and labor friendly elements of federal legislation, it was altogether more sober about the IRA; see Sunrise Movement 📷[@sunrisemvmt], "The Inflation Reduction Act Is Not the Green New Deal. It Should Be Bigger. It Should Invest in Frontline Communities. It Should Not Include Fossil Fuels. But Time Is Running out for Dems to Take Action. If They Don't Pass It Now, It May Be Years before They Get Another Chance," Tweet, Twitter, August 7, 2022, https://twitter.com/sunrisemvmt/status/1556363966452056064.

7 Aylin Woodward, "Climate Change Is Causing Birthstrikers to Refuse to Have Children," *Business Insider*, March 23, 2019, https://www.businessinsider.com/climate-change-birthstrikers-refuse-children-2019-3.

8   Woodward, "Alexandria Ocasio-Cortez."

9   Julian Borger, "Doomsday Clock Stays at Two Minutes to Midnight as Crisis Now 'New Abnormal,'" *The Guardian*, January 24, 2019, sec. World news, https://www.theguardian.com/world/2019/jan/24/doomsday-clock-2019-two-minutes-midnight-nuclear-war-new-abnormal.

10 "Are We Still 30 Years Away from Fusion Energy? Some Think the Timeline's Shrinking," Marketplace (NPR, December 23, 2022), https://www.marketplace.org/2022/12/22/are-we-still-30-years-away-from-fusion-energy-some-think-the-timelines-shrinking/.
    The presenter of this piece suggests that it will take about 15 years for fusion energy to come online. Even if this optimistic projection were to come to pass, it would take decades to roll out the systems and replace current fossil-fuel infrastructure.

11 Stacie L. Pettyjohn and Becca Wasser, "A Fight Over Taiwan Could Go Nuclear," *Foreign Affairs*, July 13, 2022, https://www.foreignaffairs.com/articles/china/2022-05-20/fight-over-taiwan-could-go-nuclear.

12 Since his early work on risk, Bostrom's work has evolved to focus technological threats sometimes at the expense of the kinds of structural threats that preoccupy the present writers. From our point of view, the value of Bostrom's early thinking is that it helps organize our thinking about extinction into firmly scientific terms. As one of Bostrom's more recent critics notes, "The 'eschatological' scenarios now being discussed are based not on the revelations of religious prophets, or secular metanarratives of human history (as in the case of Marxism), but on robust scientific conclusions defended by leading experts in fields such as climatology, ecology, epidemiology and so on." See Emile P. Torres, "Why Longtermism Is the World's Most Dangerous Secular Credo," Aeon, October 19, 2021, https://aeon.co/essays/why-longtermism-is-the-worlds-most-dangerous-secular-credo. Of course, most recent scholarship concerning the alleged Marxist historical metanarrative reveals the tenuous textual grounds upon with claims to a Marxist teleology of history rest. See especially, Marcello Musto, *The Last Years of Karl Marx, 1881–1883: An Intellectual Biography*, trans. Patrick Camiller (Stanford, California: Stanford University Press, 2020).

13 Nick Bostrom, "Existential Risks: Analyzing Human Extinction Scenarios and Related Hazards," *Journal of Evolution and Technology* 9 (March 5, 2002), https://jetpress.org/volume9/risks.html.

14 Bostrom, "Existential Risks," 2–3.

15 Bostrom, "Existential Risks," 6–7.

16 Bostrom, "Existential Risks," 9.

17 Although Bostrom's most recent thinking on existential threats focuses on the dangers of artificial intelligence, he continues to consider climate change to be among the most serious threats facing humanity. That said, he believes that "risk awareness" is growing, and somewhat optimistically notes that with "advances in knowledge, methods, and attitudes, the conditions for securing for existential risks the scrutiny they deserve are unprecedentedly propitious." See Nick Bostrom, "Existential Risk Prevention as Global Priority: Existential Risk Prevention as Global Priority," *Global Policy* 4, no. 1 (February 2013): 15–31, https://doi.org/10.1111/1758-5899.12002.

18 Bostrom, "Existential Risks," 10.

19 Bostrom, "Existential Risks," 12. In addition to the Orwell classic, any number of a series of contemporary dystopian fiction speaks to the elided "posthumanity" defining the Shriek. Netflix's very popular *Tribes of Europa* (German) and *Barrier* (Spanish) TV-series format shows are perfect exemplars of the Shriek. Science fiction-writer Kim Stanley Robinson's best-selling novel *The Ministry for the Future*,

praised by former President Obama and which we take up in the concluding chapter, verges on but optimistically pulls back from the Shriek scenario.

20 Bostrom, "Existential Risks," 13.

21 In a sense, we write in the same spirit that animates Indian novelist and social theorist, Amitav Ghosh, when he writes of his hope that out of the anti-extinction struggles, "will be born a generation that will be able to look upon the world with clearer eyes than those that preceded it; that they will be able to transcend the isolation in which humanity was entrapped in the time of its derangement; that they will rediscover their kinship with other beings, and that this vision, at once new and ancient, will find expression in a transformed and renewed art and literature." Amitav Ghosh, *The Great Derangement: Climate Change and the Unthinkable* (Chicago, IL: The University of Chicago Press, 2017), 162.

22 Noam Chomsky, *Internationalism or Extinction*, ed. Charles Derber, Suren Moodliar, and Paul Shannon, Universalizing Resistance (New York, NY: Routledge, 2020), 22.

23 Aaron Blake, "Trump's Loose Talk on Nuclear Weapons Suddenly Becomes Very Real," *Washington Post*, October 11, 2017, https://www.washingtonpost.com/news/the-fix/wp/2017/10/11/trumps-loose-rhetoric-on-nuclear-weapons-has-become-a-very-real-concern/.

24 Coral Davenport, "With Trump in Charge, Climate Change References Purged from Website," *New York Times*, January 20, 2017, https://www.nytimes.com/2017/01/20/us/politics/trump-white-house-website.html.

25 "Yale Climate Opinion Maps 2020," Yale Program on Climate Change Communication, accessed January 17, 2022, https://climatecommunication.yale.edu/visualizations-data/ycom-us/.

26 Ed Miliband, "Our Biggest Enemy Is No Longer Climate Denial but Climate Delay," *The Guardian*, July 30, 2021, sec. Opinion, https://www.theguardian.com/commentisfree/2021/jul/30/climate-denial-delay-inaction-british-government.

27 Monbiot, "The Earth."

28 Monbiot, "The Earth."

29 Greta Thunberg (quotes from Thunberg) cited on Wikipedia. Greta Thunberg, Wikipedia.

30 Naomi Klein, *This Changes Everything: Capitalism vs. the Climate* (New York, NY: Simon & Schuster, 2014).

31 Jacob Weisberg, "Ronald Reagan's Disarmament Dream," *The Atlantic*, January 1, 2016, https://www.theatlantic.com/politics/archive/2016/01/ronald-reagans-disarmament-dream/422244/.

32 Weisberg, "Ronald Reagan."

33 Yale Magrass and Charles Derber, *Glorious Causes* (New York, NY: Routledge, 2020).

34 Lawrence Goodwyn, *Democratic Promise: The Populist Moment in America* (Oxford, UK: Oxford University Press, 1976).

35 The Martin Luther King, Jr. Center for Nonviolent Social Change, The Three Evils of Society, 2015, https://www.youtube.com/watch?v=6sT9Hjh0cHM.] Though coming toward the end of King's criminally abbreviated life, this statement is consistent with his earliest expressed beliefs on capitalism. In 1951, for example, he recorded the following note: "I am convinced that capitalism has seen its best days in American, and not only in America, but in the entire world. It is a well-known fact that no social institution can survive when it has outlived its usefulness. This, capitalism has done. It has failed to meet the needs of the masses." Martin Luther King, Jr., "Notes on American Capitalism," The Martin Luther King, Jr., Research and Education Institute, January 28, 2015, https://kinginstitute.stanford.edu/king-papers/documents/notes-american-capitalism.

1 The Extinction Triangle

1 Nick Bostrom, "Existential Risks: Analyzing Human Extinction Scenarios and Related Hazards," *Journal of Evolution and Technology* 9 (March 5, 2002), https://jetpress.org/volume9/risks.html.
2 Naomi Klein, "Capitalism Killed Our Climate Momentum, Not 'Human Nature,'" *The Intercept* (blog), August 3, 2018, https://theintercept.com/2018/08/03/climate-change-new-york-times-magazine/.
3 George Monbiot, "Crisis? What Crisis?," George Monbiot, February 19, 2019, https://www.monbiot.com/2019/02/15/crisis-what-crisis/.
4 Noam Chomsky, *Internationalism or Extinction*, eds. Charles Derber, Suren Moodliar, and Paul Shannon, Universalizing Resistance (New York, NY: Routledge, 2020).
5 Carbon Brief, for example, lists nine Tipping Points pertaining to climate change that "could push parts of the Earth system into abrupt or irreversible change": Greenland ice sheet disintegration; permafrost loss; Atlantic meridional overturning circulation breakdown; Boreal forest shift; Amazon rainforest dieback; West Antarctic ice sheet disintegration; West African monsoon shift; Indian monsoon shift; coral reef die-off. "Explainer: Nine 'Tipping Points' That Could Be Triggered by Climate Change," Carbon Brief, February 10, 2020, https://www.carbonbrief.org/explainer-nine-tipping-points-that-could-be-triggered-by-climate-change.
   The Stockholm Resilience Center identifies several "planetary boundaries" that pose serious existential risks on their own. These include stratospheric ozone depletion, biodiversity loss and extinctions, release of novel entities (including chemical pollution), climate change, ocean acidification, freshwater consumption and the global hydrological cycle, land system change, biochemical (primarily nitrogen and phosphorus) flows into the biosphere and oceans, and atmospheric aerosol loading. For three of these no safe boundary has been established, two are in the high risk zone, another three are in the "increasing risk" zone, only two, freshwater use and stratospheric ozone, are in the safe zone for now. See Will Steffen et al., "Planetary Boundaries: Guiding Human Development on a Changing Planet," *Science* 347, no. 6223 (February 13, 2015): 1259855, https://doi.org/10.1126/science.1259855.
6 A. P. J. Mol, David Allan Sonnenfeld, and Gert Spaargaren, eds., *The Ecological Modernisation Reader: Environmental Reform in Theory and Practice* (London, UK and New York, NY: Routledge, 2009).
7 William A. Schwartz and Charles Derber, *Nuclear Seduction: Why the Arms Race Doesn't Matter – and What Does* (Oakland, CA: University of California Press, 2021).
8 Charles Derber, *Welcome to the Revolution: Universalizing Resistance for Social Justice and Democracy in Perilous Times* (New York, NY: Routledge, 2017).
9 Derber, *Welcome*.

2 Is Capitalism Too Hot?

1 Fiona Harvey, "Humanity Is Waging War on Nature, Says UN Secretary General," *The Guardian*, December 2, 2020, sec. Environment, https://www.theguardian.com/environment/2020/dec/02/humanity-is-waging-war-on-nature-says-un-secretary-general-antonio-guterres.
2 Roy Scranton, "I've Said Goodbye to 'Normal.' You Should, Too," *The New York Times*, January 25, 2021, sec. Opinion, https://www.nytimes.com/2021/01/25/opinion/new-normal-climate-catastrophes.html.

3 Sarah Kaplan and Andrew Ba Tran, "More Than 40 Percent of Americans Live in Counties Hit by Climate Disasters in 2021," *Washington Post*, January 5, 2022, sec. Climate & Environment, https://www.washingtonpost.com/climate-environment/2022/01/05/climate-disasters-2021-fires/.

4 Andreas Malm, *Fossil Capital: The Rise of Steam Power and the Roots of Global Warming* (London, UK and New York, NY: Verso, 2016).

5 Malm, *Fossil Capital*.

6 Malm, *Fossil Capital*.

7 Malm, *Fossil Capital*.

8 Bruce Podobnik, *Global Energy Shifts: Fostering Sustainability in a Turbulent Age* (Philadelphia, PA: Temple University Press, 2008), http://www.SLQ.eblib.com.au/patron/FullRecord.aspx?p=496402, 69.

9 David S. Painter, "Oil and World Power," *Diplomatic History* 17, no. 1 (January 1993): 159–170, https://doi.org/10.1111/j.1467-7709.1993.tb00167.x.

10 Podobnik, *Global Energy Shifts*, 88.

11 Harry Braverman, *Labor and Monopoly Capital: The Degradation of Work in the Twentieth Century*, 25th anniversary ed. (New York, NY: Monthly Review Press, 1998).

12 Braverman, *Labor and Monopoly Capitalism*.

13 Stuart Ewen, *Captains of Consciousness: Advertising and the Social Roots of the Consumer Culture*, 25. anniversary ed. (New York, NY: Basic Books, 2001).

     See also Stuart Ewen and Elizabeth Ewen, *Channels of Desire: Mass Images and the Shaping of American Consciousness*, 2nd ed. (Minneapolis, MN: University of Minnesota Press, 1992).

14 Painter, "Oil and World Power."

15 Andres Barreda, "Oil as a Blind Spot in the Rearview Mirror of the Russian Revolution" (2017).

16 Barreda, "Oil."

17 Barreda, "Oil."

18 Timothy Mitchell, *Carbon Democracy: Political Power in the Age of Oil* (London, UK: Verso, 2013). Cited by Matt Stoller, "How Coal Brought Us Democracy, and Oil Ended It: Lessons from the New Book 'Carbon Democracy,'" *Naked Capitalism* (blog), September 13, 2012, https://www.nakedcapitalism.com/2012/09/how-coal-brought-us-democracy-and-oil-ended-it-lessons-from-the-new-book-carbon-democracy.html.

19 Podobnik, *Global Energy Shifts*, 88.

20 Cited in Podobnik, *Global Energy Shifts*, 88.

21 Drew Hansen, "Unless It Changes, Capitalism Will Starve Humanity By 2050," *Forbes*, February 9, 2016, https://www.forbes.com/sites/drewhansen/2016/02/09/unless-it-changes-capitalism-will-starve-humanity-by-2050/.

22 Justin Farrell, cited in Hansen, "Unless It Changes."

23 Hansen, "Unless It Changes."

24 Ayn Rand, *The Virtue of Selfishness: A New Concept of Egoism*, Centennial ed., A Signet Book (New York, NY: Signet, [1964] 2005).

25 Rand, *The Virtue*.

26 Garrett Hardin, "The Tragedy of the Commons," *Science* 162, no. 3859 (1968): 1243–1248. Of course, notwithstanding Hardin's broad reception, he was confusing a "free-for-all" with the commons. In non-capitalist societies, where "resources" including land are shared or held in common, norms and other means of regulation emerge as communities come to steward the resources upon which their livelihoods matter. It is only in the context of a broader society organized for private profit that individuals have an incentive to exploit public goods for their exclusive benefit.

27 Naomi Klein, *This Changes Everything: Capitalism vs. the Climate* (New York, NY: Simon & Schuster, 2014), 72.

28 It bears reiterating that for Marx, the fetishism whereby individuals come to see commodities have powers of their own, going well beyond their use, is at once a social *and* psychological process grounded in the historical emergence of private property as the means by which all humanity is forced to win or access their livelihood.

29 Juliet Schor, *Born to Buy: The Commercialized Child and the New Consumer Culture* (New York, NY: Scribner, 2004).

30 Chirag Dhara and Vandana Singh, "The Delusion of Infinite Economic Growth," *Scientific American*, June 20, 2021, https://www.scientificamerican.com/article/the-delusion-of-infinite-economic growth1/.

31 Dhara and Singh, "The Delusion."

32 Dhara and Singh, "The Delusion."

33 Frances Moore Lappé, *EcoMind: Changing the Way We Think, to Create the World We Want* (New York, NY: Nation Books, 2013).

34 Dhara and Singh, "The Delusion."

35 Cited in Charles Derber, *Greed to Green: Solving Climate Change and Remaking the Economy* (Boulder, CO: Paradigm Publishers, 2010).

36 Optimistically, the commentator believes that stricter scrutiny may limit greenwashing as consumers, regulators and even shareholders demand greater transparency. See Beau River, "The Increasing Dangers of Corporate Greenwashing in the Era of Sustainability," *Forbes*, April 29, 2021, https://www.forbes.com/sites/beauriver/2021/04/29/the-increasing-dangers-of-corporate-greenwashing-in-the-era-of-sustainability/.

3 Plague for Profit

1 African American scholars and activists have long presented a perspective on the systemic character of racism and resulting role for policing. One recent work in particular seems to capture the activist and social change energy of the movements that emerged following the murder of George Floyd during the pandemic's first summer, see Mariame Kaba, *We Do This 'til We Free Us: Abolitionist Organizing and Transforming Justice*, Abolitionist Papers (Chicago, IL: Haymarket Books, 2021).

For a fuller picture of recent police violence and race, see "Fatal Police Violence by Race and State in the USA, 1980–2019: A Network Meta-Regression," *The Lancet* 398, no. 10307 (October 2, 2021): 1239–1255, https://doi.org/10.1016/S0140-6736(21)01609-3. On the structural role of policing see Alex S. Vitale, *The End of Policing* (London, UK and New York, NY: Verso, 2017).

2 Nicholas LePan, "Visualizing the History of Pandemics," Visual Capitalist, March 14, 2020, https://www.visualcapitalist.com/history-of-pandemics-deadliest/.

3 Allysia Finley, "Capitalism Is What Will Defeat Covid," *Wall Street Journal*, March 19, 2021, https://www.wsj.com/articles/capitalism-is-what-will-defeat-covid-11616192690.

4 Lepan, "Visualizing." Note: Many of the death toll numbers listed in the table are best estimates based on available research. Some, such as the Plague of Justinian and Swine Flu, are subject to debate based on new evidence.

5 Lepan's table has been updated for this total. It reflects the global toll as of February 9, 2022. "WHO Coronavirus (COVID-19) Dashboard," World Health Organization, accessed February 9, 2022, https://covid19.who.int.

6   Frederick Engels, *The Condition of the Working Class in England* (1845), https://
www.marxists.org/archive/marx/works/1845/condition-working-class/
Echoing Dickens and also using Manchester as a starting point, Engels describes the
appalling over-crowding, poor sanitation, and air pollution afflicting working-class
neighborhoods. The 24-year-old Engels then asks in his first book:

> How is it possible, under such conditions, for the lower class to be
> healthy and long lived? What else can be expected than an excessive
> mortality, an unbroken series of epidemics, a progressive deterioration
> in the physique of the working population? Let us see how the facts
> stand.
>
> That the dwellings of the workers in the worst portions of the cit-
> ies, together with the other conditions of life of this class, engender
> numerous diseases, is attested on all sides. … [L]ung diseases must be
> the inevitable consequence of such conditions, and that, indeed, cases
> of this kind are disproportionately frequent in this class. That the bad
> air of London, and especially of the working-people's districts, is in
> the highest degree favourable to the development of consumption, the
> hectic appearance of great numbers of persons sufficiently indicates.
> If one roams the streets a little in the early morning, when the multi-
> tudes are on their way to their work, one is amazed at the number of
> persons who look wholly or half-consumptive. Even in Manchester
> the people have not the same appearance; these pale, lank, narrow-
> chested, hollow-eyed ghosts, whom one passes at every step, these
> languid, flabby faces, incapable of the slightest energetic expression,
> I have seen in such startling numbers only in London, though con-
> sumption carries off a horde of victims annually in the factory towns
> of the North. [Engels, "The Condition," "Results."]

7   "Public Health in the Industrial Revolution," Schoolshistory.org.uk, accessed
February 9, 2022, https://schoolshistory.org.uk/topics/medicine-through-time/
public-health-in-the-industrial-revolution/.
8   "Public Health."
9   Kyle Harper, *Plagues upon the Earth: Disease and the Course of Human History*, The
Princeton Economic History of the Western World 46 (Princeton, NJ: Princeton
University Press, 2021), 23.
10   Charles Derber and June Sekera, "An Invisible Crisis," *Boston Globe*, January 22,
2014, sec. Opinion, https://www.bostonglobe.com/opinion/2014/01/22/the-
hidden-deficit/LMvPwkE9tPmOQcezlCTFjM/story.html.
11   Derber and Sekera, "Invisible."
12   Derber and Sekera, "Invisible."
13   Writing about the main vector of the plague, one scholar notes, "the diffusion of
the rat across Europe looks increasingly like an integral part of the Roman conquest." Quoted in Harper, "Plagues," 17.
14   CosmoLearning, "Topic: Pandemics | CosmoLearning Medicine," CosmoLearn-
ing, accessed February 20, 2022, https://cosmolearning.org/topics/pandemics/.

15 Mike Davis, *Late Victorian Holocausts: El Niño Famines and the Making of the Third World* (London, UK and New York, NY: Verso, 2017), 17–18.

16 Davis, *Holocausts*, 18. In many ways, these epidemics resembled those visited upon the indigenous peoples of the Americas by Columbus and his followers four centuries earlier. Of Portuguese expansion into Africa, Davis write, "with the emergence of drought-and-famine-related epidemics of smallpox, malaria, dysentery and sand jiggers, colonial troops made unprecedented headway against weakened populations …. He goes on to quote one observer who relates disease to the relative ease of conquest: "The debilitating effects of hunger and disease in the decade of the 1870s may go far towards explaining why the social and political tensions generated by the spread of white plantations did not explode in revolt within the Portuguese enclave" (Davis, *Holocausts*, 148).

17 Charles Derber and Yale R Magrass, *Moving beyond Fear: Upending the Security Tales in Capitalism, Fascism, and Democracy* (London, UK and New York, NY: Routledge, 2019).

18 Derber and Magrass, *Moving*, 4–5.

19 Derber and Magrass, *Moving*, 5.

20 Derber and Magrass, *Moving*, 7.

21 Rob Wallace et al., "COVID-19 and Circuits of Capital," *Monthly Review*, May 1, 2020, https://monthlyreview.org/2020/05/01/covid-19-and-circuits-of-capital/.

22 Ron Klain, Ross Anderson, and Nancy Sullivan, *Pandemics and the Existential Threat to Global Security* (Aspen, CO: Aspen Institute, 2017), https://admin.aspenideasfestival.production.a17.io/sessions/pandemics-and-the-existential-threat-to-global-security.

23 Klain, Anderson, and Sullivan, *Pandemics*.

24 Robin McKie, "Rampant Destruction of Forests 'Will Unleash More Pandemics,'" *The Guardian*, August 30, 2020, sec. Environment, https://www.theguardian.com/environment/2020/aug/30/rampant-destruction-of-forests-will-unleash-more-pandemics.

25 McKie, "Rampant Destruction."

26 McKie, "Rampant Destruction."

27 Wallace et al., "COVID-19."

28 Wallace et al., "COVID-19."

29 John Bellamy Foster and Intan Suwandi, "COVID-19 and Catastrophe Capitalism," *Monthly Review* (blog), June 1, 2020, https://monthlyreview.org/2020/06/01/covid-19-and-catastrophe-capitalism/.

30 Quoted in Foster and Suwandi, "Catastrophe Capitalism."

31 Nabil Ahmed et al., "Inequality Kills: The Unparalleled Action Needed to Combat Unprecedented Inequality in the Wake of COVID-19" (Oxfam, January 17, 2022), https://doi.org/10.21201/2022.8465.

32 Max Fisher and Emma Bubola, "As Coronavirus Deepens Inequality, Inequality Worsens Its Spread," *The New York Times*, March 15, 2020, sec. World, https://www.nytimes.com/2020/03/15/world/europe/coronavirus-inequality.html.

33 Foster and Suwandi, "Catastrophe Capitalism."

4 Bloody Money

1 Daniel Ellsberg, *The Doomsday Machine: Confessions of a Nuclear War Planner* (New York, NY: Bloomsbury, 2017), 20.

2 Ellsberg, *Doomsday*.

3 Stephen Cohen, *War with Russia: From Putin and Ukraine to Trump and Russiagate* (New York, NY: Hot Books, 2019).

4 Charles Derber and Yale Magrass, *Moving Beyond Fear: Upending Security Tales in Capitalism*, Fascism and Democracy (New York, NY: Routledge, 2018).

5 Noam Chomsky, *Internationalism or Extinction*, ed. Charles Derber, Suren Moodliar, and Paul Shannon, Universalizing Resistance (New York, NY: Routledge, 2020).

6 Much of this volatility finds its origins in European imperialism and the borders of empire cut across peoples and nations bring with them the inevitable territorial disputes. These disputes in turn are perpetuated and often exacerbated by Cold War and New Cold War rivalries. See Amy Hawkins, "The World Is Reaping the Chaos the British Empire Sowed," *Foreign Policy* (blog), accessed February 23, 2022, https://foreignpolicy.com/2019/08/13/the-world-is-reaping-the-chaos-the-british-empire-sowed/. And, Stelios Michalopoulos and Elias Papaioannou, "The Long-Run Effects of the Scramble for Africa," *American Economic Review* 106, no. 7 (July 1, 2016): 1802–1848, https://doi.org/10.1257/aer.20131311. For more comprehensive view, see Richard Gott, *Britain's Empire: Resistance, Repression and Revolt* (London, UK and New York, NY: Verso Books, 2011).

7 William A. Schwartz and Charles Derber, *Nuclear Seduction: Why the Arms Race Doesn't Matter – and What Does* (Oakland, CA: University of California Press, 1990), http://ark.cdlib.org/ark:/13030/ft1n39n7wg/.

8 "India Moves from Occupation to Annexation in Occupied Kashmir: FO," *Dunya News*, August 6, 2019, https://dunyanews.tv/en/Pakistan/503947-India-moves-occupation-annexation-occupied-Kashmir-FO-.

9 Owen B. Toon et al., "Rapidly Expanding Nuclear Arsenals in Pakistan and India Portend Regional and Global Catastrophe," *Science Advances* 5, no. 10 (October 4, 2019): eaay5478, https://doi.org/10.1126/sciadv.aay5478.

10 William and Schwartz and Charles Derber, *The Nuclear Seduction: Why the Arms Race Doesn't Matter Now – and What Does*. Berkeley, CA: University of California Press, 1988.

11 Carl Sagan cited in Matthew R. Francis, "When Carl Sagan Warned the World about Nuclear Winter," *Smithsonian Magazine*, November 15, 2017, https://www.smithsonianmag.com/science-nature/when-carl-sagan-warned-world-about-nuclear-winter-180967198/.

12 Yale Magrass and Charles Derber, *Glorious Causes: Irrationality in Capitalism*, War and Politics (New York, NY: Routledge, 2020).

13 Schwartz and Derber, Nuclear Seduction.

14 D. W. MacKenzie, "Does Capitalism Require War?" Text, Mises Institute, April 7, 2003, https://mises.org/library/does-capitalism-require-war.

15 Thomas L. Friedman, *The Lexus and the Olive Tree: Understanding Globalization*, First Picador edition (New York, NY: Picador, 2012), 30.

16 MacKenzie, "Capitalism."

17 Immanuel Maurice Wallerstein, *World-Systems Analysis: An Introduction*, (Durham, NC: Duke University Press, 2004).

18 The classic chronicler of this history is Noam Chomsky, see *The Essential Chomsky*, ed. Anthony Arnove (London, UK: Bodley Head, 2008).

19 Noam Chomsky, *Hegemony or Survival? America's Quest for Global Dominance* (London, UK: Penguin, 2004). See also Noam Chomsky, *Who Rules the World?*, First U.S. edition (New York, NY: Metropolitan Books, Henry Holt and Company, 2016).

20 Wallerstein, *World Systems*. See also Giovanni Arrighi and Beverly J. Silver, *Chaos and Governance in the Modern World System*, Contradictions of Modernity 10 (Minneapolis, MN: University of Minnesota Press, 1999). Harry Magdoff, *Imperialism:*

From the Colonial Age to the Present: Essays (New York, NY: Monthly Review Press, 1978).

21 Chomsky, *The Essential Chomsky.*

22 Arrighi and Silver, *Chaos and Governance*, 32.

23 Graham Allison, "The Thucydides Trap: Are the U.S. and China Headed for War?," The Atlantic, September 24, 2015, https://www.theatlantic.com/international/archive/2015/09/united-states-china-war-thucydides-trap/406756/.

24 Graham T. Allison, *Destined for War: Can America and China Escape Thucydides's Trap?* First Mariner Books edition 2018 (Boston, MA and New York, NY: Houghton Mifflin Harcourt, Mariner Books, 2018).

25 As we will explain in the final chapter, social movements from below and dramatic political campaigns like Upton Sinclair's End Poverty in California, helped shape Roosevelt's response and Keynesian turn.

26 Charles Derber and Yale Magrass, *Capitalism: Should You Buy It?* (New York, NY: Routledge, 2014).

27 Jonathan Nitzan, "Military Keynesianism and the Military-Industrial Complex," Real-World Economics Review Blog (blog), December 27, 2016, https://rwer.wordpress.com/2016/12/27/military-keynesianism-and-the-military-industrial-complex/.

28 Antonio Gramsci, *Prison Notebooks*, ed. Joseph A. Buttigieg, 3 vols., European Perspectives (New York, NY: Columbia University Press, 2011), 20.

29 Derber and Magrass *Beyond Fear.*

30 Derber and Magrass *Beyond Fear*, Chapter 1.

31 Magrass and Derber, *Glorious Causes.*

32 Magrass and Derber, *Glorious Causes*, Chapter 5.

33 Roxanne Roberts, "Hillary Clinton's 'Deplorables' Speech Shocked Voters Five Years Ago—but Some Feel It Was Prescient," *Washington Post*, August 31, 2021, https://www.washingtonpost.com/lifestyle/2021/08/31/deplorables-basket-hillary-clinton/.

34 This is perhaps best exemplified by his failed attempt to organize a massive Independence Day parade. See David Smith, "'A Narcissistic Travesty': Critics Savage Trump's Independence Day Jamboree," The Guardian, July 3, 2019, sec. US news, https://www.theguardian.com/us-news/2019/jul/03/donald-trump-fourth-of-july-parade-speech-independence-day.

35 Magrass and Derber, *Glorious Causes.* Introduction and Chapter 1.

36 Karl Marx and Frederick Engels, *Manifesto of the Communist Party*, 1848, https://www.marxists.org/archive/marx/works/1848/communist-manifesto/.

5 America's "Extinction Exceptionalism"

1 Richard Laycock and Catherine Choi, "Doomsday Preppers: How Many Are Preparing for the End?" *Finder*, February 18, 2021, https://www.finder.com/doomsday-prepper-statistics.

2 Noam Chomsky, *Internationalism or Extinction*, ed. Charles Derber, Suren Moodliar, and Paul Shannon, Universalizing Resistance (New York, NY: Routledge, 2020).

3 Chomsky, *Internationalism.*

4 Charles Derber, *Sociopathic Society* (New York, NY: Routledge, 2017).

5 Jeremy Rifkin, The European Dream: How Europe's Vision of the Future Is Quietly Eclipsing the American Dream (New York, NY: Jeremy P. Tarcher/Penguin, 2004).

See also George Lakey, *Viking Economics: How the Scandinavians Got It Right-and How We Can, Too*, 1st edition (Brooklyn, NY: Melville House, 2016).

6 "Off Target: Ranking of EU Countries' Ambition and Progress in Fighting Climate Change" (Brussels: Climate Action Network Europe, June 17, 2018), https:// caneurope.org/content/uploads/2018/06/CAN_Off-target_report_FIN.pdf.

In 2022, Climate Action Network (CAN) Europe, note some progress post COP26, but also expressed concern based on a February 21, 2022, EU Foreign Ministers' declaration on "EU Climate Diplomacy." Sven Harmeling, CAN Europe's International Climate Policy Coordinator, declared that EU aspirations require "that they are followed up with swift, coherent and ambitious action for scaling-up international climate finance, putting an end to finance for fossil fuels, and developing concrete partnerships for phasing down coal use and other fossil fuels."

See "CAN Europe Response: EU Foreign Affairs Minister Council Conclusions on 21 February 2022," *CAN Europe* (blog), February 23, 2022, https://caneurope. org/can-europe-response-fac-conclusions/.

7 "Off Target."
8 Rifkin, *European Dream*; Lakey, *Viking Economics*.
9 Rifkin, European Dream; Lakey, *Viking Economics*.
10 Charles Derber and Yale R. Magrass, *Morality Wars: How Empires, the Born-Again, and the Politically Correct Do Evil in the Name of Good* (London, UK and New York, NY: Routledge, 2016), https://www.taylorfrancis.com/books/e/9781315633398.
11 Avery Hartmans, "The Annual Sun Valley Conference, Known as 'summer Camp for Billionaires,' Will Return in July — and Powerful Moguls like Jeff Bezos and Mark Zuckerberg Are on the Guest List," Business Insider, accessed March 2, 2022, https://www.businessinsider.com/sun-valley-conference-returns-july-2021-after-pandemic-cancelation-2021-6.
12 Lakey, *Viking Economics*.
13 Kim Phillips-Fein, "Countervailing Powers: On John Kenneth Galbraith," *The Nation*, May 11, 2011, https://www.thenation.com/article/archive/countervailing-powers-john-kenneth-galbraith/.
14 Ronald Reagan, "Inaugural Address" (Speech, Inauguration, Washington, DC, January 20, 1981), https://www.reaganfoundation.org/media/128614/inaguration.pdf.
15 Suzanne Mettler, *The Government-Citizen Disconnect* (New York, NY: Russell Sage Foundation, 2018), https://books.google.com/books?id=CzNcDwAAQBAJ.
16 Mettler interviewed in Sean Illing, "Why so Many People Who Need the Government Hate It," *Vox*, August 17, 2018, https://www.vox.com/2018/8/17/17675100/suzanne-mettler-government-citizen-disconnect-welfare.
17 Seth Jacobson, "'No Sea Sickness so Far': Greta Thunberg Update on Atlantic Crossing," *The Observer*, August 17, 2019, sec. Environment, https://www.theguardian.com/environment/2019/aug/17/greta-thunberg-four-days-into-atlantic-crossing.

6 Molecules of Freedom?

1 George Carlin, *America*, 1971, https://genius.com/George-carlin-america-lyrics.
2 Roy Scranton, "I've Said Goodbye to 'Normal.' You Should, Too," *The New York Times*, January 25, 2021, sec. Opinion, https://www.nytimes.com/2021/01/25/opinion/new-normal-climate-catastrophes.html.
3 Noam Chomsky, *Internationalism or Extinction*, ed. Charles Derber, Suren Moodliar, and Paul Shannon, Universalizing Resistance (New York, NY: Routledge, 2020).

4 This is not to deny that proper, sustainable forest management strategies must be implemented. However, the Trump administration, responded to the fires, much as did his Australian counterpart address simultaneous fires in Australia, by taking one truth – the need for land management – to obscure the larger trust, that of catastrophic climate breakdown.

5 Union of Concerned Scientists, "Each Country's Share of CO_2 Emissions," January 14, 2022, https://www.ucsusa.org/resources/each-countrys-share-co2-emissions.

6 Table compiled from: Robbie M. Andrew, "A Comparison of Estimates of Global Carbon Dioxide Emissions from Fossil Carbon Sources," *Earth System Science Data* 12, no. 2 (June 29, 2020): 1437–1465, https://doi.org/10.5194/essd-12-1437-2020.

7 Irfan, "Why the US."

8 James Ellsmoor, "Trump Administration Rebrands Fossil Fuels As 'Molecules of U.S. Freedom,'" *Forbes*, May 30, 2019, https://www.forbes.com/sites/jamesellsmoor/2019/05/30/trump-administration-rebrands-carbon-dioxide-as-molecules-of-u-s-freedom/.

9 Joey Mendolia, "All of the Ways Scott Pruitt Changed Energy Policy," PBS NewsHour, July 5, 2018, https://www.pbs.org/newshour/nation/all-of-the-ways-embattled-epa-chief-scott-pruitt-has-changed-energy-policy.

10 Mendolia, "Scott Pruitt."

11 "DoD Releases Report on Security Implications of Climate Change," Government, U.S. Department of Defense, July 29, 2015, https://www.defense.gov/News/News-Stories/Article/Article/612710/dod-releases-report-on-security-implications-of-climate-change/.

12 "DoD Releases Report."

13 R. P. Turco et al., "Nuclear Winter: Global Consequences of Multiple Nuclear Explosions," *Science* 222, no. 4630 (December 23, 1983): 1283–1292, https://doi.org/10.1126/science.222.4630.1283.

14 Daniel Ellsberg, The Doomsday Machine. Op.cit. William Schwartz and Charles Derber, The Nuclear Seduction op.cit.

15 Neta C. Crawford, "The Defense Department Is Worried about Climate Change – and Also a Huge Carbon Emitter," The Conversation, June 12, 2019, http://theconversation.com/the-defense-department-is-worried-about-climate-change-and-also-a-huge-carbon-emitter-118017.

16 Crawford, "The Defense Department."

17 Crawford, "The Defense Department."

18 Michael T Klare, Blood and Oil: The Dangers and Consequences of America's Growing Petroleum Dependency (New York, NY: Henry Holt and Company, 2004), https://archive.org/details/bloodoildangersc0000klar.

19 Charles Derber, *The Wilding of America: Money, Mayhem, and the New American Dream*, Sixth edition (New York, NY: Worth Publishers, a Macmillan Higher Education Company, 2015). Chapter 1.

20 Derber, *The Wilding of America.*
   Charles Derber, *Sociopathic Society: A People's Sociology of the United States.* (Boulder, CO and London, UK: Paradigm Publishers, 2013).

21 Derber, The Wilding of America.
   Derber, *Sociopathic Society.*

22 Charles Derber and Yale R. Magrass, Moving beyond Fear: Upending the Security Tales in Capitalism, Fascism, and Democracy (New York, NY: Routledge, 2019). See also Yale R. Magrass and Charles Derber, Glorious Causes: The Irrationality of Capitalism, War and Politics, Universalizing Resistance Series (New York, NY: Routledge, Taylor & Francis Group, 2020).

23 Jeremy Rifkin, *The European Dream: How Europe's Vision of the Future Is Quietly Eclipsing the American Dream* (New York, NY: Jeremy P. Tarcher/Penguin, 2004).

24 Rifkin, *The European Dream.*

25 Seymour Melman, *The Permanent War Economy: American Capitalism in Decline,* A Touchstone Book (New York, NY: Simon and Schuster, 1974).

26 List of Largest Energy Companies, Wikipedia, enwikipedia.org

27 US Energy Information Administration, "What is US electricity generation by source?" eia.gov

28 Jude Clemente, "Exxon, Chevron Leading The Permian Oil and Natural Gas Surge," *Forbes,* May 1, 2019, https://www.forbes.com/sites/judeclemente/2019/05/01/exxon-chevron-leading-the-permian-oil-and-natural-gas-surge/.

29 Jude Clemente, "The Great American Oil and Natural Gas Pipeline Boom," *Forbes,* June 2019, https://www.forbes.com/sites/judeclemente/2019/08/06/the-great-american-oil-and-natural-gas-pipeline-boom/.

30 Mark Green, "The 'Amazing' U.S. Shale Revolution," American Petroleum Institute, February 12, 2019, https://www.api.org/news-policy-and-issues/blog/2019/02/12/the-amazing-us-shale-revolution.

31 "Infographic: The Climate Risks of Natural Gas," Union of Concerned Scientists, February 3, 2014, https://www.ucsusa.org/resources/climate-risks-natural-gas.

32 "Climate Risks."

33 "Climate Risks."

34 Dan Alforo, "IEA: United States to Dominate Global Oil, Natural Gas Growth Through 2025, Energy in Depth, Nov. 14, 2018, energyindepth.org.

35 Terry Gross, "'Kochland': How The Koch Brothers Changed U.S. Corporate and Political Power," *NPR,* August 13, 2019, sec. Business, https://www.npr.org/2019/08/13/750803289/kochland-how-the-koch-brothers-changed-u-s-corporate-and-political-power.

36 Gross, "'Kochland.'"

37 John Schwartz, "Fossil Fuels on Trial: New York's Lawsuit Against Exxon Begins," *The New York Times,* October 22, 2019, sec. Climate, https://www.nytimes.com/2019/10/22/climate/new-york-lawsuit-exxon.html.

38 Michael Klare, *Blood and Oil.* Charles Derber, *Greed to Green: Solving Climate Change and Remaking the Economy* (Boulder, CO: Paradigm Publishers, 2010).

39 Steven Greenhouse, *Beaten down, Worked up: The Past, Present, and Future of American Labor* (New York, NY: Penguin Random House, 2020).

40 Jeremy Rifkin, *The European Dream.*

41 Jeremy Rifkin, *The European Dream.*

7 Inconvenient Truths

1 Noah Higgins-Dunn, "The U.S. Has the Worst Coronavirus Outbreak in the World: 'The Numbers Don't Lie,' Dr. Fauci Says," *CNBC,* August 5, 2020, https://www.cnbc.com/2020/08/05/dr-fauci-agrees-the-us-has-the-worst-coronvirus-outbreak-in-the-world-the-numbers-dont-lie.html.

2 The US recorded 1.067 million fatalities followed by Brazil with nearly 690,000. "WHO Coronavirus (COVID-19) Dashboard," accessed November 28, 2022, https://covid19.who.int.

3 Brian Klaas, "Opinion | Trump's Performance on Covid-19 Looks Especially Bad Compared with the Rest of the World," *Washington Post,* July 13, 2020, https://www.washingtonpost.com/opinions/2020/07/13/trumps-performance-covid-19-looks-especially-bad-compared-with-rest-world/.

4 Ryan Grenoble, "Trump Admits He Lied About COVID-19 Threat in New Woodward Book," *Huffington Post*, September 9, 2020, https://www.huffpost.com/entry/trump-coronavirus-bob-woodward_n_5f58fd32c5b6b48507fabc99.

5 Nicholas Kristof, "Opinion | 'We'Re No. 28! And Dropping!' – The New York Times," *New York Times*, September 9, 2020, https://www.nytimes.com/2020/09/09/opinion/united-states-social-progress.html.

6 Jeneen Inrterlandi, "Can the C.D.C. Be Fixed?," *New York Times*, June 17, 2021, https://www.nytimes.com/2021/06/17/world/from-the-times-magazine-can-the-cdc-be-fixed.html.

7 Jeneen Interlandi, "Why We're Losing the Battle with Covid-19," *The New York Times*, July 14, 2020, sec. Magazine, https://www.nytimes.com/2020/07/14/magazine/covid-19-public-health-texas.html.

8 Taylor Telford, "Income Inequality in U.S. Is at a Five-Decade High, Census Data Show," *Washington Post*, September 26, 2019, https://www.washingtonpost.com/business/2019/09/26/income-inequality-america-highest-its-been-since-census-started-tracking-it-data-show/.

9 "Inequality – Income Inequality – OECD Data," *OECD*, accessed November 28, 2022, http://data.oecd.org/inequality/income-inequality.htm.

10 "The Impact of Coronavirus on the Working Poor and People of Color – The Impact of Coronavirus on the Working Poor and People of Color – United States Joint Economic Committee," Democrats Joint Economic Committee, April 24, 2020, https://www.jec.senate.gov/public/index.cfm/democrats/2020/4/black-latino-and-low-income-communities-are-disproportionately-impacted-by-the-coronavirus.

11 W. Holmes Finch and Maria E. Hernández Finch, "Poverty and Covid-19: Rates of Incidence and Deaths in the United States During the First 10 Weeks of the Pandemic," *Frontiers in Sociology* 5 (June 15, 2020): 47, https://doi.org/10.3389/fsoc.2020.00047.

12 Terry Gross, "How COVID-19 Became a 'Tremendous Windfall' for the Ultra Rich," *NPR*, December 23, 2020, sec. Business, https://www.npr.org/2020/12/23/949578530/how-covid-19-became-a-tremendous-windfall-for-the-ultra-rich.

13 Kendall Hoyt, "How World War II Spurred Vaccine Innovation," *The Conversation*, May 8, 2015, https://theconversation.com/how-world-war-ii-spurred-vaccine-innovation-39903.

14 Jeremy Rifkin, The European Dream: How Europe's Vision of the Future Is Quietly Eclipsing the American Dream (New York, NY: Jeremy P. Tarcher/Penguin, 2004).

15 Karen Alea, "I was an Evangelical Christian, And I Know Why Many of Them Resist Logic About COVID-19," *Huffington Post*, September 17, 2020, https://www.huffpost.com/entry/evangelical-christians-covid-19-pandemic_n_5f5b9875c5b6b48507ffc791.

16 Ibid.

17 Ibid.

18 The Editors, "Scientific American Endorses Joe Biden," *Scientific American*, October 1, 2020, https://doi.org/10.1038/scientificamerican1020-12.

19 Dedrick Asante-Muhammad and Chuck Collins, "Opinion: The Pandemic Is Accelerating the Racial Wealth Divide. Here's How We Turn It around," *MarketWatch*, June 27, 2020, https://www.marketwatch.com/story/the-pandemic-is-accelerating-the-racial-wealth-divide-heres-how-we-turn-it-around-2020-06-25.

20 Leonard E. Egede and Rebekah J. Walker, "Structural Racism, Social Risk Factors, and Covid-19—A Dangerous Convergence for Black Americans," *New England*

Journal of Medicine 383, no. 12 (September 17, 2020): e77, https://doi.org/10.1056/ NEJMp2023616.

21 Ibid.

22 Ed Pilkington, "Covid-19 Death Rate among African Americans and Latinos Rising Sharply," *The Guardian*, September 8, 2020, https://www. theguardian.com/world/2020/sep/08/covid-19-death-rate-african-americans-and-latinos-rising-sharply.

8 America the Not-So-Beautiful

1 William Schwartz and Charles Derber, The Nuclear Seduction. Op. cit.

2 Stockholm international Peace Research Institute, 2018, cited in List of Countries by Military Expenditures, Wikipedia.

3 David Vine, *The United States Probably Has More Foreign Military Bases than Any Other People, Nation or Empire in History*, The Nation, September 4, 2015, thenation. com.

4 Quoted in Bob Herbert, "Opinion | In America; War Games," *The New York Times*, February 22, 1998, sec. Opinion, https://www.nytimes.com/1998/02/22/ opinion/in-america-war-games.html.

5 Tomgram: Andrew Bachevich, Creating a Perpetual War Machine, TomDispatch. com, April 10, 2018, tomdispatch.com.

6 Jeremy Rifkin, The European Dream. Op. cit.

7 Noam Chomsky, The Essential Chomsky. Op. cit.

8 Yale Magrass and Charles Derber, Glorious Causes. Op. cit.

9 Daniel Ellsberg, *The Doomsday Machine: Confessions of a Nuclear War Planner* (New York, NY: Bloomberg Publishing, 2017).

10 Ibid., p. 337.

11 Ibid., p. 339.

12 Ibid., p. 319.

13 Ibid., p. 319.

14 Ibid., p. 344.

15 Mark Landler, Two and a half years into his presidency, Mr. Trump is enthusiastically calling for the toppling of one regime, in Venezuela, and energetically undermining another, in Iran. *New York Times*, May 8, 2019, nytimes.com.

16 Aaron Mehta, "Here's How Many Billions the US Will Spend on Nuclear Weapons Over the Next Decade," *Defense News,* January 24, 2019, Defensenows.com.

17 Ibid.

18 Seligman, Bryan Bender, and Connor O'Brien, "Biden Goes 'Full Steam Ahead' on Trump's Nuclear Expansion Despite Campaign Rhetoric," *Carnegie Endowment for International Peace*, June 3, 2021, https://carnegieendowment.org/2021/06/03/ biden-goes-full-steam-ahead-on-trump-s-nuclear-expansion-despite-campaign-rhetoric-pub-84684.

19 Ibid.

20 Ibid.

21 Mehdi Hassan, "Trump Wants to Make It Easier to Start a Nuclear War," *The Intercept*, February 8, 2018, https://theintercept.com/2018/02/08/donald-trump-nuclear-war/.

22 Shannon Togawa Mercer, "Document: Nuclear Posture Review 2018," Lawfare (blog), February 2, 2018, https://www.lawfareblog.com/document-nuclear-posture-review-2018.

23 Hassan, "Trump Wants to Make It Easier to Start a Nuclear War."

24 Ibid.

25 Thomas Franck, "U.S. to Release 1 Million Barrels of Oil per Day from Reserves to Help Cut Gas Prices," CNBC, March 31, 2022, https://www.cnbc.com/2022/03/31/us-to-release-1-million-barrels-of-oil-per-day-from-reserves-to-help-cut-gas-prices.html.

26 Michael T. Klare, "Ukraine's Nuclear Flashpoints," *The Nation*, April 20, 2022, https://www.thenation.com/article/world/ukraine-nuclear-war/.

27 Jonathan Steele, "Ukraine's Grim Choice: Why Surrender May Be the Honorable Option," CounterPunch.org, March 7, 2022, https://www.counterpunch.org/2022/03/07/ukraines-grim-choice-why-surrender-may-be-the-honorable-option/.

28 Steven Lee Myers and Amy Qin, "Biden Has Angered China, and Beijing Is Pushing Back," *The New York Times*, July 20, 2021, sec. World, https://www.nytimes.com/2021/07/20/world/asia/china-biden.html.

29 Ibid.

30 Daron Acemoglu, "The Dangers of Decoupling," *Project Syndicate*, July 22, 2021, https://www.project-syndicate.org/commentary/dangers-of-us-china-decoupling-by-daron-acemoglu-2021-07.

31 Ibid.

32 William J. Broad and David E. Sanger, "A 2nd New Nuclear Missile Base for China, and Many Questions About Strategy," *The New York Times*, July 26, 2021, sec. U.S., https://www.nytimes.com/2021/07/26/us/politics/china-nuclear-weapons.html.

33 Chris Buckley and Steven Lee Myers, "Biden's China Strategy Meets Resistance at the Negotiating Table," *The New York Times*, July 26, 2021, sec. World, https://www.nytimes.com/2021/07/26/world/asia/china-us-wendy-sherman.html.

9 Lessons from Abolition

1 About the 2062 Transcript

"The 2062 Transcript" appeared quite suddenly. Beginning as joke among undergrad engineers at Peter H. Clark Institute of Technology (PHCI) just outside Jackson, MS, something curious was emerging. Asking what happens to a letter on a computer screen after someone erases it, drinking buddies' banter turned into the kind of earnest, after-midnight conversations that roam across ideas and disciplines. What do you mean? Well, here's the thing: say you typed "1" and then hit the backspace or delete key, what happens to the "1"? It turns out that the deleted letters actually do have "afterlives." From software companies monitoring their operating systems, to hidden NSA and GCHQ operatives, to hackers tracking corporations, and to low-rent private detectives and jealous lovers, it seems nearly everyone tracks every keystroke and these live out invisible afterlives in ever-growing digital archives – ones quite invisible, embedded as they are in a mass of physical hardware, the sterile places where the cloud becomes a thing, one among a vast array of server farms scattered across and above the planet, materializing itself as temperature controlled encasements of aluminum, exotic minerals, and silicon. Above all else, however, the archives have an energy footprint, every deleted character, it turns out, is still an energy consumer, and will be long after our earthly bodies return their energy and matter to the cosmos.

But the PHCI students weren't concerned about philosophical problem of the deleted character's afterlife. Instead, they were teasing a friend from the Great Lakes region in Africa, "the Maasai," as they called him after the Nilotic peoples of his home village. Never failing to complain about his fellow students' energy extravagant lifestyle, "the Maasai" pointed out that his community uses less energy than a deleted character!

Then the banter became speculative: what if we wrote an AI script that "scraped," i.e., pulled data out of, those archives? The script could aim at discovering every single deleted character, every aborted upload, and every email recalled by its sender. We could then ask the AI what all this assortment means. More philosophically, the script is effectively asking, are there any cumulative patterns or even meanings in these paths not chosen?

And so they hacked and coded their way to thousands of lines of code calling still other millions of lines of prewritten or computer-generated code and libraries. Then they figured out how to take the passive code, still resident on their computers, and engineer it into something that could replicate and copy itself onto other computers in order that it may inspect all the files resident there, on those other computers. Yes, they created a virus.

The code then databased and indexed what they found, processing not only *what* they found, but also *how* they found it. In effect, the code would be learning how it could learn more, better, and faster. To increase their computing power to process all this new information and generate succeeding generations of code, they developed an address book identifying all of idle or idling computers from which they could borrow of few cycles of processing power. Next, they instructed it to compare their findings and unearth patterns with existing real-world texts composed by humans. The ever-more sophisticated code, essentially now a feral beast sustaining itself off whatever resources it found, using those in turn to seek more, more, always seeking more, and it seemed that deleted characters were an inexhaustible resource.

Periodically the code phoned home. At least it would message or email its original creators with interesting findings, ones that resembled real-world texts. Eventually, the code rewrote its messaging instructions, nowadays it was rasterizing brilliant images inspired by Kandinsky, Pemba, and Matisse. In the beginning, the PHCI drinking buddies would gather to read the AI's cute haikus and what appeared to be especially witty tweets about recognizable people and events, ones that the AI discovered or rather extrapolated in a bizarrely social form of "co-authorship" (assuming that word could be applied to the multiple and diversely intentioned source data and the resulting composite creation). But soon, more elaborate texts emerged – cute ditties followed by dirty, then hilarious limericks. Newer, more complex emails start to arrive. Now they were looking more and more like formal academic texts, novellas, and even epic poems. With each leap in sophistication came ever larger readerships and audiences, quickly eclipsing the PHCI's Reddit group to envelope unknowably large networks of networks – all awaiting the AI's next creation.

Then IT appeared, "the 2062 transcript" was the title. Even if it appeared to be coherent – seeming also to accurately portray and even dovetail with the conversation of the day – IT, the transcript, had a strange status: an artificial intelligence extracted it from zettabytes of data using algorithms that were well beyond the comprehension of the original authors who wrote the initial code. And so what was it? A message from the future? An apocryphal text? Whatever IT was, it certainly moved the needle as people stopped debating its origins and turned their attention to debating its prescriptions.

10 Front for Survival

1 MM clarifies later: For example, those parts of the working class that were also oppressed by virtue of their region, nationality, gender or race may see universalist framings as denying their particular situations. This was all the more true because the most exploited and oppressed parts of the working class often formed communities that were on the climate frontlines – those experiencing climate breakdown's impacts earlier and more intensely than the rest of humanity. In many but by no means all cases, this differential experience of climate and social realities points to a different kind of politics than one focusing on elections and instead to ones with localist framings and strategies for meeting immediate needs. Of course, you can see why I emphasize intra-working-class problem solving given that people had to work with each other to develop a sense of the universal rather than simply asserting a universal and letting the chips fall where they may!

Sunkara offered us a universalist framing, but as I have explained, it did not recognize how to get to the universalist frame. Do people suddenly wake up out of a siloed identity politics frame of mind and become universalists? Similarly, Snyder, whom I mentioned later, failed to show me how to go from my immediate personal predispositions to a collective identity or collective action. There were other approaches popular at the global level and in certain regions. For example, arising out of indigenous movements, there were many collectivist projects that recognized a multiverse, as opposed to a universe, and formulated as "One No" (to capitalism) and "Many Yeses" (to alternative forms of social organization and world views). But these too did not offer us an agency or method for dialogues and action in the face of truly desperate circumstances. And here's where the principles of the Slender Path begin to emerge.

2 MM returned to the topic of class-like divisions in a postinterview note: Now this too may sound common sensical, but reigning theories of class from really bright thinker-activists often had a sectarian quality at the time. For example, an important and very influential working-class leader Jane McAlevey taught generations of activists to turn to the organic leaders of the working class for wisdom and direction and for developing forms of participation that enabled working-class people to develop their demands. Not controversial, then or now. But she also challenged middle-class activists and radicals who sought to mobilize the working class (as opposed to organize them). This propensity for mobilization, or worse, advocacy, in her reading led to working-class apathy and failed campaigns. Another thinker very influenced by her thinking and one who influenced sectors of the socialist movement looking for certainty in uncertain times was Matt Huber, an energy expert and geographer. He too bemoaned the intrusion of what he saw as the professional managerial class (PMC) into working-class movements and especially the environmental movement. While very sympathetic to both Huber and McAlevey's concerns, I felt that their class analysis failed to grasp the dynamic character of the working class and contradictory nature of the so-called PMC.

For the Slender Path to emerge, that is for us to realize the principle upon which we may move forward and stave off extinction, we needed a different form of class analysis that sought out how build on the strengths and insights of the various parts of the working class and put those into dialogue with one another. What Huber and McAlevey were calling the PMC – which had conceptual roots in the 1970s sociology of people like the Ehrenreichs and also the sociologist Alvin Gouldner but went back much further into the reformist thinking of Eduard Bernstein – was actually a composite of many different kinds of "professionals" – in my view highly paid workers with certain skills that include those for coordinating production and interfacing with other institutions. Their numbers and internal self-identity as a class was extremely variable over time and from place to place. Moreover, many of their organizations, sometimes non-profit entities, employed many people who carried out knowledge functions but who were intellectual workers in their own right. What the alleged PMCs, the intellectual workers, and often also union bureaucrats, and the like had in common is that their locations gave them a peek at the whole – including our existential threats. What was therefore pivotal was the merging of their knowledges with that of the rest of the working class. And these intellectuals, or better phrased, workers doing knowledge work had developed vital tools for address our existential threats.

For example, in the course of the international Framework Convention on Climate Change's work, different kinds of scenario planning and modeling frameworks were developed to understand the policy options available to humanity. These modeling tools proved essential to developing discussion about local policy choices and program designs. Ironically, one set, called Shared Socioeconomic Pathways, emerged out of the British bureaucracy. Ideas about "Circular Economics," that emphasized sustainability over profits had similar origins. For those of us operating in working-class communities, our work was to pull in these diverse sources of knowledge and working power and to articulate which ones worked for us as a whole.

3 MM adds: To give you one example of this revolution in values and the matter of degrowth. Few matters are as critical to our daily lives as the food we eat. A critical thinker, Francis Moore Lappé helped foster a veritable cultural revolution, one which linked our individual choices to the global systems of production. Her bestselling book, *Diet for a Small Planet*, was a half century old by the twenties. Her work and the movements that it inspired helped us understand that the vast majority of our agricultural land was used to produce food that really provided less than a fifth of the calories we were consuming. This contradiction, at a time when agricultural land could serve broader social goals – for example, regenerative agriculture to sequester carbon, was critical consciousness raising tool. It reframes questions about the kind of growth and global priorities that we shared. The tacit "we" in this matter was not a clumping of individuals but humanity as a whole. No longer were we considering the topic of a "we" that is an aggregation of individual choices. The "we" was a global actor in the making, a polity if you will that was and is debating the question of what type of growth "we" need. While many radicals, ones who were very conscious of our global extinction threats, had written off these kinds of cultural questions as, "non-class" or "lifestyle" questions, or worse, problems of the "cultural elite," the topic very quickly merged with projects in the Global South concerning production and diet. This also addressed inner-city questions over health and diet, ones in which the most exploited parts of the working class were being subjugated to corporate interests in the marketing of processed foods and industrial agriculture. As people recognized the links to how rural and ex-urban working people were dealing with their crises, matters of agricultural policy and investments helped us recognize the potential for cross-cutting coalitions within the global, national and regional working classes began to emerge. Degrowth, though not framed as such, helped us understand the importance of

qualitative change as opposed to the cancerous focus on perpetual and infinite growth.

In fact, in the late teens, Lappé could proudly point to an electoral campaign in rural Maine. She noted that a young woman, a rarity among elected officials, campaigned for and won election to the state legislature of the grounds of a "Green New Deal for Maine." While some people saw "the deal" as emblematic of a growth agenda, it became very clear that the legislator was interested in "quality" jobs, not "more" jobs, ones that ensured more public goods for Maine-ers and beyond.

Other examples abounded. Some urban activists found ways to radically reduce the waste inherent in commercial food production and the hospitality sector by developing the necessary institutions to reprocess food and create a more circular public goods "economics" – all of this required non-market, local governance and institution building as well as an organized consciousness of what we produce, consume and waste collectively. Previously, only the capitalists had such a "total" overview, one exercised through their investment function and one which failed to address our shared interests. In this context, growth came to refer to our values and our sophistication in coming to know what counted and what should not. Capitalist growth came to be questioned, in its place came both a revival of both new and age-old demands for equality, autonomy and self-realization, demands which simply did not compute in terms of the still-reigning neoliberal individualism.

Index